CHINA AND THE WTO

China and the WTO
Why Multilateralism Still Matters

Petros C. Mavroidis and André Sapir

PRINCETON UNIVERSITY PRESS

PRINCETON AND OXFORD

Published by Princeton University Press
41 William Street, Princeton, New Jersey 08540
6 Oxford Street, Woodstock, Oxfordshire OX20 1TR

press.princeton.edu

Library of Congress Control Number: 2020947118
ISBN 9780691206592
ISBN (ebook) 9780691206608

British Library Cataloging-in-Publication Data is available

Editorial: Hannah Paul and Josh Drake
Production Editorial: Nathan Carr
Jacket/Cover Design: Jessica Massabrook
Production: Erin Suydam
Publicity: Kate Hensley and Kate Farquhar-Thomson

This book has been composed in Adobe Text Pro and Gotham

Printed on acid-free paper. ∞

Printed in the United States of America

10 9 8 7 6 5 4 3 2 1

CONTENTS

PREFACE

The story of China's participation in the World Trade Organization (WTO) is one of rapid passage from euphoria to angst. In 2001, its accession to the WTO added one of the last big missing pieces to complete the puzzle of world trade integration. By admitting China, home to a quarter of the world's population, the WTO finally justified the "W" in its title, but it also opened the door to the unknown.

Never before had the WTO or its predecessor, the General Agreement on Tariffs and Trade (GATT), admitted a member so big and with an economic system so different from the liberal market economy system upon which they are predicated. When it joined the WTO, China was in transition from a non-market to a market economy but not to a liberal market economy as some Western leaders blinded by the "end of history" narrative may have believed or hoped. China only pledged to become a socialist market economy. Slowly, Western leaders have understood what this means, and they are worried.

We are worried too. The size and rapid growth of China were bound to generate a backlash from trading partners, especially the United States, which is concerned about losing its status as the most powerful country in the world. Like others, we had hoped that the WTO would be able to mediate these inevitable tensions and avoid an escalation. Unfortunately, the mismatch between the current WTO framework and the Chinese system has undermined the WTO's ability to play its role. Worse, this situation has encouraged the United States, under the leadership of Donald Trump, to seek redress against China's behavior outside the WTO framework. This situation is untenable. Something must give. Either China or the WTO must change. Otherwise the WTO system will not survive.

This worry is what motivated us to write this book. As academics who have spent our lives studying the international trade system—Petros as a law professor at Columbia Law School and André as an economics professor and fellow at an economic think tank in Brussels—we wanted to understand how the GATT and then the WTO had dealt with earlier accessions of new members with different economic systems and what lessons history may hold for the current tensions with China.

We draw two main lessons from our reading of history. One is that the United States cannot handle China the way it handled Japan in the past, when it also threatened U.S. economic hegemony.

The other lesson is that China and the WTO cannot sit idle and do nothing about the gap between the Chinese economic system and the WTO system. True, China does not violate WTO rules more than any other WTO member. And when it is told by WTO judges that it has violated international rules, it takes appropriate measures to correct its domestic rules. Yet, because of its idiosyncratic economic system, China clearly violates the spirit of the WTO, which was not conceived to have a socialist country as one of its largest members, and now also the world's largest goods exporter. This probably explains the Trump administration's unilateral aggression against China, since one can only litigate at the WTO against the application of the written rules, not their spirit. And since unilateral pushback by the U.S. administration against China has not succeeded and will not succeed, the United States is tempted to undo the WTO system altogether. But this would plunge the world back into the somber days before the creation of the rules-based multilateral system.

We contend that recommitting to multilateralism is the only viable solution to extricate Beijing and Washington from their trade conflict, which risks escalating into a full-blown war. A bilateral deal between China and the United States is neither realistic nor desirable. It is unrealistic because the two parties are engaged in a conflict that goes far beyond trade and neither will be ready to make concessions to the other for fear that it will weaken its global geopolitical standing. And it is undesirable because any bilateral trade deal that would be acceptable to the two parties would inevitably come at the expense of other countries.

A multilateral solution would also have the advantage that it would address a problem that is not unique to China, although it is uniquely acute in the case of China because of its size. State-owned enterprises (SOEs), a feature of China's socialist market economy regime, entered the trade lexicon with China's accession to the WTO, but they exist everywhere. In fact, they were quite prevalent in the early days of the GATT in many of its members. Yet, SOEs did not pose a problem to the trading system at the time because all its members shared (or at least accepted) the liberal understanding that was implicit in the GATT, a reflection of the fact that its main architects were Americans and British. Today, the situation is different. SOEs play an important role in China and some other WTO members that do not adhere to the liberal understanding that remains implicit in the WTO regime.

To retain its principles and yet accommodate China, the WTO needs to translate some of its implicit liberal understanding into explicit treaty language. We advance specific proposals to this effect, which, if adopted, would induce China to change its economic behavior, although it would retain its economic regime. In our view, therefore, the solution to the problem posed by China to the international trading system is not to demand a change in its economic regime but to induce a change in its economic behavior. Less than that would threaten the survival of the WTO.

To do all this, powerful countries need to the bury the hatchet of aggression, to undo what they have been doing recently. They need to rekindle with cooperative spirits, with leaders who understand what is at stake and will seize the moment. The world is experiencing a clash between a descending and an ascending power, a Thucydides trap. It is up to the world community to escape this trap scot-free. The recent doom and gloom in which the world community has found itself because of the COVID-19 pandemic can be reversed if the world community practices what academics like ourselves have been preaching: a return to the table of negotiations with a view to a multilateral agreement.

ACKNOWLEDGMENTS

A book is a collective effort, and this one is no exception. We have relied on friends and experts to review our work and guide us through a process that took well beyond the time that we had originally allocated to it for completion. It might sound cliché, and yet it is totally true that without the active support of various individuals, this project, which started as a private conversation between the two of us, would have never seen the light of day in its present form.

We would like to start by thanking our "teina," Jeremy Stewart, who was supposed to act as research assistant but ended up being much more than that. He served as sounding board first, and as correcting board subsequently, to the various ideas discussed in the pages that follow.

Going back to the early days of this project, we relied heavily on Shohei Nishimura and Fumihiko Okumura, who have helped us put together the data for Japan. David Weinstein graciously shared with us his immense expertise on Japan. Lenka Sustrova provided us with valuable information regarding the accession of Czechoslovakia to the GATT. With their support, we managed to functionalize the two axes of this volume, the comparison of the Chinese accession with that of Japan and with that of the Eastern Bloc countries that had joined the GATT previously.

We also turned to national delegates who took an active role in the negotiation leading to the accession of China to the WTO. Mogens Peter Carl, Karl Falkenberg, and Patrick A. Low never tired of responding to our numerous questions regarding the process of accession. Peter Williams spared no effort in sharing with us his unique experience regarding accessions to the GATT/WTO in general and enabled us to draw parallels between the multiple accession procedures that we discuss in this volume.

Various individuals helped us understand narrower questions that we needed to address in order to complete our work: Curtis Milhaupt, on SOEs (state-owned enterprises), Michel Kostecki, on East-West relations, and Pierre Sauvé, on the OECD's aborted Multilateral Agreement on Investment, whereas Marco C.E.J. Bronckers, Carlo-Maria Cantore, Rodd Izadnia, Wolf Meier-Ewert, Rajan Sabitha Rani Neeraj, and Jasper-Martijn Wauters generously responded to dozens of queries regarding WTO law.

As usual, we counted on Claus-Dieter Ehlermann, Kirtikumar Mehta, and Damien J. Neven, long-time friends and mentors, to guide us through the intricacies of antitrust enforcement. Alan Winters shared his thoughts on the relationship between trade and national security and helped us streamline our thinking in this respect.

Gary Hufbauer read what we thought was the final draft of this work. His astute remarks helped us realize that it was not as ready to be published as we might have thought. His many challenging suggestions have found their way into this volume, and we are thankful that he took the time to read our work so carefully and comment on it in detail.

We first circulated the core ideas permeating this volume as a Bruegel Working Paper, and we must thank Guntram Wolff and Maria Demertzis both for providing us with useful comments and for generously hosting our endeavors.

To test our ideas, we decided to discuss them in various forums. Christiane Daleiden organized the first meeting with a few EU delegates to the WTO to discuss the original idea and have a first reaction by seasoned trade experts. Denis Redonnet then arranged, in February 2019, an informal gathering in the Directorate General for Trade of the European Commission in Brussels, where we presented the first draft of this volume and received valuable feedback. Doug Nelson and Bernard Hoekman organized two wonderful conferences at Tulane University on May 12–13, 2019, and the European University Institute in Florence on July 10, 2019, where we presented this volume and benefited from very helpful comments. We also presented the ideas in this volume at the WTO Public Forum on October 9, 2019. We would like to thank the participants in all these events, particularly Chad P. Bown. We also discussed our work at a seminar at Columbia Law School on October 14, 2019, and benefited enormously from comments offered by Jagdish Bhagwati, Merit Janow, and Tom Zeiler. The audience at the World Trade Forum held in Bern on October 25, 2019, also offered valuable feedback. Lastly, the reviewers of the book for Princeton University Press made very helpful comments and suggestions on different drafts.

Our editor at Princeton University Press, Hannah Paul, exceeded our expectations by guiding us smoothly through the publication process and turning a few ideas into the current volume, which also benefited from great suggestions by Jim Ashton, our developmental editor. Jennifer Backer provided superb (and very patient) copyediting. We are most thankful and appreciative to all of them for their efforts and suggestions.

ABBREVIATIONS

APEC Asia-Pacific Economic Cooperation

ATF Agreement on Trade Facilitation

BIT bilateral investment treaty

CCP Chinese Communist Party

CEECS Central and Eastern European countries

CFIUS Committee on Foreign Investment in the United States

CJEU Court of Justice of the European Union

CPTPP Comprehensive and Progressive Agreement for Trans-Pacific Partnership

DOC Department of Commerce

DSB Dispute Settlement Body

DSU Dispute Settlement Understanding

EC European Community

EU European Union

FDI foreign direct investment

FTA free trade agreement

GATS General Agreement on Trade in Services

GATT General Agreement on Tariffs and Trade

GDP gross domestic product

GPA Agreement on Government Procurement

IMF International Monetary Fund

IP intellectual property

ITA Information Technology Agreement

ITO International Trade Organization

MFN	most-favored nation
NAFTA	North Atlantic Free Trade Agreement
NDRC	National Development and Reform Commission
NME	non-market economy
NTB	non-tariff barrier
NVC	nonviolation complaint
OECD	Organisation for Economic Cooperation and Development
RBP	restrictive business practice
SASAC	State-Owned Assets Supervision and Administration Commission
SCAP	Supreme Commander of Allied Powers
SCM AGREEMENT	Agreement on Subsidies and Countervailing Measures
SCOC	state capital operation company
SEZ	special economic zone
SG AGREEMENT	Agreement on Safeguards
SIE	state-invested enterprise
SII	Structural Impediments Initiative
SOCB	state-owned commercial bank
SOE	state-owned enterprise
SOFI	state-owned financial institution
STC	state-trading country
STE	state-trading enterprise
TFEU	Treaty on the Functioning of the European Union
TIER	Technology Import Export Regulation
TISA	Trade in Services Agreement
TPP	Trans-Pacific Partnership
TPRM	Trade Policy Review Mechanism
TRIMS AGREEMENT	Agreement on Trade-Related Investment Measures
TRIPS AGREEMENT	Agreement on Trade-Related Aspects of Intellectual Property Rights

TRM   transitional review mechanism

TRQ   tariff-rate quota

TT   technology transfer

USMCA   United States-Mexico-Canada Agreement

USTR   United States Trade Representative

VER   voluntary export restraint

WTO   World Trade Organization

WTO AGREEMENT   Agreement Establishing the World Trade Organization

CHINA AND THE WTO

Introduction

China's accession to the World Trade Organization (WTO) has presented the increasingly globalized economic system with a conundrum. Are the contributions of China's high-growth, export-oriented economy a win-win—an unalloyed benefit for both the People's Republic and its trading partners? Or, as seems increasingly to be the prevailing opinion, has China's markedly different economic system, combined with its perceived tendency to bend or even break the rules of international trade, made it a problem that needs solving?

China's participation in the WTO has provided it with almost uninhibited access in 163 markets, the United States among them, and China has profited immensely from its participation in the world trading system. Recording unprecedented growth rates, it has transformed itself from a low-income, developing country to a global power in one generation. This is not, of course, due solely to its trade performance; China has long been a central player in global geopolitics and its economic potential has loomed large throughout East Asia and, indeed, the rest of the world. In recent years, that potential has been realized as China has profited from globalization to become a trade powerhouse. Its export-led growth model has perfectly positioned it to take advantage of the elimination of trade barriers for its products worldwide.

The rest of the world has profited from China's growth as well—at least in part. China's unprecedented export growth has benefited foreign consumers and stimulated capital gains for foreign investors. And yet, the silver

1

lining of cheap Chinese consumer goods and corporate capital gains is tinged with gray. Accusations have surfaced and proliferated that China's success is due not only to its industry but also to other factors, and most notably, the suggestion that it simply does not play by the rules, whether by engaging in illegal subsidization or by counterfeiting, as just two examples. Such accusations are probably expressed most vociferously in Washington, D.C., but not only there. With varying degrees of vehemence, many of China's trading partners, especially the big players like the United States, the European Union, and Canada, have voiced their views of China's trading practices that range from general concern to pointed critique. Typically, these voices have criticized the extent of state involvement in the Chinese economy and argued for stricter enforcement of the current multilateral rules regulating international trade.

The Trump administration has preferred to take justice into its own hands. President Trump's decision to "take on" China has been making headlines since the summer of 2019, accompanied by a roller coaster of announcements of tariffs on specific products, followed by the imposition of some of them, retaliation by China, subsequent announcements veering toward peaceful resolution of the dispute, then renewed belligerence, and finally a deal. These are not dull times, as far as international trade news is concerned.

Of course, we are not here to judge the usefulness of similar tactics (antics?) when it comes to possible political exploitation. Our interests instead are the repercussions that similar actions have on the multilateral edifice of international trade. To us, what matters most is whether this is the most appropriate way to resolve the China issues.

But the world is not unanimous in criticizing China's trading practices. For one, there is a silent majority of trading nations, the smaller players, who have other fish to fry. Israel, for example, has not joined the chorus of critics. And then there are those, such as economist Dani Rodrik (2018), who claim that the current situation should not be of concern to the WTO at all, as China, its idiosyncratic elements notwithstanding, should simply be accommodated within the four corners of the current multilateral edifice. All the more so, the argument goes, since China's growth has contributed to the growth of many other nations. The world trade community, stakeholders and academics alike, have advanced various proposals to address the China problem. Some say, "Do nothing." Others advocate increased and stronger enforcement of existing rules. Still others insist, "Hit them where it hurts."

But to reach a long-term solution, we first have to decide if China is, in fact, acting outside the legitimate practices of world trade. In other words, what exactly is the "China problem"?

The China Problem: Myth and Reality

If China plays by the book, then there should be no problem—its trade practices, alien as they might appear to some since they are not consonant with trade practices followed by most market economies, should be accommodated like any other country's. But considered from another angle, China must be doing something wrong; otherwise there would be nothing to complain about—"Where there is smoke, there is fire," as the old adage has it. In the pages that follow, we understand the "China problem" as the sum of claims that various trading nations (and most comprehensively and loudly the United States) have mapped out.

A major difficulty in assessing the situation is that this problem is a moving target—claims continually appear, disappear, and reappear again. Let us take the accusation that China is a currency manipulator as just one example. The Trump administration branded China a manipulator, the president withdrew the accusation a few months later, he reintroduced it once again sometime later, and then the administration succeeded in reaching a deal with China.

Two complaints, however, surface with some regularity and have withstood the test of time: that Chinese state-owned enterprises (SOEs) benefit from unfair trade advantages and that Chinese companies (both private and state owned) impose forced technology transfer (TT) deals on foreign businesses as a condition for accessing the Chinese market. In this volume, we focus on these two claims, which are central both to the way the Chinese economic system operates and to the difficulty that foreign economic operators encounter in their dealings with Chinese firms inside and outside China.

How to Deal with China?

Essentially, we argue that the courses of action advanced to deal with the "China problem" are inappropriate or, at best, only partly efficient. We explain why bilateral solutions only advance short-term, narrow interests aiming to redress trade imbalances as opposed to systemic interests that address the cause of concern or effect change in the medium term. The world trading community's interests would be better served by a different approach—namely, amending the current trade law regime and bringing it into line with the original "liberal understanding" of the General Agreement on Tariffs and Trade (GATT). In our view, only a legislative amendment will allow the WTO membership to solve the problems posed by SOEs and forced TT. Implicitly, thus, we believe that there is merit in the concerns raised. We also believe, though, that the eventual solution to the current problems should not be China-specific. Concerns about SOEs and forced TT are not unique to China. Similar problems exist with regard to other current or potential WTO members. Multilateral solutions are, therefore, necessary. We argue that China, because of its size, simply exacerbated a problem that already existed.

To avoid misunderstandings as to the scope of our endeavor, we should emphasize that we do not purport to offer a complete blueprint to reform the WTO in all its dimensions. We leave this much-needed, but ambitious, task to others. Our goal is more modest. We seek simply to propose WTO reforms that we consider essential to lessen the tensions in the trading system arising from China's size and the nature of its economic system.

In the pages that follow, we will argue against the two extreme solutions to the "China problem": unilateral measures against China to force a change of its economic regime on the one hand, and staying idle on the other. We concede that some of the concerns raised can be addressed through more active enforcement of the current WTO regime. When we say that some of the concerns about China can be handled effectively within the four corners of the existing WTO regime, we adhere to the view expressed elsewhere that a stricter enforcement of the Protocol of Accession for China might yield satisfactory results.

The bulk of the other concerns can only be addressed if new obligations are added to the current WTO regime. This is, in our view, particularly important, for even if we can imagine how a well-intentioned, imaginative WTO judgment might deflate the current state of uneasiness, such a judgment would be case specific. Furthermore, decisions made by WTO judges carry less weight than formal legislative amendments. In an era of doubt as to the legitimacy of the WTO Appellate Body, it is probably wiser (even though, we readily admit, more cumbersome) to opt for legislative solutions.

The GATT/WTO is, of course, the (legal) benchmark to judge the adequacy of the existing regime to address the two concerns mentioned above. As we explain in chapter 5 in detail, the GATT is an incomplete contract regulating trade transactions based on a "liberal understanding" of the law and economy.[1] Suffice it to state for now that the GATT was part of the wider International Trade Organization (ITO) project, which contained disciplines on both state and private restraints to trade. The GATT was a chapter of the ITO (Chapter IV) and regulated only state barriers to trade.

The GATT entered into force on January 1, 1948, while awaiting the advent of the ITO. Even though the formal negotiation of all issues involved had been finalized, the treaty repeatedly failed to get through the U.S. Congress, and no other nation was prepared to ratify it without U.S. approval. Politics got in the way, and the ITO never saw the light of day. It never will, as the WTO has taken its place. The GATT disciplines, nevertheless, were part and parcel of a wider understanding on how to liberalize trade, which is predicated on respect for private rights and limited and controlled state intervention in the economy. This was explicitly contracted in the ITO, as we show in chapter 5.

But the obligations that were explicitly contracted in the ITO were almost never explicitly incorporated in the GATT text. Article XXIX is an exception, even though it only requests a best endeavor to observe the obligations. The implicit, rather than explicit, adherence to the ITO obligations on private rights and limited state intervention constitutes the "liberal understanding" of the GATT.

The GATT "liberal understanding" implicitly assumes that in all GATT/WTO members

- laws, contracts, and property rights will be enforced;
- the state will not undo contractual promises regarding trade liberalization through favoritism (pecuniary or otherwise) toward domestic agents; and
- investment will be liberalized.

None of this was ever translated into legal language in the GATT/WTO agreements, but it formed the essential background against which the multilateral trading system has been operating since its inception in 1948. All

---

1. In order to avoid any misunderstanding, we do not use the term "liberal understanding" throughout this volume in its possible ideological connotation. We use it simply, as equivalent to "market economy." Market economies of course differ in the way they approach social policies, among other things. But they all share one common element: they represent an economic system, where (economic) decisions and the ensuing pricing of goods and services are, for all practical purposes, determined by the interactions of private individuals, citizens, and businesses alike. Government interventions are meant to address market failures and not to dictate the way each and every transaction in the economy should take place.

the big players shared (or at least accepted) the liberal understanding of the law and economy. In Ruggie's (1982) account, this was the era of "embedded liberalism," the post–World War II era, where states were putting together an international system supporting free trade and market economies, while acknowledging the right to regulate in order to combat unemployment and support welfare policies at home. One might add that this was the quintessential reason why the multilateral rules operated so smoothly, despite the increasing number and heterogeneity of GATT/WTO members.

China was not the first, and it will likely not be the last, country to join the GATT/WTO with an economic system different from the liberal system that the main incumbent members have adopted. The GATT had to face a somewhat similar situation when socialist, non-market countries from Central and Eastern Europe joined the club. But these countries were small, and it was relatively easy to negotiate their accession through existing protocols, which imposed specific obligations on the acceding countries. Furthermore, their subsequent transformation into market economies linked to their accession to the European Union removed whatever problems might have existed during their initial years of participation in the world trading system.

Even when Japan wanted to join—a much bigger economy in which the state played a crucial role, even though it was not centrally planned—the GATT liberal understanding was not questioned. Japan was an outlier; it was far from sharing the liberal understanding when it joined the GATT under the protective aegis of the United States. This changed relatively soon afterward, when Japan acceded to the Organisation for Economic Cooperation and Development (OECD) a few years after it had joined the GATT. Through (or because of) its OECD membership, it endorsed the liberal understanding and aligned its regulatory regime to that of the Western countries that dominated the GATT.

India and Brazil, two large and important original signatories that might have been a thorn in the system's side, always accepted the GATT's basic tenets, each gradually welcoming the liberal understanding and thus avoiding clashes with other GATT/WTO members as their economies grew over time. India first in 1991, with the economic reform operated by Prime Ministers Rao and Singh, and Brazil with the adoption of Plano Real of 1994, steered by Presidents Franco and Cardoso, abandoned the heavily interventionist policies of the past and espoused the principles and practices of market economics for good.

In short, until the accession of China, the multilateral trading system was able to cope with increasing variety in economic systems among its members with little difficulty. This was either because new members were fairly small or, if they were larger economies, because they shared (or subsequently accepted) the liberal understanding that was implicit in the original GATT text and that reflected the fact that its main architects were from the United States or Great Britain.[2]

This time, it is different. China is neither small nor willing to reform its one-party political system and everything it entails in terms of state participation in the working of the economy, as many of its partners had hoped it would have done within a relatively short period of time after joining the WTO.

Outline of the Book

Chapter 1 serves as background information so that the reader can better appreciate the concerns voiced against China. In this chapter, we provide some data regarding the development of the Chinese economy in recent years and discuss the reactions of the world community to the new situation. We will highlight the worldwide euphoria when China entered the WTO frame, the antithesis of the more recent dysphoria that is gaining pace across the industrialized world.

In chapter 2, we begin by examining the claims against China presented by the U.S. authorities (based on discussions in the Trilateral group, where officials of the European Union, Japan, and the United States participate), the most vehement critics of Chinese policies, and then focus on the central issues: SOEs and TT, which lie at the core of complaints against China's trade and investment regime. They represent the high-priority items for the Trilateral group[3] but also for a few others and are therefore salient concerns of all of China's major trading partners.

---

2. See Irwin, Mavroidis, and Sykes 2008 and Tumlir 1984. Japan presented the world trading regime with challenges as a result of its monumental growth rates in the 1960s and 1970s. Complaints against Japan were raised not only at the moment it acceded to the GATT but also a few years after it had joined. Already at the moment of its accession, it managed to provoke a record number of invocations of the non-application clause. Eventually, however, Japan became "one of us," and its ascension to Quad status is the best proof to this effect. We will discuss the Japanese problem in detail.

3. Following the decision of the European Union, Japan, and the United States (the "Trilateral"), during the 11th WTO Ministerial Conference of the WTO, to work together and confront China, they have been focusing on these two issues. See USTR, Joint Statement by the United States, European Union, and Japan at MC 11, December 12, 2017; USTR, Joint Statement of the Trilateral Meeting of the Trade Ministers of the United States, European Union and Japan, May 23, 2019.

Most importantly, by addressing these two concerns, we will be in a position to understand whether the current legal regime applicable to China (that is, the multilateral trade law as reflected in the WTO agreements that bind all WTO members including China, and the Chinese Protocol of Accession, which contains China-specific obligations) suffices to address the concerns raised. If the answer to this question is yes, then we need to explore the reasons for underenforcement. If the answer is no, then we need to ask why the current regime is inadequate and what can be done about it. To determine the answer, we analyze SOEs and TT in terms of the legal regime applicable to China—the multilateral rules as well as the Chinese Protocol of Accession. The combination of these rules provides a benchmark for assessing the ability of China's current regime to deal effectively with the concerns voiced by the international community.

Our conclusion? In a nutshell, the current WTO rules on SOEs could, in principle, resolve at least some of the concerns raised by the United States and China's other trading partners, but such a resolution requires a more imaginative interpretation of the existing rules than the WTO has thus far been willing to concede. This entails a reorientation of the current case law, a demanding exercise by any account. Therefore, in our view, a clarification of the rules on SOEs, inspired by existing regulatory solutions at the bilateral and plurilateral level, would go a long way toward addressing the current concerns. A legislative amendment would, by spelling out the details, preempt discretion by the WTO judges and avoid the risk of unsatisfactory outcomes due to unclear rules. In other words, clearing up some of the haziness that has plagued rulings related to SOEs will go a long way toward bringing China into alignment with the goals and policies of the WTO.

With respect to TT, the situation is different: the current rules are not adequate to address the friction over forced TTs. This is largely because requests for TT by private agents are not covered in the current WTO agreements, since these agreements do not deal with private trade deals but exclusively with state barriers to trade. Since similar requests could occur elsewhere as well (and not only in China), an expansion of current agreements to include private TT deals is necessary. But such an expansion raises an important issue: if the concern about TT is new—that is, if it postdates the WTO members' negotiation with China that led to the conclusion of the Protocol of Accession—then it needs to be addressed now for the first time. If, conversely, the concern predates the negotiation, why has it not been addressed before? Is the concern about TT a new issue, specific to China? If these concerns have caused problems before, why were they not addressed? Where did the system go wrong? Whatever the answer, we believe that only a negotiation of new rules can help solve the problem of private impediments to trade.

That private impediments could hinder trade liberalization was, of course, common knowledge when the GATT was being negotiated. Therefore, as we will show in more detail later, the ITO, under the aegis of which the GATT was originally supposed to come, contained a chapter dealing with multilateral responses to restrictive business practices (RBPs) by private agents. The degree of state involvement in the workings of the economy varies across trading nations. In principle, however, the original members shared a commitment to the market economy, and thus private impediments would be addressed by domestic competition laws.

The introduction of competition discipline in China is quite recent, and even today, China remains a country with substantial state involvement in the workings of the national economy. Countries with similar substantial involvement, ranging from Japan of the 1950s to Soviet bloc countries like Hungary and Poland, joined the GATT before China did. The parallels with their accession processes are not only relevant but warranted indeed.

For these reasons, in chapter 3, we will be discussing the experience of countries with similarities to China and the ways their accession processes unfolded. We will see that China presented the incumbents with a novel issue: even among similarly situated countries, China was something new. Before its accession, GATT incumbents had only dealt with small countries with heavy state involvement in the economy (like Hungary and Poland) or with big countries with less pronounced state involvement in the market (like Japan) but never with such a huge country that had, at the same time, such extensive state control over its economy.

In the same chapter, we will provide a more detailed discussion of the Japanese accession to the GATT, a choice predicated on a variety of reasons. For starters, the reaction to China's participation in the WTO is reminiscent of the hostility toward the accession of Japan to the GATT in the 1950s and the subsequent attempts to resolve the "Japan problem." Recent complaints against China are very similar to earlier complaints against Japan. Almost identical arguments were raised against the destructive nature of the Japanese "mercantilist trade and investment regime." Furthermore, reliable historical accounts[4] support the argument that Japan's organization of its economy was one of the paradigms that Chairman Deng, the

---

4. Vogel (2011; 2019) has analyzed this issue probably more comprehensively than anyone else.

man credited with the transformation of the Chinese economy, aspired to emulate.

Japan has, of course, fully integrated into the ranks of the Western world. This does not, however, mean that, as in the case of Japan, one should expect changes in China soon—we will, in fact, demonstrate the opposite. We want to show the differences between the two countries and why the factors that influenced the transformation of Japan into a market economy are absent in China. We will explore the differences and the similarities between the two situations and draw conclusions.

Other countries with different economic systems have largely aligned themselves with the global trading system, of course, but China differs from these as well. For example, in the WTO era incumbents did have to face a request for accession by Russia and some other ex–Soviet bloc countries that have not joined the European Union and by Arab countries with heavy state involvement in the workings of their economies. Both sets of countries, however, are closer to the smaller ex–Soviet bloc countries that had joined the GATT than they are to China. As a result, although some lessons can be drawn from earlier experiences, the reader should not expect "lock, stock, and barrel" types of solutions here. China is singular, and it requires singular responses. In chapters 4 and 5, we focus on these responses—the courses of action advanced elsewhere, both by the United States and by academia.

In chapter 4, we will be dealing with unilateral threats and tariff increases as the "stick" meant to induce cooperative behavior by China. Relying on the existing research by Bown (2019) and Amiti, Redding, and Weinstein (2019), among others, we will explain why this strategy has already proved to be inefficient. But this is not the end of the story; if similar courses of action are followed in the future as well, countries confronting China risk facing countermeasures and a further weakening of the multilateral regime.

Finally, we will also examine the limits of enforcement of the current regime. Our main conclusion is that where clear rules have been agreed upon (as in the case of regulation of export taxes), complainants against China have scored their biggest victories. Imaginative proposals, such as that of Jennifer Hillman (2018), to pursue nonviolation complaints (NVCs) against China, a legal instrument of ambiguous efficacy anyway, are, in our view, not a recipe for success.

In chapter 5, we will address the thesis of Dani Rodrik (2018) according to which the WTO regime should accommodate players with divergent preferences when it comes to regulating their national economy. Consequently, the argument goes, the world trading community should stay idle and desist from trying to persuade China to change. We disagree. By doing nothing, problems will persist, and, more important, it is not true that the GATT/WTO regime was designed to fit every country—it is predicated on the "liberal understanding" that we discussed earlier.

Why, then, did the Protocol of Accession not include terms inspired from this "liberal understanding," which could have been tailor-made for China? In part, we will argue, there was exuberance—the widespread expectation that China would quickly transform into a market economy. In part, it was because there is only so much one can achieve through a Protocol of Accession.

The GATT/WTO regime was not designed with countries like China in mind. The framers of the GATT all shared the quintessential characteristics of market economies. This is what the implicit "liberal understanding" of the GATT amounts to. On the other hand, Protocols of Accession cannot serve as a means to impose choices regarding the organization of a country's national economy. To prove this point, we will investigate the statutory language regarding the objective function of Protocols of Accession as well as their practice. We will explain why, the legitimacy of claims regarding underenforcement of the Chinese Protocol of Accession notwithstanding, transforming China into a market economy through its Protocol of Accession was legally and policy-wise not an option. It is in this context that we will compare China's Protocol of Accession to the WTO with earlier GATT accession protocols for countries with significant state involvement in their trade regime.

Our discussion of the issues up to this point will lead us to conclude that none of the courses of action proposed so far can help the world trading community solve the "China problem." If the world trading community is serious about addressing SOEs and forced TT, then it would be well-advised to change its course of action.

Chapter 6 offers proposals on how to improve WTO rules to deal with China (and other countries with some similar features). We will consider what is actually possible—rather than ideal—in terms of legislative reforms, borrowing from existing examples to which China is most likely to acquiesce rather than devising new rules altogether. Our proposals are counterpoints to the two radically opposed solutions that have been put forward to deal with the existing clashes between the WTO regime and China's economic regime: on the one hand, demands that China radically change its economic regime to conform to Western ideals; on the other, that the WTO stay out of the controversy and that its members accept that they must accommodate China's state-controlled economy. We reject both of these proposals.

We argue that there is a third way that is more promising. In order to retain its principles and yet accommodate China, the WTO needs to translate parts of its implicit liberal understanding into explicit treaty language. We advance specific proposals to this effect that, if adopted, would induce China to change its economic behavior even as it retains its economic regime. In other words, the solution to the problem posed by China to the international trading system is not to demand a change in its economic regime but to induce a change in its economic behavior. In particular, we envisage a situation where China is able to retain its SOEs but where they behave in a market-friendly manner.

We will discuss separately, in chapter 7, the recent pushback against market-oriented reforms that President Xi has masterminded and executed. China today seems a long way from the aspirations to transform into a market economy by 2016 that accompanied its accession process. It is, in our view, an additional reason to strengthen the current multilateral framework so that it acts as a counterbalancing force to constituencies arguing for heavier state (i.e., Chinese Communist Party [CP]) involvement in the economy. If the framework is not strengthened, it may be too late to forestall the CP from instituting even stricter state controls than already exist in China.

Our volume ends with a call for renewed commitment to multilateralism. Unilateral action has increasingly proved to be ineffective. It is time to try the carrot instead of the stick. We do not intend to discuss all the mishaps that the world trading system is currently experiencing, but we would be remiss if we turned a blind eye to the fact that China is a contributing factor.

Globalization has seemed for years to be a fact of life—a new fundamental and permanent foundation for the world economy. But China's accession to the WTO has revealed potential cracks in that foundation. As Bown and Irwin conclude in their excellent article:

> The fall of the Berlin Wall and the collapse of communism opened up Eastern Europe and the former Soviet Union to global markets. The reforms of Deng Xiaoping did the same for China. But only in the unipolar moment, which began in 2001, when China joined the WTO, were open markets truly global. Now, the period of global capitalism may be coming to an end. What many thought was the new normal may turn out to have been a brief aberration. (2019, 136)

If there is still some hope to prove this (increasingly realistic) statement wrong, we argue, it is through a return to the values that helped establish the post–World War II multilateral edifice. Although in this book we concentrate narrowly on the "China problem," it is not a problem that is self-contained. Instead, it has profound implications for the economic ties that bind countries together in a globalized world—or the barriers that thrust them apart. In short, we view this work as a contribution to the much larger project of reinvigorating the multilateral regime.

1

The Rise and Rise of China

(AND WHAT SHOULD BE DONE ABOUT IT)

> But the shore will never look more attractive than it is now. A man
> may stand here and put all the world behind him.
> —HENRY DAVID THOREAU

On November 11, 2001, the day after the WTO membership unanimously
approved the admission of China to the organization as its 143rd member,
Mike Moore, the WTO director-general, said that this day would be remem-
bered as "one of the most significant events of the 21st century for China,
the WTO, and the world."[1] This view was widely shared around the world.

Thoreau's windswept confidence in new vistas captures the euphoria
surrounding China's accession to the WTO to perfection: a widespread
feeling of optimism that the world trading community had turned a corner.
The end of communism in Europe had begun the process of integrating
the Soviet bloc into the world economy. Now the accession of China to
the WTO, the culmination of a long process that had started in the late
1970s to early 1980s with the reform agenda of Chairman Deng Xiaoping,
continued that integration and seemed to justify the exuberance of economic observers.

1. https://www.wto.org/english/news_e/spmm_e/spmm37_e.htm.

In Washington, D.C., in a statement welcoming China into the international trading system, President George W. Bush said that "we look forward to the great benefits we know that greater trade will bring to all our peoples."[2] The European reaction echoed this sentiment:

15. In reality, China's accession can only lock in and deepen market reforms, empowering those in the leadership who support further and faster moves towards economic freedom. The opening up of telecommunications, the internet and satellite services will inevitably expose the Chinese people to information, ideas and debate from around the world. The rule of law will be strengthened as China finds herself obliged to play by the global trade rules. The spillover of economic freedom and respect for commercial law into the political and social sphere will be gradual, but the contribution made by WTO entry will be positive. Many human rights activists and members of the foreign policy community agree that bringing China into the world trading system will be a push in the right direction in these spheres also.[3]

Western exuberance was echoed within China as well. In Beijing, the government-run newspaper, the *People's Daily*, proclaimed in a front-page editorial that "this is a historic moment in China's reform and opening-up and the process of modernisation."[4]

There was, to be sure, reason to celebrate. Blustein cites interviews he conducted with high-ranking trade policy experts that underscore this universal feeling of great achievement. For example, one expert looked confidently at the road ahead: "Their [i.e., China's] policies will align with ours—not over months, but it's going to happen. There was great confidence in that. And if you're confident about the endpoint, it allows you to be more patient about missteps along the way" (2019, 123). As Blustein summed it up excitedly, "With the inclusion of China, a nation of 1.25 billion at the time, the 'W' in the trade body's acronym attained validity that it previously lacked" (4).

The mood was celebratory among the delegations present at the WTO General Council meeting with China. Was it justified? Looking back, one wonders whether the negotiators had thought beyond China's accession

2. President Bush did not, however, make a priority out of China. As Baker (1995) explains in his very insightful account, the pivoting toward Asia began with the Obama administration. It was, in fact, an acknowledgment that China now occupied an important position in world affairs.

3. European Commission 2001.

4. http://news.bbc.co.uk/2/hi/business/1702241.stm.

to the difficult process of actually integrating its vastly different economy into the WTO's system. Their feeling of accomplishment was, perhaps, not sustainable.

The Process of China's Accession to the WTO

China was one of the original contracting parties to the GATT in 1947, but its status was deactivated in 1950 after the formation of the People's Republic. For the next three decades, China had practically no contact with the GATT. The situation changed in the late 1970s and early 1980s, following Deng Xiaoping's economic reforms. Deng first politically transformed China, then liberalized its economy unilaterally through his decision to open the door to China's participation in the Asia-Pacific Economic Cooperation (APEC), and, finally, knocked on the door of the GATT itself.

TRANSFORMATION STARTS AT HOME

Deng's strategy, aptly described by Lardy (2002), Vogel (2011), and Kroeber (2016), consisted of two pillars: reform and opening (*gaige kaifang*). The phrase he and other reformers used to describe *gaige kaifang* was "crossing the river by feeling for the stones." They would embark on this exercise through trial and error, feeling their way partially blind through unfamiliar territory.[5]

Deng was a pragmatist. Vogel notes (2019, 426) that one of his favorite mottoes was Mao's dictum "seek truth from facts." He could be blunt when criticizing China's failures to address basic human needs; he was eager to borrow ideas from others when warranted, if he thought they had something to offer. He did not shy away from bold decisions on sensitive issues as he pursued his goal of gearing the Chinese economy toward efficiency.

Accounts about China's reforms start from Deng's chairmanship. And of course, it is only fair to give Deng the lion's share of credit for China's reform process. Nevertheless, as Gewirtz (2017) correctly underscores, Hua Guofeng and Hu Yaobang, a Deng protégé, had been promoting reform even before Deng acceded to the chairmanship. But Deng co-opted and expanded their originally hesitant reforms. He buried the hatchet with Japan by signing

---

5. In his wonderful account of Deng's economic thinking and how it managed to influence the reform policies of China, Gewirtz (2017) mentions that this term captures the essence of China's reform process.

the 1978 Treaty of Peace and Friendship, and having appeased his neighbors, he turned to the world.[6]

He looked into Singapore's and Japan's experiences in Asia[7] and learned from Western countries as well.[8] He asked for technological assistance, for example, from the Japan External Trade Organization (JETRO), as he did from various Western establishments. Dozens of scientific and technical delegations visited China, and slowly Chinese entrepreneurs and bureaucrats and increasingly even Chinese students visited the West. One thing was clear to him: China could and should work to join the world economy by loosening the iron grip of the state on certain economic sectors.

Farming was the first sector to privatize, as Kroeber explains in his authoritative short history of China's transformation (2016, 27ff.). This was not a paradox. Speaking in 1979, Chen Yun, the head of the China Development Bank, mentioned that of the 900 million people then living in China, 80 percent were farmers, and they were poor.[9] Change had to start there. Originally, the most common privatized firm was a household enterprise (*getihu*), which by law could not comprise more than seven employees. This is, of course, a far cry from the size of today's Chinese behemoths.

In the 1980s, rural reform picked up speed and was implemented by Township and Village Enterprises (TVEs). Unlike SOEs, which originally

6. Vogel (2019) mentions as a corollary of the return to the renewed friendly relations between the two countries (the new era starting probably with the 1962 Liao-Takasaki trade agreement, which was rescinded, only to resurface with the normalization of relations in 1972) the establishment of the China-Japan Working Group for Exchange of Economic Information, which held its first meeting in 1981 and has continued to meet every year with the exception of 2013–14, when tensions between the two countries over the Senkaku/Diaoyu Islands could not be overcome. Vogel also notes that Japan, unlike other countries, was unwilling to impose severe sanctions against China following the Tiananmen tragedy; Japanese prime minister Kaifu was the first to visit China after the event (2019, 355).

7. Vogel brings to light a point that analysts often miss (2019, viiff.). China and Japan have the longest-standing historical contact of any other dyad of countries. They have been interacting for over 1,500 years.

8. We are mindful that the West/non-West divide might be too harsh and risks being perceived as a clumsy shorthand here. We are further aware that state intervention is present in both Western and (and principally so) non-Western countries. We understand the divide to refer to the (relative) presence in Western countries and the (relative) absence in non-Western countries of checks and balances on state intervention in the economy. There are SOEs, for example, in the European Union, but they must observe the EU competition and state aids law. This is not the case with respect to SOEs in non-Western countries. We will use the juxtaposition West/non-West in the rest of this volume as a shortcut to denote the relative degree of state intervention in the economy.

9. Vogel 2011, 429. Chow (2018) provides a succinct survey of agricultural reform in China and what it meant from a social welfare perspective.

were entirely statist entities, TVEs could adjust to market conditions. They were a huge success and arguably provided the impetus for the gradual transformation of SOEs as well.[10]

The next step was the establishment of special economic zones (SEZs), in which trade and investment were liberalized and a strong emphasis on building infrastructure paved the way for the change. Having collected evidence from eighty-odd countries that had implemented SEZs, China embarked on a similar adventure in 1980—the culmination of Deng's experiments. The idea was that SEZs would be given enough flexibility to effectively be regulated by the market. They would be free-trade areas, where goods would be imported without being subjected to tariffs and would be reexported following transformation in the SEZ. Guangdong (Canton), Fujian, Shenzen, and Zuhai were the first four SEZs, and their success was phenomenal. The combination of developing country labor costs and rich country infrastructure led unavoidably to the Chinese export-led growth model.[11] Uninhibited access to the world markets was the next logical frontier.

Deng faced criticism from various directions, the economic success of the experiment notwithstanding. In Guangdong and Fujian especially, to bring transaction costs as low as possible, local officials saw the value of establishing "one-stop shops," where investors and traders alike could procure all the necessary information regarding the transactions they were involved in. It did not take long for the most conservative sections within the party to react, attempting to thwart the opening up of the economy. Guangdong and Fujian officials had to tread very carefully in order to assure foreigners that it was business as usual while not arousing the reactionary forces in Beijing. Was China about to change?[12]

---

10. Vogel 2011, 445ff. In fact, SOEs were allowed to adopt a dual-pricing system. After they had met their obligations (sale of goods at a rate fixed by the government), they could sell their remaining products at market rates. Eventually, the former element was relaxed (at least for some SOEs) and the latter strengthened; see Vogel 2011, 460ff., especially 470ff., where he explains how Deng managed to remove various price controls.

11. Kroeber 2016, 45ff.

12. Chinese officials were facing suspicion abroad. McGregor mentions a meeting between Chen Yuan and Tom Robinson, a well-known political scientist, at the Washington, D.C., Cosmos Club in the 1980s when, faced with "intrusive" questions by the latter regarding the incompatibility of the reform program with the prevailing Chinese communist ideology, Chen Yuan responded, "We are the Communist Party, and we will define what communism is" (2010, 37). At the same time, Chinese officials had to keep a poker face at home and pretend nothing much was changing. Vogel mentions that, in order to avoid enabling SEZs to become agents for widespread change, Chen Yun insisted that they be called special economic zones as opposed to special zones (2011, 402). It was the same Chen Yun who had argued in favor of keeping the number of SEZs to four, for fear that their expansion would turn China into a capitalist entity; see Vogel 2011, 412ff.

According to Vogel, Deng managed to find a compromise (2011, 420ff.). Although fourteen coastal states received authorization to open their own SEZs, Deng reassured the party that there was no risk that China would become a capitalist country. While his decision to move China toward market liberalization was clear for all to see, Deng was equally clear on another issue: institutions had to be built to support the market opening, and the Chinese Communist Party should manage the process.[13] The party would, in his conception, be the pillar upon which an economic transformation could stand. Deng was apparently convinced that the party could continue to operate as it always had, the transformation notwithstanding. Deng scoffed at the broader transformation happening in the Soviet Union at the same time; in his view, Mikhail Gorbachev had abdicated the necessarily central role of the party in his haste to liberalize. Vogel quotes Deng's son relaying the Chinese leader's opinion: "my father thinks Gorbachev is an idiot."[14]

Deng could not understand the lack of perspective in the Russian leader's model to call for transformation of the economy without ensuring the central role of the party first. He presciently predicted that the people would remove Gorbachev, which, more or less, eventually happened. Deng wanted to avoid a similar fate. Preserving the role of the party was a priority. We cannot underscore this point enough. It is, in our view, the source of the grievances that many WTO incumbents have raised in recent years against China, and we will be returning to it in various places in this volume.[15] Martin and Bach (1998) explain that China initiated important reforms in the realm of state trading because of the anticipated accession to the WTO. Sixteen foreign trade corporations (FTCs) had practically monopolized import and export trade before Chairman Deng's reforms. Their number increased substantially as a result of reforms (with exceptions in some farm goods and oil), eventually eliminated exchange rate distortions, and allowed prices to become a decisive factor in resource allocation.

13. Vogel (2011) provides a thorough development of this point in his unparalleled account of Deng's policies.

14. Vogel 2011, 423. The appreciation for the role of the party is not the only thing Chairman Deng did not share with the Soviet and eventually Russian leadership. He was no fan of the "shock therapy" practiced in Russia either and this without the benefit of hindsight. Goldman underscores that, unlike Russia, China was crossing the stream "one stone at a time" and did not rush into massive privatization of formerly state-owned property (2003, 66ff.). In fact, the very existence of SOEs in massive scale, a hybrid form, is proof of this deliberate choice.

15. Vogel cites a memo by Tip O'Neill, then Speaker of the House, stating that "Deng had absolutely no doubt that, at least for China, the separation of powers was a terribly inefficient way to run a country, something China should avoid" (2011, 342).

Deng's commitment to push on with reforms impressed many outsiders. Vogel explains in detail how Robert McNamara, then president of the World Bank, overruled even the pleas of his country of origin, the United States, and accelerated the process of China's entry into the Bank (2011, 456ff.). In an unprecedented move, he assembled a large group of China specialists who traveled to China on a three-month study tour aiming to acclimatize Bank officials to the idiosyncratic elements of the Chinese economy.[16] This was a firm signal that the international community was embracing the reforms. It seemed only a matter of time before China would rejoin the GATT. But there was a necessary intermediate stage: China had to integrate itself into an important regional trading coalition, the APEC. This was an important proving ground for a newly liberalized China, and, as it turned out, its participation in APEC was not without friction.

We should keep in mind that the reform agenda came at a cost. Deng might have paid less of a price in terms of political capital than a democratically elected president would have, but, undeniably, there was a cost. Zhang, Zhang, and Wan (1998) estimated that the cost of market-opening measures as a result of accession to the WTO in the short run would be substantial in terms of job loss. However, they estimated the medium-run benefits at around $35 billion. Reality proved that they erred on the pessimistic side. China has won more.

LOVE THY NEIGHBOR

APEC was launched in Seoul in 1989, and China had not been invited to join along with the original members. As Clintworth (1995) correctly observes, however, China was too important to be ignored. It received an invitation in 1990 and joined one year later.

---

16. It was a two-way street. China sent people abroad to study how reform occurred in various Eastern European countries. Some were Chinese officials, and some were private citizens, as Hvistendahl (2020) documents. China also invited experts ranging from Janos Kornai, a Hungarian reform-minded economist, to Nobel prize winners Kenneth Arrow, Lawrence Klein, and Milton Friedman to spend time in China and educate the bureaucracy on the feasibility of reforms and the most appropriate way forward. Gewirtz (2017) makes a persuasive case that people like Kornai exerted most of the influence on the thinking of Chinese bureaucrats, not superstar economists like Friedman. Chinese, in this line of argument, felt they had more in common with economists who participated in transforming former communist economists than with experts imbued with Western liberalism. The apex of contacts was the Bashan Conference (1985), a six-day international symposium on macroeconomic management, where various Chinese and foreign economists discussed the ideal relationship between the state and the market.

At the time, China's relations with the GATT were in limbo. China had already made one request to rejoin the multilateral trading system, in 1986. That year, Arthur Dunkel, who was the head of the GATT, visited China and had a series of talks with the Chinese bureaucracy about what needed to be done—the prerequisites, so to speak, for China to rejoin the GATT. But these initial discussions did not yield much.

Dunkel's visit to China followed a successful trip by Åke Lindén, his Swedish advisor and legal counsel to the GATT, who had been to China in 1984 to start paving the way toward accession. In preparation for its accession to the GATT, China adopted important legislative initiatives such as revised customs regulation and tariffs. The Chinese Ministry of Foreign Economic Relations and Trade (MOFERT), already established in 1982, agreed to give up its monopoly on foreign trade in 1984 and to allow trade to occur through licensed trading agencies, the precursors to the opening of trading rights. Furthermore, two GATT study groups were established, one in Shanghai and the other in Beijing, with the purpose of acclimatizing Chinese officials and the business community to the upcoming reality. China was entering a new phase, and the GATT was part of the openness strategy, which also included membership in the International Monetary Fund (IMF) and the World Bank. It is accession to the GATT, though, that was expected to have the biggest impact on the Chinese economy. When Zhao Ziyang, general secretary of the party (1987–89), met Dunkel in 1986, he tried to explain to him how the concept of a "planned commodity economy," introduced in 1984, could fit with the market-oriented GATT.[17]

The process of accession almost immediately stalled and was, in effect, frozen completely after the tragic events in Tiananmen in 1989. It took three years for negotiations to restart, even unofficially. China joined the APEC in 1992, at a time when it was still negotiating accession into the GATT/WTO.

Drysdale and Hardwick (2018) underscore the two major benefits that China derived from its participation in the APEC. First, APEC participation led China to adopt its first serious trade liberalization measures. The APEC served, in a way, as the antechamber for China's eventual entry into the multilateral trade club. Second, at that time, and because of the events in Tiananmen, China's leaders could not have taken it for granted that they would enter the GATT stage without facing the objections of some GATT members. China had to build alliances and persuade countries that they would become good GATT citizens. Through its participation in the APEC,

17. Jakobson and Oksenberg (1990, 86ff., 147ff.) discuss these issues in great detail.

China built such momentum. Its neighbors, the other APEC members, would soon be supportive of its request to join the GATT.

NEXT STOP, GENEVA: CHINA'S GATT STATUS

After seeking and obtaining observer status at the GATT, China informed the director-general, in a communication dated July 10, 1986, that it had decided to "seek the resumption of its status as a contracting party to GATT" and was prepared "to enter into negotiations with GATT contracting parties" toward this end. Chinese leaders saw an opportunity to take advantage of trade liberalization among GATT members, but they needed GATT status to do it. Their request deserves to be quoted at length:

> China is currently pursuing the basic national policy of opening to the outside world and revitalizing the domestic economy and will adhere to it in the years to come. It is the firm belief of the Government of the People's Republic of China that the ongoing process of economic reform will contribute to the expansion of economic and trade relations with the contracting parties, and that the participation of China as a contracting party in the work of the GATT will further the objectives of the General Agreement. China is a developing country. The Chinese Government expects to receive treatment equivalent to that accorded to other developing contracting parties. China is prepared to enter into negotiations with GATT contracting parties on the resumption of its status as a contracting party. To this end, it will provide information on its economic system and foreign trade regime. I shall feel obliged if you could transmit this request of the Government of the People's Republic of China to the contracting parties for their consideration.[18]

China's declaration left no one in doubt that it wanted to reenter the world trading regime as a developing country. By that time (1986), a few developed nations had put into place Generalized System of Preferences (GSP) schemes, whereby they provided developing countries with tariff preferences. China signaled that it did not want to miss out on this opportunity. On the other hand, the emphasis on reentry (which may have suggested that it wanted to take back its seat at the GATT without offering trade concessions) was, of course, inconsequential, since China had, as the quoted passage makes clear, agreed to start negotiations anew.

18. GATT Doc. L/6017, July 14, 1986.

The Chinese hierarchy further underscored that it was fully prepared to join the WTO thanks to the market-opening initiatives that it had undertaken. They were, it seems, implying that they accepted that pre-Deng China was not fit for this purpose. This is an important admission, and we will return to this issue later when discussing the implicit liberal understanding of the GATT.

Accession to the GATT was the big prize that China was after. If it had succeeded, it would have sent the world community a strong signal that, in the words of Liang (2002), China was a "responsible stakeholder."

JOINING THE WTO

In March 1987, the GATT established a Working Party on China's Status as a Contracting Party, which met on twenty occasions between 1987 and 1995 without reaching an agreement. In the meantime, the GATT had given way to the WTO, the successor world trading organization. China dutifully modified its request for an application for accession to the WTO, and the GATT Working Party was converted into a Working Party on the Accession of China to the WTO. It met eighteen more times between 1995 and 2001, when it finally issued a report including a Draft Protocol on the Accession of the People's Republic of China. The protocol outlined the terms and conditions for the accession of China to the WTO. The committee had given China the thumbs-up.

Halverson (2004), Liang (2002), and various contributors to the work by Cass, Williams, and Barker (2013) provide a very detailed account of China's negotiation process. It was not a smooth ride by any stretch of the imagination. Liang, in particular, discusses the issues involved, the ups and downs during the process, and the role the Chinese hierarchy was called to play, as well as various anecdotes concerning bilateral requests and offers between China and its major trading partners that influenced the eventual outcome. Drama persisted until the very last stages of the negotiations, as Gertler (2003) explains in his detailed account.

The report of the Working Party makes it clear that the main factor behind the protracted negotiations was the special nature of China's foreign trade regime. The China regime, when compared to those prevailing in most of the WTO members, was idiosyncratic and, for incumbents, a major cause for concern. In an introductory statement to the report, the representative from China attempted to downplay these idiosyncrasies, insisting on the primacy of the market reforms already undertaken:

Since 1979, China had been progressively reforming its economic system, with the objective of establishing and improving the socialist market economy. . . . State-owned enterprises had been reformed by a clear definition of property rights and responsibilities, a separation of government from enterprise, and scientific management. A modern enterprise system had been created for the state-owned sector, and the latter was gradually getting on the track of growth through independent operation, responsible for its own profits and losses. A nation-wide unified and open market system had been developed. An improved macroeconomic regulatory system used indirect means and market forces to play a central role in economic management and the allocation of resources. . . . Further liberalization of pricing policy had resulted in the majority of consumer and producer products being subject to market prices. The market now played a much more significant role in boosting supply and meeting demand.[19]

Other members of the Working Party were not necessarily buying this explanation. In a review of China's situation, they expressed numerous concerns about specific aspects of its foreign trade regime, including:

- the application of the principle of non-discrimination in relation to foreign individuals and enterprises (whether wholly or partly foreign funded);[20]
- the continuing governmental influence and guidance of the decisions and activities of [state-owned and state-invested] enterprises relating to the purchase and sale of goods and services . . . [and] about laws, regulations and measures in China affecting the transfer of technology, in particular in the context of investment decisions;[21]
- the special features of China's economy, in its present state of reform, [which] still created the potential for a certain level of trade distorting subsidization;[22] and
- the lack of transparency regarding the laws, regulations and other measures that applied to matters covered in the WTO Agreement and the Draft Protocol.[23]

19. WTO Doc. WT/ACC/CHN/49 at §6.
20. WTO Doc. WT/ACC/CHN/49 at §15.
21. WTO Doc. WT/ACC/CHN/49 at §§44 and 48.
22. WTO Doc. WT/ACC/CHN/49 at §171.
23. WTO Doc. WT/ACC/CHN/49 at §324.

At the time that China entered the WTO, therefore, there was a clear aware-ness that China needed to continue to further its reforms. But, crucially, the vast majority of observers believed that accession to the WTO would, in itself, accelerate these reforms.

China, on the other hand, managed to get its priorities right. It under-stood that although all incumbent members had to agree to its accession to the WTO, the road to Geneva would be greatly facilitated if it could first reach an agreement with the United States, and it began to work toward that end. Negotiations between the two countries culminated with the signing of the U.S.-China Bilateral Agreement: many of the items featured in the Chinese WTO Protocol of Accession had already found their way into this bilateral contract. The two legal documents are not coextensive, however. Since other members added requests, the Protocol of Accession encom-passed the agreement reached bilaterally with the United States as well as a few more items.

The signing of the U.S.-China Bilateral Agreement was not a foregone conclusion. Following Premier Zhu Rongji's visit to the United States in January 1999, and his meetings with President Clinton and Federal Reserve Chairman Alan Greenspan, a deal seemed possible in April 1999, but, ulti-mately, it proved elusive. Blustein notes that it took six days and nights of acrimonious negotiations in Beijing to clinch the definitive deal between the United States and China (2019, 15ff.). Although it is beyond the pur-pose and scope of this volume to provide a detailed, analytical account of the U.S.-China agreement, some of its features are worth recounting since they highlight the dominant thinking at that time in the world economic community: that China was on its way to becoming a market economy and that there was no turning back. A brief perusal of the official summary of the agreement[24] leaves us in no doubt that the U.S. focus was on obtaining concessions in specific areas. There was undoubtedly discussion on issues of a more "systemic" nature as well.

One wonders, however, whether the signatories should have been as optimistic that the agreement was as far-reaching as they thought it to be. Regarding the treatment of SOEs, for example, the U.S. officials declared in an almost triumphant mood in the official summary: "We have clarified the status of state-owned and state-invested enterprises under the WTO

24. https://clintonwhitehouse4.archives.gov/WH/New/WTO-Conf-1999/factsheets/fs-006.html. Bhala (2000) provides a very comprehensive account of the agreement. Compare Drezner 2000.

Agreement on Subsidies and Countervailing Measures. This will help ensure that we can effectively apply our trade law to these enterprises when it is appropriate to do so." Charlene Barshefsky, the United States Trade Representative (USTR) at that time, amplified this statement during the hearing before the House Ways and Means Committee organized to discuss the bilateral agreement. In her response to a question posed by Representative Phil Crane of Illinois, she stated: "We have firm commitments from China with respect to the manner in which State trading enterprises will conduct their business, that is to say on commercial terms. But we have expanded the definition of State enterprise to include not only State trading enterprises, not only State-owned enterprises, but most importantly, State-invested enterprises."[25] Barshefsky was equally sanguine regarding the other major issue we discuss in this volume, forced transfer of technology. The hearing before the House Ways and Means Committee organized to discuss the bilateral agreement provides clear evidence to this effect. In response to questions asked by Representative Charles Rangel of New York, she said: "We do not want [the] Chinese to be able to have a system that drains jobs or technology from the United States as a condition of doing business in China or as a condition of importing into China or as a condition of investing in China if companies want to invest. So, forced technology transfer will be prohibited."[26] Barshefsky was, in effect, saying that China would agree to ban transfer of technology. But Barshefsky was speaking about actions by the Chinese state, not about the actions of private business. Little did she know, at the time at least, that the distinction between public and private was not siloed as far as China was concerned; there was in fact osmosis between the two, as requests by the U.S. private sector subsequently made clear.[27]

The belief that China was genuinely changing may well have guided this and similar reactions. Indeed, various members of Congress underscored China's changing nature during that hearing, none more clearly than Representative James P. Moran of Virginia:

> There is danger in viewing China through the snapshot of today's headlines. To look only at China in the present is to see a nation beset with

25. Hearing before the Committee on Ways and Means, HR, 106th Cong., 2nd Sess., February 16, 2000, Serial 106–78 (Washington, DC: US GPO).

26. Hearing before the Committee on Ways and Means, HR, 106th Cong., 2nd Sess., February 16, 2000, Serial 106–78 (Washington, DC: US GPO).

27. Blustein notes that Barshefsky, now in private practice, has been unapologetic about the deal ever since, claiming "we were as comprehensive as we could have been at the time" (2019, 60).

human rights abuses, municipal corruption and inefficiency. To look at China over the span of twenty years or even five years is to see a dynamic nation moving inexorably toward a market-oriented economy and genuine reform. With economic change will come prosperity, and with this broader prosperity the people will demand political change.[28]

The participants at the hearing were almost unanimous in sharing this belief. The only dissident was Chuck Mack, a leader of the International Brotherhood of Teamsters, who underscored China's poor human rights record and the potential for job losses in the United States as a result of the Chinese accession to the WTO.[29] His voice, nevertheless, was not enough to spoil the celebrations.

The Chinese leadership prompted this type of thinking. Premier Rongji made all the right noises in 1999 when he visited the United States, reassuring his audiences that China would implement necessary market reforms within five years.[30] Interaction between Western economists and the Chinese leadership, detailed by Gewirtz (2017), added to the reigning optimism that China was indeed changing. Meanwhile, the U.S.-China Business Council, a group consisting of more than 200 multinationals with operations in China, and the U.S.-China Chamber of Commerce, with over 250 members from a variety of industries, spearheaded the business rapprochement with China, publishing annual surveys about China's practices and raising awareness about the opportunities for, as well as the challenges of, foreign investment in the Chinese market.

The U.S.-China agreement was naturally about economic and trade issues and did not extend to other areas of concern of the U.S. administration and American society, such as the protection of human rights. Charlene Barshefsky left no one in doubt in this respect, when during the hearing before the House Ways and Means Committee mentioned earlier she stated:

> Of course this agreement is not a human rights policy in and of itself. Change in China will only come through a combination of internal pressure and external validation of those who struggle for political voice. . . . But this agreement does represent a remarkable victory for economic reformers within China and for our own efforts to give the Chinese

28. Hearing before the Committee on Ways and Means, HR, 106th Cong., 2nd Sess., February 16, 2000, Serial 106–78 (Washington, DC: US GPO).

29. Hearing before the Committee on Ways and Means, HR, 106th Cong., 2nd Sess., February 16, 2000, Serial 106–78 (Washington, DC: US GPO).

30. Blustein 2019, 13ff.

people more control over their own destiny and more ability to meet and exchange ideas with the outside world. And thus, a number of leading Chinese and Hong Kong advocates of democracy endorse WTO membership . . . not only for its economic value, but as a foundation for broader future reform.[31]

Her statement demonstrates, nevertheless, that, in the prevailing thinking at the time, economic reform would ultimately lead to political reform as well. This optimism has been disproven so far, as we will see in subsequent chapters, even though other means were employed to this effect. President Clinton spearheaded, along with his Chinese counterpart, the "rule of law initiative," aiming to promote cooperation in the field of law. The noble intentions notwithstanding, this initiative has not led to anything concrete.[32] In the rush to profit from an open-market future in China, human rights took a distant second place.

The U.S.-China agreement was a milestone, even though, as Gertler (2003) points out, a few hurdles on the way to accession still remained. China managed to conclude agreements with the European Union, Japan, and the other WTO incumbents and joined the WTO as its 143rd member. All but one WTO member welcomed China into the multilateral trading system. The one exception was El Salvador, which decided to invoke the non-application clause for a few years, as we will explain later. There is no evidence of coordination across incumbents regarding their wish list of requests from China. Suffice it to say for now that China was not put under collective pressure. Instead, it faced a series of bilateral negotiations, which, upon successful completion, opened the WTO door.[33] If economic reform

31. Hearing before the Committee on Ways and Means, HR, 106th Cong., 2nd Sess., February 16, 2000, Serial 106–78 (Washington, DC: US GPO).

32. Gewirtz (2003), a Yale Law School professor on leave at the U.S. Department of State from 1997 to 1998 to work on an official U.S.-China initiative to promote the rule of law, has honestly admitted as much.

33. There was no serious WTO-wide discussion on the effects of the Chinese regime on the WTO system. The working assumption was that change, and for some shift-paradigmatic change, was about to happen. No one entertained or wanted to entertain the thought that China might stop reforms or even roll them back. There were some critical and/or skeptical voices to be sure, usually in academia. Lighthizer (2010), the current USTR, has claimed that many experts did not sufficiently account for China's commitment to mercantilism. Steinberg (1997), for example, had argued that China's accession was likely to weaken the WTO system. Ostry (2003) questioned whether China could ever meet the elaborate WTO transparency obligations, whereas Herzstein (1999), a former undersecretary for international trade in the Department of Commerce during the Carter administration, claimed that eliminating tariffs would not amount to much. According

was to lead to political reform, it would definitely not result from a coordinated strategy among other WTO members. It would instead depend on economic and social pressures within China—and Chinese assurances that it would happen.

The WTO Has Been Good to China

Fast-forward to today. China's achievements since it joined the WTO have been truly remarkable. In 2001, it was the sixth largest exporter of goods in the world (fourth, if the European Union [EU] is counted as one unit). By 2009, it became the world's largest exporter, surpassing the EU bloc as of 2014. According to World Bank data, China's exports increased by almost 30 percent every year between 2001 (the year of its accession to the WTO) and 2006.[34]

China's rapid export growth has been accompanied by equally meteoric growth in production and income. According to IMF data, in 2001 China's GDP amounted to barely 13 percent of the GDP of the United States. By 2014, this figure surpassed 60 percent, a threshold that, according to Campbell and Sullivan (2019), no U.S. adversary had ever reached. At the same time, China's per capita income (measured in current international dollars) moved rapidly up the ranks, from the level of Sudan in 2001 to the level of Brazil in 2016.[35]

And China is still growing, of course. In the words of Nicholas Lardy, a well-known China expert:

> The world has never seen anything like the rise of China from an impoverished and politically unsteady country in 1978 to a confident and ambitious superpower 40 years later. Its economy has grown faster for longer than any other country on record, persistently defying widespread warnings of a drastic slowdown that was supposedly to occur at any moment. (2019, 1)[36]

---

to him, China's domestic market was quite statist, and unless statism had been dealt a blow, the market would never be open to foreign goods, services, and investment.

34. https://data.worldbank.org/indicator/NE.EXP.GNFS.CD?locations=CN. And this is not all, even though these numbers are quite breathtaking. The World Bank mentions that China can double its GDP simply by catching up to OECD countries in its total factor productivity (TFP). In addition, it remains quite distant from the global technology frontier and thus the potential for growth should not be underestimated (2019b, ivff.).

35. https://www.imf.org/external/pubs/ft/weo/2019/02/weodata/index.aspx.

36. The World Bank reclassified China from a lower- to upper-middle-income country in 2011.

China's pace of growth is equally astounding when put into historical perspective. Allison offers an appropriate illustration to this effect:

> If the US were a corporation, it would have accounted for 50% of the global economic market in the years immediately after World War II. By 1980, that had declined to 22 percent. Three decades of double-digit Chinese growth has reduced that US share to 16 percent today. If current trends continue, the US share of global economic output will decline further over the next three decades to 11 percent. Over the same period, China's share of the global economy will have soared from 2 percent in 1980 to 18 percent in 1986, well on its way to 30 percent in 2040. (2017, xvi–xvii)

China has become the manufacturing powerhouse of the world in no time. When Deng visited Japan in 1978, Vogel notes, China had not even started building its first high-speed railway (2019, 340). By 2015, it would have more than 12,000 miles of high-speed railway—more than the rest of the world combined. Allison quotes Kevin Rudd, the former Australian prime minister and a China expert, describing the Chinese explosion as "the English Industrial Revolution and the global information revolution combusting simultaneously and compressed into not 300 years, but 30" (2017, 13).

Accession to the WTO has certainly been a decisive factor in this success story. Brandt et al. (2017) and Feng, Li, and Swenson (2017) find strong evidence that WTO accession improved the performance of Chinese manufacturing firms. Wu (2018) cites evidence that Chinese exports grew from $266 billion in 2001 to $2.3 trillion in 2015.[37] China could and did profit from uninhibited access to 163 foreign markets and was now in a position to sign preferential deals with some of them. The years of uncertainty surrounding its market access, especially to the United States, were long gone.

Finally, Chow (2018) cites econometric evidence that opening the door of the WTO added 1 percentage point to China's GDP growth during the first years following its accession. China had, to an extent, specialized in areas where it had comparative advantage and further profited from the enhanced competition that it was now facing through its participation in international markets.

---

37. Vogel, who, like many others, agrees, provides additional arguments in support of these figures (2019, 370ff.).

The Positives and Negatives of China's Growth

The rapid emergence of China as the world's largest producer and exporter of goods (primarily manufactured goods) has been generally welcomed by consumers and its trading partners around the world. At the same time, it was bound to create tensions with trading partners and the trading system as a whole, due to China's unusual domestic economic system—which might seem to some to give it unfair advantages.

On the one hand, China's growth is welcomed, even celebrated, since China's growth is good news for the rest of the world. In fact, some China experts, including Lardy (2019), have been torn between two opposite ideas. Should the world community aim to tame China (and thus imperil world growth) or let China's growth continue unobstructed and unregulated (and then be prepared to deal with the resulting adverse effects in various economies)? McMahon (2018) is torn as well, pointing to the growth weakness of both the European Union and the United States but also to the fact that China's growth, like Japan's in the early 1980s, may be unsustainable because it is built on massive debt. The implication is that growth should not be imperiled, but the question of what to do about the potential negative consequences of Chinese economic leadership remains unanswered. Even though there are good reasons suggesting that the growth rates of the last years are not sustainable in the short to medium run,[38] tensions between China and its trading partners emerged quickly and remain. China's growth cannot continue at the same pace without it eventually threatening the current hegemons.

Growth, yes, but not too much of it, in other words. What we care about in this volume, though, are the "growth ingredients." Those who feel dubious about China's success complain about its unorthodox methods. To them, the Chinese path to growth over the past half century is unwelcome.

Tensions between China and its major trading partners have been especially acute for three distinct reasons. First, China has posed a challenge to the functioning of the trading system because of the special nature of its

---

38. Lardy cites the World Bank estimates for growth in China, of 6.3 and 6.2 percent, respectively, for 2019 and 2020 (2019, 2). Cooper (2018) echoes these numbers, citing the Chinese government's predictions for a "new normal" annual growth of around 7 percent, as opposed to 9–10 percent in the previous years: the five-year plan (2016–20) forecasts growth of 6.5 percent. These numbers are, of course, not at all a "hard landing," as Perkins (2018) observes. The IMF reports similar figures, predicting an additional slowdown by 2023, when growth should be around 5.5 percent. All Western economies would be happy with half this growth, of course.

domestic economic system, which the country's ruling Communist Party describes as a "socialist market economy" but others (mainly, but not only, outside China) call "state capitalism." The hope that China would relax state control of its economy as a result of its accession to the WTO has remained unfulfilled. The WTO is not a safe, where the changes necessary for members to operate as liberal market economies are "locked in" and must be observed.

The special nature of China's economic system along with the country's sheer size explain why the negotiations for China's accession to the GATT/WTO were long and difficult.[39] They explain even better why problems have arisen following the conclusion of the accession negotiations, precisely because of the inability of the WTO to dictate changes in the manner in which the Chinese domestic economy should be run. We should add here that, as Patterson has astutely argued (2018, 2ff.), the success that China has enjoyed in the WTO has strengthened the belief of the Chinese people in the party and has consolidated and legitimized its presence in the country.

The GATT/WTO regime was able to accommodate centrally planned economies, but, as we will see in chapter 3, these economies have had to walk on a tightrope. Their size and de facto irrelevance in international trade were the excuse incumbents needed to avoid resolving potential problems. Because of its size, China is a different story. The problems it poses cannot wait for a solution any longer. The longer the wait, the more difficult it will be to find a solution.

The second source of tension—appearing soon after China had joined the WTO—was that the world economy was hit by a global financial crisis and a recession, which affected China very differently than it did its main trading partners. During 2008 and 2009, the EU, Japan, and the United States suffered a cumulative GDP contraction of, respectively, 3.5, 6.5, and 2.6 percent, while China's GDP expanded by 18.8 percent. And though many believe that China saved the world from a much deeper recession by expanding its internal demand, others see this period as a turning point, when China decisively overtook some advanced economies in terms of production and economic power.[40]

39. Kroeber quotes Premier Wen Jiabao stating the following about the impact that China's size has on issues that it (and the world community) has been confronting: "When you multiply any problem by China's population, it is a very big problem. But when you divide it by China's population, it becomes very small" (2016, 21).

40. In November 2008 the Chinese government did introduce a stimulus package worth 4 trillion renminbi, the equivalent of 14 percent of the Chinese GDP at the time.

The third reason for tension between China and its trading partners is the state of the world trading system itself and its difficulty in adapting to the new economic and political reality. This point requires some elaboration, as it involves both the changing identity of the membership of the global trade community (especially its leaders) and an evolving trade agenda, which, with the passage of time, becomes increasingly difficult to manage. And to make matters even more complicated, there is an additional aggravating factor resulting from the combination of changing membership and an altered agenda, as a steadily more heterogeneous membership is called on to address hard-to-handle behind-the-border trade impediments.

At its creation in 1947, the GATT had 23 signatories, but two clearly dominated the system: the United States and the United Kingdom. These two countries were the main players until the Kennedy Round in 1964–67. The European Union (then the European Economic Community) succeeded the United Kingdom and provided the second important pillar next to the United States, the economic prowess of which ensured that its leadership would continue unabated.

The transatlantic partners were, of course, in agreement as to their understanding of trade liberalization. Over the years, the number and heterogeneity of signatories expanded a great deal, but the system remained dominated by a small group of like-minded Western countries, the "Quad"—an informal group comprising the trade ministers of Canada, the European Union, Japan, and the United States, which met at least once a year starting in 1982.

Canada was an original GATT signatory, and Japan, as we will see in more detail, had by that time become practically "Westernized." As a result, the Quad was a rather homogeneous construct enjoying substantial geographic representativeness, and it steered the world trading regime to the successful negotiation of the Tokyo and Uruguay rounds. These two rounds completed the tariff agenda by reducing tariffs to near insignificance and laid the groundwork for the negotiation of non-tariff barriers (NTBs).

Soon after the WTO was established in 1995, and following the rise of new emerging economies, things changed. The "old Quad" did not comprise the most representative players anymore, and it did not include the most important either. It was soon replaced by a "new Quad," now comprising the European Union, the United States, Brazil, and India. The latter two were the leading developing countries in the WTO, and developing countries had by that time vastly outnumbered their developed counterparts in the multilateral trade institution. In part due to the unprecedented trade liberalization generated by the new agreements, they had joined the growth bandwagon as well.

There was a downside. The "new Quad" was not the "old Quad" in terms of homogeneity. The "new Quad" could not function as the antechamber for whatever would be submitted to the table of negotiations where the whole WTO membership would be convened. Neither could it harmoniously decide the emerging trade agenda.

Therefore, when China joined the WTO it became part of an institution that was led by a group of countries that did not see eye to eye on the key issues regarding further trade integration. China also joined the leaders' group on some occasions (even though, formally, it never became a member of the "new Quad") and has been increasingly central to all important WTO questions ever since.

Heterogeneity at the helm did not help in addressing the problems posed by China following its accession to the WTO. It is not accidental that the China issues had been discussed in the relatively homogeneous Trilateral (composed of the EU, Japan, and the United States) and not in the substantially more heterogeneous "new Quad" (where India and Brazil had replaced Canada and Japan at the table with the EU and the United States).

Moving to the evolving trade agenda, it is appropriate to underscore that the GATT was remarkably successful in eliminating import and export quotas and reducing tariffs. This success has also been its curse. Having lowered at-the-border measures, the GATT turned to behind-the-border measures (such as government procurement, subsidies, and technical regulations), which now became much more visible forms of trade barriers than they had been before. The GATT made some headway in taming behind-the-border measures, but their nature made them ill-suited to substantial progress among a large and increasingly heterogeneous group of countries.

Immediately before China's accession, the WTO had scored some important victories with the successful conclusion of the so-called extended negotiations under the General Agreement on Trade in Services (GATS; telecoms, financial services) and the Information Technology Agreements (ITA I and II). Both the Agreement on Trade Facilitation (ATF) and the Aid for Trade initiative were also crucial, highlighting the role of the WTO in decreasing trading costs for developing countries. The WTO also managed to contain protectionism following the 2008 financial crisis. Bown (2011) thoroughly researched the worldwide reaction to the great recession and concluded that it did not lead to massive recourse to protectionism. In his account, respect for the WTO legal regime was an important contributing factor to this outcome.[41] And this is where the buck stopped.

Unlike tariffs, NTBs (behind-the-border measures)[42] cannot be gradually reduced, for very often they are necessary to address market failures. Regulation must be tolerated because it is often indeed warranted. Furthermore, what is warranted continues to be largely a matter of national preference. The only integrating discipline on which all WTO members could agree was nondiscrimination. But nondiscrimination does not guarantee market access, since the latter is conditional upon satisfying requirements unilaterally set by the importing members.

The WTO has, to be sure, carried on with its efforts along these lines. It has continued to confront behind-the-border measures, but the further increase in the number (currently 164) and heterogeneity of members and the fact that the power to set the agenda has shifted from the old (homogeneous) Quad to the new (heterogeneous) Quad have proved formidable difficulties. "Deep integration" (e.g., mutual recognition or harmonization of national regulations) is out of the question for such a heterogeneous group of countries, which have divergent preferences and capabilities. Unfortunately, if deep integration is absent, it is hard to go beyond "lip service" when dealing with regulation-imbued NTBs.

More than forty years after the end of the Tokyo Round, the first round that placed NTBs on the multilateral agenda, the world community is still beating around the bush on this issue. The difference between then and now is that during the Tokyo Round a "club approach" was favored: willing participants would move ahead, even if some chose to stay behind. The Uruguay Round marked the return to an "everyone through the door" approach—all signatories were required, by adhering to the various WTO agreements, to adopt the same agenda regarding NTBs. Leaders at Uruguay described their endeavor as a "single undertaking." But progress thus far has been anything but single-minded.

In conclusion, when the trade agenda focused essentially on reducing the level of customs duties, it could have afforded having a heterogeneous

41. In later research, Bown (2018) confirms that there is no evidence that the G20 (Group of 20) economies made significant changes to their applied import tariffs during the period between 2010 and 2016. However, he also finds a modest increase in import protection arising through changes in how countries have applied temporary trade barriers of antidumping, countervailing duties, and safeguards.

42. We use the terms NTBs (non-tariff barriers) and behind-the-border barriers as synonyms.

leadership, though it certainly benefited from having a homogeneous leadership (a hegemon). Alas, now that the trade agenda has moved to addressing NTBs, it does not have this luxury anymore.

China thus entered the world trade community at a moment of regulatory stalemate. Without clear progress on the question of NTBs, concerns about SOEs and TT could never be effectively addressed.

Furthermore, the WTO has failed to meaningfully advance the trade agenda with new liberalization or trade rules.[43] Ever since the Kennedy Round, the multilateral system successfully concluded comprehensive trade rounds every ten years or so. This was not the case after the Uruguay Round, which took eight years to complete—longer than any round prior to it. The risk of total failure appeared a few times, most prominently following the unsuccessful Brussels Ministerial Conference in 2001. Several new agreements were concluded, and the world trading regime added disciplines in trade in services and trade-related intellectual property rights, areas that had never been discussed multilaterally before and where the WTO was institutionally "innocent," to say the least. And yet, only six years later, it embarked on a new comprehensive round—the Doha Round—focusing on an issue where, yet again, the WTO had limited expertise. Complicating things further, the newly acceded China was a full-fledged member this time. The writing was probably on the wall regarding the eventual failure of the whole enterprise, but no one wanted to take a dispassionate stance at that moment.

One wonders whether the initiation of the Doha Round, the undeniable interest in the issue notwithstanding, occurred at the most appropriate moment, or even whether it had been carefully planned. Instead of wrapping up the unfinished business of the Uruguay Round and focusing on serious implementation of whatever had been concluded, the trading partners chose to move on to something different. It embarked on a new attempt to summit the Everest of global trade instead of further exploring a route it had already marked out. It did so, furthermore, when it was clear that there was no hegemon behind the makeshift, improvised Doha agenda. The cherry on top was the Doha participants' insistence on confronting problems that

---

43. There are, of course, dozens of ongoing negotiations taking place under the aegis of the WTO, their subject matter ranging from non-agricultural market access to digital trade. A brief perusal of the WTO's website provides ample evidence to this effect. Nothing concrete has come out of these initiatives, though, other than two tariff-reducing agreements (ITA I and II and the Agreement on Trade Facilitation).

the WTO has neither the expertise nor the mandate to solve—namely, the wider development agenda.

The ongoing malaise surrounding the Doha Round should, consequently, not come as a surprise. It has not helped the WTO: indeed, it has actually reduced its policy relevance. A weaker WTO was emerging only a few years after it had reached its apex with the conclusion of the Uruguay Round.

The accession of China to the WTO coincided with the initiation of the Doha Round. Resources were invested in the Doha Round instead of into the implementation of the terms agreed for China's accession (an unprecedented event of monumental proportions) or the faithful implementation of the still recently concluded Uruguay Round. Against this backdrop, the mounting challenges that China represented for the world trading system culminated in a crisis, with no institutional assessment of the situation by the WTO. There is no WTO response, so far, to the question "What is the problem with China?" In fact, there is no WTO discussion on this subject at all.

And here we are now, facing a deadlock in the Doha Round, a moribund round for a few years already, and a worldwide uneasiness regarding China's participation in the WTO as well. In short, the world trading regime is struggling to cope with its new agenda. The impossibility of addressing NTBs effectively and the absence of leadership thanks to the heterogeneity of the current WTO membership help explain why this has been the case. China entered the WTO, contributed to its heterogeneity, destabilized the quest for leadership (because of its size, which cannot be overlooked), and made it even more difficult for the already shaky WTO to deliver on its agenda.

To be fair, other events did not help either. In July 2008, the WTO membership had managed to put together a package (the "July package") that, if adopted, could have changed the course of events. Alas, it was not to be. The world trading community came quite close to agreeing, in principle, to a downsized Doha agenda, but events conspired (for reasons outside the purview of this volume) to preclude that possibility. And around that time, the financial crisis hit the United States and the European Union, the undisputed leaders of the pack, in quick succession. China, meanwhile, emerged unscathed.

2

Complaints against China

(EUPHORIA EXITS AND DYSPHORIA ENTERS)

The true sign of intelligence is not knowledge, but imagination.
—ALBERT EINSTEIN

After their Trilateral meeting in September 2018, the trade ministers of the European Union, the United States, and Japan (respectively China's first, second, and third largest trading partners) issued a joint statement voicing their concern about "third countries" (without explicitly mentioning China) that maintain "non-market oriented policies and practices," develop "State Owned Enterprises into national champions," and "require or pressure technology transfer from foreign companies to domestic companies."[1] This came only a few weeks after the United States had unilaterally imposed duties on Chinese products above and beyond what is permissible under WTO rules in order to pressure China to change its behavior. Was this, perhaps, a signal that the honeymoon period was over for China?

By joining the WTO, China had also joined numerous multilateral agreements regulating trade in goods and services and trade-related intellectual property rights. It also promised to join one plurilateral agreement, the Agreement on Government Procurement (GPA), a promise that has yet to

---

1. Joint Statement on Trilateral Meeting of the Trade Ministers of the United States, Japan, and the European Union, New York, September 25, 2018.

be fulfilled. In WTO parlance, multilateral and plurilateral agreements are usually referred to as "covered agreements." The Protocol of Accession was supposed to deal with concerns that could not be addressed within the four corners of the existing WTO covered agreements.[2]

Since China has not joined the GPA or any other plurilateral agreement so far, it is the combination of the multilateral agreements and the terms and conditions agreed in the Protocol of Accession that provide the legal benchmark against which to discuss the consistency of Chinese trade practices, including with respect to their SOEs and forced TT. In *China–Raw Materials*, the Appellate Body made it clear that Protocols of Accession are justiciable.[3] Consequently, to the extent that China has agreed to specific obligations in its protocol, it is liable to being brought before a WTO panel if there is disagreement as to whether it has lived up to its contractual obligations.

The Protocol of Accession addressed the concerns raised about China's trade practices in different ways. The overarching hope, of course, was that China would transform itself into a proper market economy. With respect to antidumping, a concrete date (2016) was agreed upon as to when there should be no automatic presumption that China could be treated as a non-market economy (NME).

Today, nearly twenty years after its accession to the WTO, China is still a socialist economy. The Chinese state continues to maintain a heavy hand in the country's economy and, consequently, its trade regime. Coupled with the fact that China has become the world's largest or second largest country in the world in terms of GDP (depending on how GDP is compared across countries), this situation has irritated its main trading partners, who have made their exasperation plain. Blustein mentions that as of 2002, almost immediately after China's accession, the United States asserted that China had not complied with various obligations it had assumed, ranging from commitments under the Agreement on Agriculture to transparency-related provisions (2019, 71ff.).

Such disagreements have led to the submission of disputes under both the multilateral agreements and the Protocol of Accession. Whereas the content of the multilateral agreements is the same for all WTO members, idiosyncratic terms and conditions characterize each individual Protocol

---

2. Several contributions in Toohey, Picker, and Greenacre 2015 discuss the influence that the WTO has exerted on China and its legal regime. In a parallel publication, Wang (2015) discusses the way China has implemented the obligations assumed through its accession to the WTO.

3. Mavroidis (2016) discusses in detail both issues in chapters 9 and 4 of volume 1, respectively.

of Accession. We will thus first briefly describe the content of the Chinese Protocol of Accession before discussing the disputes raised against China so far. It is against this backdrop that we will entertain our discussion regarding the adequacy of the current regime to deal with the complaints about SOEs and forced TT. In order to fully understand the complexities of disagreements over SOEs and forced TT, it is crucial to examine the underlying dispute settlement practices and the relevant clarifications that case law has contributed.

China's Protocol of Accession

When issued, the Chinese Protocol of Accession was the lengthiest and most detailed protocol to date. This was no accident. WTO signatories hoped that its inclusiveness would bind China to change, that a document that was both comprehensive and detailed in the particulars would force the Chinese to adapt to an open-market economy. Twenty years later, this hope seems to have been misplaced, and the Chinese protocol looks more and more like a missed opportunity. So what went wrong?

The Protocol of Accession was meant to bridge the gap between the place where China was, when it acceded to the WTO, and where it should be going. As with previous accessions, incumbents introduced various idiosyncratic obligations in China's protocol, all of them country specific. There is an upside and a downside associated with this approach. The upside is that Protocols of Accession can better adjust to idiosyncratic elements of individual members. The downside is that because they are customized, the functionality of specific clauses suffers, especially as they might be relevant to others as well.

It is instructive to compare the hurdles China faced to enter the WTO with the requirements for ex–Soviet bloc countries, with their similarly state-dominated economies, to sign on to the GATT. China's Protocol of Accession to the WTO contains obligations both similar to and different from those in the Protocols of Accession to the GATT for the ex–Soviet bloc countries. What is similar is the possibility for WTO members to treat China as an NME for the purpose of Article VI of the GATT and to apply safeguards on conditions less stringent than those embedded in Article XIX.[4]

---

4. Articles VI and XIX of the GATT permit a WTO member to restrict imports in case of dumping or subsidy (VI) or import surges (XIX) and if its domestic industry has suffered damage.

There are three differences between the respective Protocols of Accession for China and the ex–Soviet bloc countries. First, China's flexibility regarding Articles VI and XIX was limited in terms of time. Fifteen years after the accession of China to the WTO (that is, by December 2016), the deadline by which China could still be an NME had passed. This date was imported verbatim from the U.S.-China Bilateral Agreement of November 16, 1999. The U.S. administration believed that this was a realistic deadline for China to meet its obligation to transform into a full-fledged market economy.[5]

The 2016 deadline inserted in the Protocol of Accession should be understood as a presumption and nothing more. Consequently, as Mavroidis and Janow (2017) have argued, WTO members can lawfully continue to treat China as an NME even after 2016, but if they do, they must construct a basis for that designation. In other words, the onus is on other countries to demonstrate why China is an NME; they cannot simply presume that this is the case.

Second, unlike the ex–Soviet bloc countries when they acceded to the GATT, China was not obliged to meet certain import targets in its Protocols of Accession. China was thus, in this respect, treated like any other WTO member. It would bind its customs duties, and, for the rest, the market would take care of the volumes of trade that would go through its customs. Third, China had to accept some additional obligations regarding SOEs, intellectual property rights protection, and technology transfer (which we discuss in detail later in this chapter).

SOEs IN CHINA'S PROTOCOL OF ACCESSION

Chinese government interference in its economy was a major issue of concern for key negotiators who tried to introduce language in the final text to try to tame the involvement of the state in the working of the economy. The SOE issue is not as well-defined as it might appear to be at first glance. In fact, the very nature of a state-owned enterprise is debatable, and its definitions have metastasized among international organizations.

The manner in which Article XIX has been interpreted in case law has made it practically impossible for WTO members to successfully invoke the safeguard clause. Sykes (2006) has contributed the most comprehensive critique to this effect.

5. https://clintonwhitehouse4.archives.gov/textonly/WH/New/WTO-Conf-1999/factsheets/fs-006.html; http://images.mofcom.gov.cn/wto2/201712/20171213174424357.pdf.

To begin with, there is no specific definition of an SOE in China's Protocol of Accession; negotiators might have felt that any definition would be elusive, since various criteria (precise ones, like *ownership*, but also less precise ones, like *influence*) could usefully be employed. Opting for a precise criterion might have led to underinclusiveness, whereas opting for a less precise criterion would simply transpose the definition of SOEs from the legislative (Protocol of Accession) to the judiciary (WTO panels). Thus, while the Protocol of Accession does mention both SOEs and SIEs (state-invested enterprises), it does not define them.[6] Some reports by WTO panels distinguish SOEs from SIEs, with the latter covering entities where the state has limited ownership. In fact, many institutions and international organizations do not define SOEs, leaving it to case-by-case assessments. There are exceptions. The OECD understands SOEs as entities where the state exercises ownership. Raballand et al. (2015) employ three criteria in defining SOEs: control by the state, legal separation from the state, and the provision of both financial and non-financial services. The World Bank Independent Evaluation Group (IEG) has endorsed this definition.[7]

For the purposes of our discussion concerning the treatment of SOEs under the WTO, a definition would have been helpful, but its absence is not the end of the story. The pertinent legal question is whether SOEs should be considered "public bodies" (the term appearing in the WTO SCM [Subsidies and Countervailing Measures] Agreement) or not. If yes, then, as per the disciplines of the SCM Agreement, their actions could result in subsidies. If not, then the SCM Agreement would be irrelevant.[8]

A 2018 World Bank report (World Bank 2018b) discussing the historical evolution of SOEs and their present configuration indicates that, initially at least, SOEs were entities in the service of the state. They would be assigned tasks that would promote state objectives and would operate without necessarily paying attention to commercial considerations. Profit for the owners of these entities was secondary to state aggrandizement. This lack of a profit motive was possible because SOEs benefited from what has been termed a "soft budget constraint."[9] They knew that even if things did not go well, they could always rely on the state to take care of whatever financial issues they

6. WTO Doc. WT/ACC/CHN/49, October 1, 2001, 8ff.

7. World Bank 2018b. See, on this point, Lefebvre, Rocha, and Ruta 2019.

8. Hoekman and Nelson (2020) advance similar thinking, regretting the fact that the current SCM Agreement does not sufficiently take into account SOEs.

9. Song (2018, 347) cites the first appearance and usage of this term.

might be facing. The quid pro quo, of course, was that SOEs knew that they had to function as the arm of the state in the national economy.

CORPORATIZATION AND PRIVATIZATION OF SOEs

The first important change in the nature of SOEs in China came in 1987, with the introduction of the "contract responsibility system."[10] Briefly, the idea was that SOEs would enter into an agreement with the state outlining what they would provide and the tax burden they would shoulder. Beyond that, they were free to make profits and distribute them as they deemed appropriate.

Because of social pressure, Chow (2018) notes, SOEs were reluctant to distribute profits to their senior management. Most of the profits would go to the workforce. Anticipating that this would be the case, senior management lacked the incentives to invest time and effort in improving the SOEs they were called to manage. The "contract responsibility system" did guarantee some income to the state but fell short of modernizing SOEs and preparing them for the harsh international competition they would be called to face post-accession to the GATT/WTO.

In the 1990s, SOEs were corporatized. The term "corporatization" denotes the transformation of a government entity into a separate legal entity. Typically, the government cedes autonomy to the management of the corporatized entity, but in China's case, management autonomy was a point of contention.

The wider picture is worth recounting briefly. Financially distressed SOEs exited the market through either mergers or bankruptcy. The number of SOEs was thus consolidated to just above one hundred. With respect to state-owned commercial banks (SOCBs), China eventually ended up with the "Big Four" (the Agricultural Bank of China, the Bank of China, the China Construction Bank, and the Commercial Bank of China), which collectively control 50 percent of all China loans.[11] While large SOEs were corporatized, smaller SOEs did not follow this route and instead were privatized. Corporatization should not be confused with privatization; the degree of government intervention is not symmetric in the two cases. Corporatization is the process of transforming state assets into corporations, which could

---

10. Chow (2018) and Song (2018) offer useful explanations of this institution.

11. Cheng (2014), Cousin (2007), and Luo (2016) discuss the evolution of the Chinese banking system.

still be influenced by the state. Privatization, on the other hand, entails the delinking of the entity from state influence.

The Chinese government established the State-Owned Assets Supervision and Administration Commission (SASAC), operating under the State Council, to oversee the process of consolidation of SOEs, the corporatization of the bigger among them and the privatization of the smaller players. In addition, the SASAC essentially administers SOEs that have not been privatized by appointing directors, among other things.[12]

Those in the senior management of an SOE, as Cousin (2007) perceptively argues, have conflicting incentives. On the one hand, they must be loyal to the government, since they have been appointed by it. A higher position in the bureaucracy could depend on the loyalty managers have shown to the party officials who appointed them. On the other hand, senior managers must compete vigorously in the market against each other. Loyalty to government to advance official goals and intense market competition are not easily reconcilable, of course. The result has not been satisfactory from an efficiency perspective, and various World Bank reports (2018a, 2018b) provide strong evidence that this is the case.

SOEs are, of course, not exclusive to China. They exist around the world, and we will discuss some of them in chapter 3. There is one key difference, though, between China's SOEs and those in the rest of the world. In OECD countries, SOEs represent 15 percent of GDP. In transition economies, they represent 20 to 30 percent. China is by far the leader of this pack, owing 30 percent of its GDP to SOEs.[13]

---

12. The SASAC was established in 2003 and was tasked with improving the performance of SOEs. Initially modeled after Temasek, Singapore's SASAC equivalent, it adopted a more hands-on approach with respect to the day-to-day management of companies in its portfolio. Indeed, Puchniak and Lan (2017) and Milhaupt and Pargendler (2017) underscore Temasek's commercial orientation and independence from political influence. This is not the case for the SASAC. There are no firewalls between the SASAC and Chinese political institutions. Many of the top managers appointed in SOEs were also members of the party. The *dangjian* movement, to which we will refer in our concluding section (the reestablishment of the preeminence of the Chinese Communist Party in the economic life of the country), is the formalization of the enhanced role that the party has enjoyed in economic life. More recently, the Organization Department of the Communist Party (and not the SASAC) continues to appoint the top management. The SASAC is today described as the world's largest holding company, controlling over three-fifths of China's non-financial companies. Following a series of mergers that it instigated, the total number of companies under its purview is about one hundred. See Lardy 2019, 86ff. Compare the analysis of Kroeber (2016, 95ff.).

13. World Bank 2018b.

Concerns about China's lack of antitrust statutes at the time of its accession to the WTO also added to the seriousness of the situation.[14] There was widespread concern about both the size of SOEs and the role the SASAC was playing in the Chinese economy, as well as the ensuing need to discipline SOEs through the Protocol of Accession. For example, alignment with international prices was explicitly inserted in the protocol out of fear that, because of the involvement of the SASAC in running the economy, domestic prices in China might never become internationally competitive market prices.

Regardless, especially following President Xi's reforms, no one can dispute the nature of heavy state involvement in the operation of China's economy. Furthermore, after Xi's reforms, state involvement has metastasized. China is now becoming familiar with state capital operation companies (SCOCs) and state capital investment companies (SCICs); 142 of them operate at the provincial level and 11 nationwide.[15] But this is not all. There are SOCBs, as we have already stated, and state-owned financial institutions (SOFIs), which have expanded since the global financial crisis.[16] SOFIs are usually controlled by Huijin, an investment company owned by the Chinese government. Finally, there are financial enterprises directly supervised by the Ministry of Finance (MOF) as well. The state was omnipresent in the national economy when China was acceding to the WTO, and its influence continues to spread.

PROTECTING INTELLECTUAL PROPERTY RIGHTS IN THE PROTOCOL OF ACCESSION

It is no surprise that protection of intellectual property (IP) rights was very high on the agenda of the WTO members negotiating China's accession. Indeed, even today, despite commitments made during the accession process and ever-increasing expertise in the protection of IP rights, the situation is far from idyllic. There are cases where rights-holders have voiced their concerns but also instances where they have preferred to stay silent and avoid facing possible countermeasures. Blustein provides examples of both cases (2019, 120ff.).

Japan's Kawasaki is perhaps the most high-profile example of the former. Having participated in a consortium with Alstom (France), Bombardier

14. The China Anti-Monopoly Law was enacted in 2007. Concerns about antitrust enforcement persist to this day; see https://www.uschina.org/reports/competition-policy-and-enforcement-china.

15. World Bank 2018b.

16. World Bank 2018b.

(Canada), and Siemens (Germany), selling equipment to China and help-ing the Chinese build their own high-speed train, Kawasaki subsequently claimed that China was copying their patented goods even though con-tractual agreements had been signed to prevent this. By contrast, Siemens preferred to keep quiet on this issue to avoid jeopardizing its position in the Chinese market.[17]

Zhang and Cao (2019) conducted an empirical survey of patent enforce-ment before Chinese courts (which, as we will see later, oversee the enforce-ment of IP-related disputes through commitments that China has under-taken following its accession to the WTO) in Beijing between 2004 and 2011. Zhang and Cao conclude that foreigners were more likely to prevail in similar disputes before the court. Nevertheless, the damages adjudicated are persistently low, particularly by Western standards, largely owing to a lack of expertise in the Chinese courts when it comes to calculating the amount of compensation in similar cases.

There is not much that can be done in terms of an international agree-ment to address similar deficiencies; the onus is on China to adequately train its personnel. International agreements can, of course, provide a standard template for such decision-making protocols, but someone in China will ulti-mately be called upon to effectively implement them. Simply adjudicating such disagreements on a state-by-state basis only replaces one set of prob-lems with another: assigning the jurisdiction to international adjudication is not unproblematic. First, private agents would have to persuade their own national government to take the case against China to a WTO panel, since the WTO is a government-to-government court where private parties have no standing. Governments, of course, litigate differently than private agents and might be tempted to fend off cases if, in equilibrium, the interests of other private agents matter more to them. Second, private agents would have to await the outcome following a rather lengthy adjudication process, which can often last four to five years. Finally, since remedies in the WTO are prospective, they would not receive compensation for past damages.

In sum, going to the WTO for support with IP complaints is not a very attractive option for private entities, and submitting to Chinese courts is no panacea either. Private agents are thus between a rock and a hard place.

In its WTO accession, China did commit to protecting IP rights, an area of major concern for Western economies. Furthermore, in this context, it is

17. See also the story concerning Dongfeng, a Chinese SOE, and Nissan, the Japanese car-maker, in McGregor 2010, 216ff.

not the disrespect of IP rights that was of greatest concern to incumbents. It was also the way forced TT was operating in China. The Protocol of Accession could only address forced TT attributable to the Chinese state, not to private entities. Some disciplines agreed to address the former but not the latter issue. Alas, these disciplines did not (and could not) go far enough to meet all concerns, as we explain in what follows, even though the size of the problem cannot be underestimated.

The Size of the Problem

There are dozens of studies that try to quantify the problem of IP rights in China. To do so effectively, a reasonable counterfactual needs to be constructed, and the assumptions here matter a lot. Remember, one plausible explanation for why Chinese courts tend to underestimate the costs of IP rights violations to rights-holders is that the courts are undertrained. It would be cavalier to dismiss similar explanations out of hand because it is undeniable that Chinese institutions (courts included) were unprepared to deal with the protection of IP rights when the legislative framework was lacking in the first place.

There are, of course, other possible explanations. Branstetter (2018) cites a fair number of experts who have reported cases where Chinese companies, either by forming cartels to this effect or simply by heeding their government's wishes, have conditioned access to the Chinese market for foreign companies upon the prior transfer of technology. Branstetter also cites (2018, 2) several studies that estimate the loss in income for rights-holders. The numbers are staggering: damages in the order of tens of billions or even hundreds of billions of U.S. dollars. Under the circumstances, one can easily understand why forced TT has become a high-priority issue.

The Attractiveness of Going Solo (and Why We Disagree)

Part of the reason why President Trump has imposed tariffs on Chinese products has to do with China's practices with respect to forced TT (we explain our disagreement with this approach in chapter 4). Branstetter (2018) has proposed a different, more efficient way to deal with China. He has argued for smart sanctions against China, which will not suffer from the inefficiencies of tariff impositions. More specifically, he would like to see the United States impose targeted sanctions against Chinese companies directly involved in forced TT.

According to Branstetter, the Committee on Foreign Investment in the United States (CFIUS), which scrutinizes foreign direct investment (FDI) in the United States, could play a key role in this endeavor. CFIUS could stop investment entry in the U.S. market to all Chinese companies that had previously engaged in forced TT in the Chinese market, if it was in possession of information to this effect (i.e., that they had engaged previously in forced TT). Still, even though this proposal is for various reasons superior to the tariff hikes imposed by the Trump administration, it would still not adequately address all the issues that fall under the heading "forced TT."

For starters, CFIUS would deal with U.S. interests only. What is the incentive for CFIUS to ban Chinese companies from the U.S. market if they had, for example, forced a European company to TT? Furthermore, would similar actions be considered legitimate retaliation? Forced TT is in violation of WTO law only if it is attributable to the Chinese authorities. Private behavior is not sanctioned under WTO law. The WTO disciplines only address behavior attributed to one of its signatories, that is, states and customs territories with sovereignty over the exercise of their trade policy. The WTO has no mandate to discipline private behavior. This is the realm of competition law, an area where the WTO has no competence.

WTO Disputes against China

Various WTO members have been complainants against China, the United States predominating. In what follows, we concentrate on cases where China appeared as a respondent in WTO litigation (China's disputes where it acted as complainant are of no interest to this study).

Since its accession to the WTO, China has been a defendant in 44 cases, of which 6 have been settled or terminated and 12 are still in consultation. Some of the cases have remained at the consultation stage for a long time, without the complainant submitting a request for the establishment of a panel. We could consider them as abandoned cases, but since the Dispute Settlement Understanding (DSU)—the WTO agreement that regulates the administration of disputes—does not impose a deadline by which requests for consultations must proceed to the panel stage, they are technically still in process. Of the remaining 26 cases, 21 have been adjudicated while 5 are pending.[18]

Twenty-seven of the 44 disputes against China have included at least one claim that China has violated its Protocol of Accession. In the overwhelming

---

18. Of these 5 cases, panels have been established but not yet composed in 2 cases and panels composed in the 3 other cases.

majority of such cases, complainants invoked the Protocol of Accession as an additional basis for complaints falling under the multilateral agreements. With respect to export taxes, and some cases relating to IP rights, the Protocol of Accession served as the primary legal basis for the complaints lodged. This is so because, in these cases, China accepted obligations that other WTO members had not accepted. However, as we will explain in chapter 5, China went further than other WTO members in areas covered by WTO law, but it did not accept obligations, which are not germane to the WTO contract.

Using the subject matter of each dispute as a benchmark, we divide the 21 adjudicated cases as follows:

- Seven concern trade defense measures by China against imports of various products (from the EU, the United States, Canada, and Japan). The WTO members that suffered similar impositions complained that China had violated its obligations under the WTO when having recourse to antidumping and other measures.
- Six concern duties on exports of various basic products (to the EU, the United States, Japan, and Mexico). The argument in these cases has been that China had imposed export duties when it was illegal to have done so.
- Two concern measures affecting production or imports of agricultural goods (with the United States).
- Three concern measures affecting imports of auto parts (from the EU, the United States, and Canada).
- One concerns measures affecting electronic payment services, the argument being that China had acted in violation of its obligations under the GATS.
- One concerns the protection and enforcement of IP rights.
- One concerns trading rights and distribution services for certain media products.

If we use the subject matter of complaints as the criterion in dividing up the cases, we observe that China has been the respondent in:

- 4 out of a total of 41 WTO disputes classified as TRIPS (trade-related aspects of intellectual property rights) disputes;
- 22 out of a total of 127 WTO subsidy disputes (with only 2 concerning SOEs); and
- 6 out of a total of 6 WTO disputes classified as exports-restrictions related.

Although nothing in the findings of these cases sheds interpretative light on the adequacy of the existing regime to address concerns about SOEs and forced TT, it is important to note that China lost in all 21 cases and has complied with the Dispute Settlement Body (DSB) recommendations in all cases. China has behaved like a good WTO citizen every time it has had to address adverse rulings by panels and/or the WTO Appellate Body. Occasionally, academics have voiced the argument that China has not fully complied with adverse rulings. Maybe so. What is clear, though, is that, so far, no WTO member has requested authorization to impose countermeasures against China for failure to implement rulings during the reasonable period at its disposal. At the very least, the presumption of compliance should be in favor of China.[19]

The discussion so far leaves us perplexed to say the least. We observed only four cases where China was found in violation of its WTO obligations concerning IP protection: once under the TRIPS Agreement, and three times under its Protocol of Accession. If China lived up to its reputation as the prime violator of IP rights, there should be many more such cases. Going strictly by the number of TRIPS-related disputes, China does not in fact deserve the reputation of a perpetrator.[20]

Equally paradoxical is this: Since most of the time China is accused of interfering too much in the marketplace, why has China not been the subject of WTO complaints with respect to this issue more often?

Has the World Trading Community Taken It Easy on China?

China entered the WTO seven years after the European Union and the United States. The European Union has been a respondent on 98 cases from January 1, 1995, until July 15, 2020 (our cut-off date), whereas the number

19. In fact, from early on, Chinese delegates adopted a very measured style when participating in WTO committees, and China did not make any waves. Various contributions in Gao and Lewis 2005 support this view. The one case where most commentators agree that implementation by China has been inadequate is *China–Electronic Payments and Services*, regarding China's openness to foreign credit cards. Visa and Mastercard continued to complain that, after the end of the process, they still could not manage to make headway in the Chinese market. Nevertheless, the United States did not request authorization to adopt countermeasures against China for failing to implement the WTO rulings. See the detailed analysis of this dispute by Hoekman and Meagher (2014). For a more recent analysis, see Zhou and Gao 2020.

20. There are reasons to feel cautiously optimistic that things have changed, as the recent dispute between Huawei and Samsung adjudicated before a Chinese court shows, where the Chinese and Korean giants were embroiled in a dispute regarding protection of IP rights. See the summary of the dispute in https://www.theglobeandmail.com/business/article-huawei-patent -case-shows-chinese-courts-rising-clout-2/.

for the United States for the same period is 167. China, on the other hand, has been asked to defend its measures on only 44 occasions. This is quite low—unexpectedly low.

Furthermore, China has implemented all findings where it has been pronounced guilty of violating WTO law. There has never been a case where China refused to implement and the original complainant requested authorization to impose countermeasures. This is normal, as few could have seriously threatened China when retaliating against it. But if China violates the WTO ad nauseam, why not introduce more complaints? The record shows that it implements adverse rulings. The hypothesis that China has delivered on its WTO obligations must be excluded; otherwise, why all the fuss?

The numbers do tell a story here, which needs to be further examined. Forty-four disputes in the last nineteen years means that, were we to hypothetically consider China an original member, the number of disputes would be closer to 60. This number is far lower than the actual number of disputes in which the EU or the United States has been a respondent.

It is, of course, a quixotic test to predict when disputes will arise in equilibrium. No less an authority than John Leddy has noted (1958; attributing the statement to de Scitovsky) that trade disputes can be the result of broader issues of political economy and, more specifically, contract incompleteness, in the model developed by Horn, Maggi, and Staiger (2010). The problem is that we cannot distinguish the wheat from the chaff, assuming the former scenario qualifies as chaff and the latter as wheat. These are very often cases of private information, where the party owning such information has little if any incentive to reveal its true motives.

Against this background, Horn, Mavroidis, and Nordstrøm (2005) have claimed that an individual WTO member's share of international trade should be the best predictor of the number of disputes in which they find themselves engaged. In their model, the probability of encountering illegal trade barriers is constant across trading nations. Therefore, the share of export trade emerges as a key explanatory variable for the overall number of disputes per WTO member. Using this benchmark, the number of disputes to which China is a party is abnormally low. Why has this been the case?

In principle, there are two diametrically opposed explanations. It could be that China is a good WTO citizen that faithfully implements obligations it assumes. This is probably a weak explanation for various reasons. For one thing, case law, to which we will turn shortly, has interpreted the very same legal provisions in a contradictory manner. We will refer, in this context, to the understanding of the term "public body," which has been interpreted in different ways in cases involving China. The more recent case law has adopted a rather expansive understanding of the term, allowing even private entities, under certain conditions, to be considered public bodies. Case law thus initially adopted a rather restrictive and subsequently a rather expansive definition of the term "public body." Had more recent case law been adopted at the time when the very first dispute was litigated, the number of disputes might have multiplied, since many might have been dissuaded by earlier case law to lodge disputes.

Furthermore, there is still the feeling in some quarters that China does not play by the rules. Although the United States has been the most active complainant against China (with 23 out of 44 total cases and 10 out of the 21 adjudicated cases) and has been very successful in its disputes (with a victory in every adjudicated case), it has also been extremely frustrated with the DSB process. During the 2018 Trade Policy Review of China, the U.S. ambassador to the WTO said:

> The WTO's dispute settlement mechanism is not designed to address a situation in which a WTO Member has opted for state-led trade and investment policies that prevail over market forces and that pursues policies guided by mercantilism rather than global economic cooperation. Rather, it is narrowly targeted at disputes where one Member believes that another Member has adopted a measure or taken an action that violates a WTO obligation. While some Chinese measures have been found by WTO panels or the Appellate Body to run afoul of China's WTO obligations, fundamental problems remain unaddressed as many of the most significant Chinese policies and practices are not directly disciplined by WTO rules or the additional commitments that China made in its Protocol of Accession.[21]

Given this situation the United States has looked for alternative ways to deal with its two main complaints about China: the role of SOEs and forced TT. The first alternative, imagined by President Obama, was the Trans-Pacific Partnership Agreement. The second is Section 301, which has been revived by President Trump. We will return to them later.

And, of course, it is not only the United States that has taken this view. As we have already stated, the Trilateral has been quite vocal in this respect as well, and other countries have also expressed or at least implied more measured concern.

---

21. WTO Doc. WT/TPR/M/375 at §4.109.

It could also be that China's trading partners are underenforcing their rights, fearing exclusion from the lucrative Chinese market. There is some anecdotal evidence pointing to underenforcement, but, of course, it is hard to prove its precise ambit.[22] Once again, companies with a presence in the Chinese market that have information about China's objectionable practices are reluctant to share it. Without solid evidence, it is difficult to state whether we are facing a case of underenforcement at all, for it is impossible to establish what the appropriate benchmark—the appropriate level of enforcement, that is—should be.

Incomplete contracts could also be a reason for the puzzling lack of complaints against China. As we will see later in this chapter, China has agreed to abstain from actions leading to forced TT. What is the quantum of proof required, though, to demonstrate that certain behavior is attributed to China? The law is silent on this issue, and case law leaves a lot to be desired in terms of clarity on this score.[23] Risk-averse agents might prefer to litigate in areas where agreed obligations are quite clear and the risk of error is, consequently, small. This largely explains why there are many "trigger-happy" complainants challenging the consistency of Chinese export taxes with the Protocol of Accession, an area where China has assumed clear-cut obligations.

Recall that the disciplines on transfer of technology do not bind private parties. What are, then, the evidentiary requirements that must be met for a complainant to show that collective refusal to enter into joint ventures absent of TT is the result of state interference that China promised to eradicate? To play it safe, panels might prefer to avoid prejudging the issue and leave it to future trade negotiators to draft and craft more precise language. It is not accidental, we believe, that the cleanest victories that complainants have scored when litigating against China are in the area of export restrictions (taxes), where the agreed obligations are unambiguous.

What is the level of independence of domestic tribunals established and tasked to enforce the TRIPS+ provisions in the Protocol of Accession?

22. Blustein mentions Gamesa, a producer of wind turbines, which saw its market share in China dwindle because of local content requirements (2019, 122ff.). Still, the market loss notwithstanding, Gamesa opted for inaction against China in order to preserve its position in the Chinese market. In a similar vein, Blustein mentions that Qualcomm was prepared to pay a fine of $1 billion, of questionable legitimacy, in order to avoid creating additional waves with the Chinese antitrust authorities (184ff.).

23. See the discussion in Mavroidis 2016, vol. 1, chap. 2, comparing the treatment of burden of production of proof in *Japan–Trade in Semiconductors* and in *Argentina–Hides and Leather*.

Litigating in areas where contractual language is ambiguous might prove a perilous endeavor. Panels might find arguments in this context a long shot.

Inaction could also be attributable to more mundane reasons. Western companies participating in global value chains might, in the name of the cheap Chinese inputs they incorporate, be willing to turn a blind eye to business-unfriendly behavior.[24] Or, they might feel that by alerting their sovereigns to infractions, they risk their place in the lucrative Chinese market. Or they might even be offered preferential entry in the Chinese market for their investment. The sky is the limit when one is looking for explanations for the lack of enforcement. It is clear, however, that whenever China assumed clear-cut obligations, as in the case of export taxes, complainants did have frequent recourse to WTO adjudication and scored important victories.

So, what is to be done under the circumstances? How can we correct the enforcement deficit? To be sure, we do not subscribe to the view that the Protocol of Accession is optimal. A few things could have been done better, and we will be referring to a couple of issues, which, in our view, were dealt with in a more efficient manner in the Trans-Pacific Partnership (TPP) Agreement, renamed the Comprehensive and Progressive Agreement for Trans-Pacific Partnership (CPTPP) after the U.S. withdrawal from TPP. In this realm, negotiators had, of course, the luxury to agree on issues that could eventually influence China without China being in a position to influence the negotiation itself, since it had not been invited to participate.

But we also do not believe that inciting risky litigation could solve the problem.[25] Litigation has yielded results viewed as satisfactory by complainants predominantly in cases where China has accepted clear and unambiguous obligations. Creating clear obligations could be accomplished by adding a chapter on SOEs to the current SCM Agreement. By contrast, for TT, to the extent that it is private behavior that we are after, a new framework would need to be negotiated.

Dealing with China beyond WTO Disputes

Following the lead of the Obama administration, a few trading nations negotiated TPP. The unspoken truth is that this was a way to corner China without providing it with a forum to express its views on the issues covered.

---

24. Blanchard, Bown, and Johnson (2017) have expressed views on this score.

25. Hence, we disagree with Bacchus, Lester, and Zhu, who argue that greater utilization of the WTO dispute process, even without changing some of its rules, would go a long way "to press China to fulfil its promises and become more market-oriented" (2018, 11).

The implicit rationale for it was dissatisfaction with the way China-specific issues had been addressed in the Protocol of Accession.

More recently, the Trump administration has adopted a highly belligerent strategy. It has unilaterally lashed out against China without observing the disciplines of the WTO. In April 1945, Churchill said to Sir Alan Brooke, chief of the Imperial General Staff, "There is only one thing worse than fighting with allies, and that is fighting without them!" The attitude of the Trump administration is quite reminiscent of this.

TPP: Where Persuasion and Cooperation Yield Encouraging Outcomes

One attempt to find an alternative, or perhaps a complement, to the multilateral track was the TPP negotiated during the Obama presidency. The TPP Agreement between the United States, Japan, and ten other Pacific Rim countries (Australia, Brunei, Canada, Chile, Malaysia, Mexico, New Zealand, Peru, Singapore, and Vietnam) signed on February 4, 2016, was an important strategic and political success for President Obama, as it was for the other leaders, especially Japanese prime minister Shinzo Abe.

The deal, which was still awaiting ratification by Congress at the end of the Obama presidency, covered 40 percent of the global economy. Its intent was to create an economic bloc with reduced trade barriers to the flow of goods, services, and data, and with new standards and rules for investment, the environment, labor, IP rights protection, and state-owned enterprises.

The TPP Agreement was the economic centerpiece of President Obama's "pivot" to Asia, which was designed to counter the rise of China in the Pacific and beyond. As the president stated on the signing of the agreement: "TPP allows America, and not countries like China, to write the rules of the road in the 21st century, which is especially important in a region as dynamic as the Asia-Pacific."[26] Among its key features was Chapter 17, which dealt with the regulation of SOEs in a comprehensive manner. In fact, the level of detail is a few standard deviations beyond and above what had been incorporated in the Chinese Protocol of Accession on this score.

Since it was negotiated without the participation of China, Chapter 17 reflects the first-best approach of the TPP partners toward the Chinese SOEs, the implicit target of their contractual arrangement. We will discuss Chapter 17 in detail in chapter 6, where we will present our solutions to the China issues, since, in our view, it provides a very appropriate regulatory

---

26. Statement by the President on the Signing of the Trans-Pacific Partnership, February 3, 2016.

paradigm of how to deal with SOEs. Unfortunately, American policymakers quickly abandoned the TPP after the election of Donald Trump; one of his first acts in office was to fulfill his campaign promise to withdraw the United States from the TPP Agreement. He has not changed his mind about this, at least not so far.

Bilateral Measures (Section 301)

Instead, Trump has revived the use of Section 301 of the U.S. Trade Act of 1974, which gives the president wide latitude to take action, including imposing protective tariffs against perceived trade infractions, as a lever to try to force domestic changes in China. This policy turn recalls the actions of George H. W. Bush in 1989, when the United States named Japan an unfair trading nation, thus paving the way for the Structural Impediments Initiative (SII) negotiations.

Section 301 was used extensively during the 1980s and 1990s, not only against Japan but also against other U.S. trading partners in order to open their markets and to exert pressure on them to observe their obligations vis-à-vis U.S. IP rights-holders. With the conclusion of the Uruguay Round negotiations in 1994 and the establishment of the WTO, Section 301 remained on the statute books but was downgraded to an instrument of diplomatic protection.[27]

The reason, as discussed by Bown (2017), is twofold. First, the WTO adopted new multilateral disciplines in areas of central commercial interest for the United States, such as the GATS Agreement for services and the TRIPS Agreement for IP rights. Second, with the creation of the Appellate Body and the introduction of remedies in cases of noncompliance with DSB rulings, the new dispute settlement system became far more constraining than the relatively toothless GATT system that the United States had long been complaining about. The main reason, we believe, that led to a change in the U.S. attitude was that the WTO Dispute Settlement Understanding (DSU) had emulated the statutory deadlines for resolving disputes that existed in the U.S. Section 301. Fast relief was thus now a very realistic

---

27. Nonetheless, Section 301 has continued to serve as an instrument at the disposal of private parties, which have no standing before the WTO courts, to alert the U.S. government of foreign trade practices that hurt them. It serves the same purpose, therefore, as the EU Trade Barriers Regulation. And, viewed from a U.S.-centric (as opposed to cosmopolitan) perspective, Section 301 has served the U.S. interests quite well, as the studies by Bayard and Elliott (1994) and Schoppa (1997) show.

prospect. Furthermore, the respondent could no longer block access to justice (what in DSU parlance is known as "negative consensus").

Although there was criticism from Washington about how well the WTO dispute settlement system worked, on the whole it seemed to provide a satisfactory (from the U.S. viewpoint) alternative to the unilateral Section 301 process. In fact, according to Bown (2017), Section 301 was never used by the United States after the advent of the WTO and before the Trump presidency. Trump's decision in August 2017 to ask the USTR to launch a Section 301 investigation into "China's acts, policies, and practices related to technology transfer, intellectual property, and innovation" was, therefore, a genuine sea change compared to the U.S. attitude with regard to this issue during the previous twenty-two years.[28]

In March 2018, the USTR advised President Trump that the Section 301 investigation revealed the following:

First, China uses foreign ownership restrictions, including joint venture requirements, equity limitations, and other investment restrictions, to require or pressure technology transfer from U.S. companies to Chinese entities. China also uses administrative review and licensing procedures to require or pressure technology transfer, which, inter alia, undermines the value of U.S. investments and technology and weakens the global competitiveness of U.S. firms.

Second, China imposes substantial restrictions on, and intervenes in, U.S. firms' investments and activities, including through restrictions on technology licensing terms. These restrictions deprive U.S. technology owners of the ability to bargain and set market-based terms for technology transfer. As a result, U.S. companies seeking to license technologies must do so on terms that unfairly favour Chinese recipients.

Third, China directs and facilitates the systematic investment in, and acquisition of, U.S. companies and assets by Chinese companies to obtain cutting-edge technologies and intellectual property and to generate large-scale technology transfer in industries deemed important by Chinese government industrial plans.

Fourth, China conducts and supports unauthorized intrusions into, and theft from, the computer networks of U.S. companies. These actions provide the Chinese government with unauthorized access

---

28. The difference, thus, between this invocation of Section 301 and prior invocations is that this time the U.S. administration was acting on its own initiative and not acting on a request by the private sector.

to intellectual property, trade secrets, or confidential business information, including technical data, negotiating positions, and sensitive and proprietary internal business communications, and they also support China's strategic development goals, including its science and technology advancement, military modernization, and economic development.[29]

Based upon these findings, Trump directed the USTR to increase tariffs on goods originating in China. The amount of Chinese imports facing additional duties was initially set at $50 billion and was later raised to $250 billion. In retaliation the Chinese government initially announced additional duties on U.S. imports worth $50 billion, an amount later raised to $110 billion. These amounts have been revised several times ever since, and, most likely, we have not seen the end of this saga.

Thirty years ago, after Japan was named an unfair trading nation, President George H. W. Bush decided not to impose additional duties but instead launched the SII talks. President Trump has imposed duties and has participated in (fruitless, so far) talks with China. Clearly U.S.-China relations today are very different from what U.S.-Japan relations were decades ago. At that time the United States and Japan were simply accusing each other of attacking one another. Today, the United States and China are in a trade war affecting more than 50 percent of their bilateral goods trade.[30] Furthermore, the Japanese recession had some appreciable impact on the rest of the world but certainly no cataclysmic effects. In the post–financial

29. Presidential Memorandum on the Actions by the United States Related to the Section 301 Investigation, issued on March 22, 2018.

30. In 2017, the United States imported $520 billion of Chinese goods and exported $190 billion of goods to China. The trade measures announced in 2018 cover, therefore, 50 percent of U.S. imports from China and more than 50 percent of Chinese imports from the United States. Amiti, Redding, and Weinstein (2019) discuss the U.S. retaliation, which resulted in a unilateral increase of tariffs on goods originating in China, as well as who bears the costs of the unilateral increase in tariffs by the Trump administration and why it risks being counterproductive. Levy (2019) provides a critical assessment of the whole episode. Shan (2019) shows that trade wars have exacerbated the U.S. trade deficit, mainly because there are no substitutes for Chinese exports to the United States and it is difficult to relocate Chinese production participating in global value chains (GVCs). For some serious analysts, like Allison, the true question will be whether the United States and China can avoid what he has termed Thucydides's trap, that is, a full-fledged war, and not a mere trade altercation. Allison defines Thucydides's trap as "the severe structural stress caused when a rising power threatens to upend a ruling one. In such conditions, not just extraordinary, unexpected events, but even ordinary flashpoints of foreign affairs, can trigger large-scale conflict" (2017, 29).

crisis years, Chinese growth has been the motor for world growth. Slowing it down would undoubtedly have more of an impact on the rest of the world as well.

President Trump's strategy has not paid off thus far, mostly because it cannot address the underlying issues in bilateral trade between the United States and China, especially SOEs and forced TT. After exploring these underlying issues further, we will return to the U.S.-China trade dispute in chapter 4, where we explain why, in our view, multilateralism continues to be the best course of action.

The Two Key Complaints: SOEs and Forced TT

The two key complaints of interest to us are SOEs and forced TT. Our aim is to evaluate how much can be done to address these concerns within the existing international trade regime. If we are led to conclude that both concerns can be effectively addressed under the current rules, then the question becomes, why haven't they been addressed? If nothing can be done about these issues under current rules, we need to ask whether the adjudicating bodies have erred by not properly interpreting the relevant rules, or, conversely, whether law has made no provision for transactions involving SOEs or forced TT.

SOEs are, of course, present in many countries, not just in China. In fact, state-trading enterprises (STEs), which have been regulated by the GATT since 1947, are a form of SOEs, albeit with limited scope. A few countries that have acceded to the WTO (after the conclusion of the Uruguay Round agreements) have maintained SOEs in their sovereignty that extend beyond state trading. This is the case not only in centrally planned economies like Vietnam, and to some extent China, but also in some Arab countries. But even incumbents like the EU are home to companies that exhibit characteristics resembling those of SOEs (e.g., public undertakings, companies with special or exclusive rights, as per the ex-Article 90 of the European Community Treaty).

The ubiquity of SOEs operating in China is what makes the difference. In the Western world, STEs or undertakings with special or exclusive rights are the exception in an otherwise market economy. Conversely, the Chinese state is omnipresent in its economy, either by owning (totally or partially) economic operators or by influencing decisions made by completely private operators. As a result, rivalry in the market is heavily influenced by state decisions. More to the point, it means that trade might suffer due to state decisions made for political reasons. In China, the market economy is subservient to the needs of the state.

The Agreement on Subsidies and Countervailing Measures (SCM) is the legal instrument in the WTO context that most drastically calls for a halt to government intervention. And yet, surprisingly, this agreement does not explicitly mention SOEs. The SCM aims to discipline financial contributions by public bodies to the extent that they confer benefits to specific recipients. Arguably, SOEs could be considered "public bodies," the subject matter of the SCM, but, as previously discussed, the understanding of this term has caused considerable acrimony.

SOEs could also come under the discipline of Article XVII of the GATT, which regulates the behavior of STEs. SOEs cover, of course, a wider remit than STEs (which are limited to trading activities), and hence, the legal discipline imposed on the latter can only partially address concerns originating in the behavior of the former. Trade is a small part of the activities of SOEs.

Note, finally, that SOEs have been regulated in various Protocols of Accession, but the substantive content of their disciplining is not identical across the various protocols. We thus risk having one sauce for the goose and another for the gander. Even though all SOEs are not created equal, and differences across them can and do exist because of idiosyncratic elements of national regulation, some generally available benchmarks should not be hard to design. Discipline—the sauce—should be applied with equity and fairness. We believe, along with others, that it is high time the SCM Agreement seriously addresses this issue. Suffice it to state for now that it is simply inefficient to address it only through Protocols of Accession, as is the case today.

Technology transfer (TT) is a different matter. The issue is only partly addressed, sometimes directly and sometimes indirectly, in various WTO agreements. The GATT and similar multilateral agreements regulating trade in goods do not cover investment and as a result do not address transfer of technology as a precondition for opening up to investment. Trade-related investment measures (TRIMS), on the other hand, the name notwithstanding, do not deal with foreign direct investment (FDI). TRIMS simply outlaw local content and export performance requirements, two measures that aim to incentivize traders to favor domestic goods (and markets).

On the other hand, the GATS is a multilateral agreement, the only one that covers investment—and only with respect to trade in services and to the extent that WTO members have voluntarily agreed to enter into specific commitments under Mode 3.[31] Members are, in principle, free to opt out and avoid making market-opening commitments. And in any case, it cannot be applied to trade in goods. Finally, the TRIPS Agreement has something to say on this score as well, albeit tangentially so, as a means to ensure protection of intellectual property rights.

Prima facie, therefore, it seems that some TT can be addressed in part through more active enforcement of the existing framework (TRIPS, and GATS, if commitments have been entered). But the current framework is not sufficient; at the very least, an amendment of the current regime is necessary to address TT in the realm of goods.

Trade and investment are, of course, both complements and substitutes, and a multilateral agreement on investment has been in the works for some time without materializing into anything concrete. China's practices on this score, because of their consequential impact, make this a high-priority issue.

In this section, we discuss complaints relating to Chinese SOEs and forced TT. We first examine China's WTO obligations under the WTO Agreement and the Protocol of Accession. We then discuss the formal WTO disputes initiated by the Trilateral members against China and their outcome. Based on this analysis, we will be in a position to cement our thesis that legislative amendments are warranted to address the worries (complaints) expressed so far against Chinese practices in these two areas.

SOEs and forced TT constitute the two main claims, as we have argued, in the sense that there is to an extent consensus across the WTO membership that something needs to be done on these two fronts in order to address the resulting trade imbalances. Concentrating on these two complaints helps us analytically as well: these two issues capture almost to perfection the hybrid nature of "public-private partnership" that permeates the Chinese economy and has given rise to the vast majority of complaints raised against China since its accession.

To be sure, various other complaints against China have also been raised, and we are not suggesting that they are less important than those revolving around SOEs and TT. But delving into their details would add nothing from our analytical perspective. However, they do underscore the intertwining of public policy ordering of preferences with the workings of the private economy, the main focus of our attention, and thus deserve some attention

---

31. Mode 3 covers establishment, that is, FDI by services suppliers.

in context. Following a brief discussion of these other kinds of claims, we will return to SOEs and forced TT.

THE OTHER CLAIMS

The initial euphoria about China's accession to the WTO gradually ceded its place to a generalized dysphoria, first in the United States but increasingly spreading across the Atlantic to Europe and beyond. Complaints against China were not restricted to SOEs and TT, however. In fact, other types of claims multiplied.

Crucially, the effects of China's export-led growth model on jobs, as well as its alleged currency manipulation, dominated the criticism. President Trump has been a leading voice of this critique. Equally important, though, is the critique concerning the perceived imbalance of the system: while China can profit from open markets abroad, it has not done correspondingly enough to offer adequate access to foreign companies.

Finally, various WTO members have voiced concern about China's reluctance to join the WTO Agreement on Government Procurement (GPA), even though it had promised to do so when acceding to the WTO.

We take these points in turn.

China's Exports and Effects on Jobs

One of the first concerns raised after China's entry to the WTO was that its unprecedented volumes of exports have exacerbated unemployment in its main export markets, most notably the United States.[32] These accusations have continued to multiply, and some reputed economists have joined the chorus. Autor, Dorn, and Hanson (2013) were the first to comprehensively discuss the employment effects of China's export-led growth strategy on the U.S. job market and have painted a rather equivocal picture. In their account, the increase of Chinese imports in the U.S. market has led to the unemployment of many low-skilled U.S. workers.

Candidate Trump called China's accession to the WTO "disastrous" and "terrible" and the "greatest jobs theft in history."[33] Such claims appear to be vastly overstated and should not be taken at face value, especially since

32. Holslag (2019) makes a similar case for the EU. Even though we do not subscribe to his analysis and especially not to his policy conclusions, he does cite sources deploring the negative effects of Chinese imports on jobs in the EU. Nevertheless, he also notes that some EU members have profited immensely from Chinese FDI, including through job creation.

33. Speech at Alumisource, Moneseen, Pennsylvania, June 28, 2016, quoted in Blustein 2019, 19.

they also are likely just a rallying cry for Trump's domestic political base. Many analysts, most notably Hufbauer and Lu (2017), have distanced themselves from this view and, responding to Autor and colleagues rather than to Trump, have claimed that the numbers have been exaggerated.[34] Even more to the point, Feenstra and Sasahara (2018) have shown that the net effect of U.S.-China trade on employment is positive for the U.S. economy, if the service industry is taken into account.

In any case, the WTO regime as it currently exists has instruments available to it to address similar phenomena. GATT Article XIX offers the most appropriate safeguard to this effect. In fact, it was designed to provide an escape route from GATT obligations when imports surge in unanticipated ways and negatively affect employment in the import market. Furthermore, until 2016, WTO members could also implement a China-specific safeguard to undo similar employment effects in their domestic market, even if the more onerous conditions of Article XIX were not met.

China: A Currency Manipulator?

During the 2016 presidential campaign, Trump pledged to label China a "currency manipulator" on his first day in office. But in an interview with the *Wall Street Journal* in April 2017, he changed his mind. "They're not currency manipulators," he said, reflecting the latest U.S. Treasury Department's finding in its annual report on foreign exchange policies of major trading partners. At the time of this writing, President Trump's position on the yuan-dollar exchange rate has altered once again, and China has been branded a currency manipulator anew. It seems, for now at least, unlikely that he will seek an agreement with China similar to the 1985 Plaza agreement with Japan, which together with the 1991 Structural Impediments Initiative (SII) agreement resulted in a significant reduction in Japan's exports to, and increase in its imports from, the United States.[35] We cannot exclude the possibility that, in the near future, the mercurial U.S. president might change his mind once again. Still, a few words are in order so that the essence of this complaint is properly understood from a trade perspective, even though this is not a concern that is shared by the Trilateral or the global

---

34. There are other benefits to consumers beyond inexpensive Chinese goods. Jaravel and Sager (2019) estimate that import penetration from China has led to a decline of 1.91 percent in consumer prices.

35. Note that this is not the first controversy regarding currency controls by China. Before acceding to the GATT, China had a dual currency system in place, aiming to boost its export-led growth model, which it agreed to abolish; see Brown 1994.

community for that matter (a part of which has engaged in similar tactics in the past).

It is a commonplace that undervaluation of the national currency is a boost to exports. The GATT framers were mindful of that and took some institutional precautions to address this eventuality. The key word in this sentence is "some." Why didn't they prescribe *decisive* measures to address the potential for currency manipulation? The GATT/WTO is, of course, a *trade* contract, and so the question of whether or not a currency is correctly valued goes beyond its purview. Instead, it falls squarely under the aegis of a different institution, the IMF. An agreement to this effect was signed between the WTO and the IMF in December 1996.[36]

Prior to the IMF-WTO agreement, there was confusion as to which institution decides what. Article XV.4 of the GATT addressed the issue of currency manipulation. This provision requested that GATT/WTO members not frustrate trade flows through currency manipulations. This provision reads:

> Contracting parties shall not, by exchange action, frustrate* the intent of the provisions of this Agreement, nor, by trade action, the intent of the provisions of the Articles of Agreement of the International Monetary Fund.

The term "frustrate" is accompanied by an asterisk, which refers to the Interpretative Note and its provision, which reads:

> The word "frustrate" is intended to indicate, for example, that infringements of the letter of any Article of this Agreement by exchange action shall not be regarded as a violation of that Article if, in practice, there is no appreciable departure from the intent of the Article. Thus, a contracting party which, as part of its exchange control operated in accordance with the Articles of Agreement of the International Monetary Fund, requires payment to be received for its exports in its own currency or in the currency of one or more members of the International Monetary Fund will not thereby be deemed to contravene Article XI or Article XIII. Another example would be that of a contracting party which specifies on an import licence the country from which the goods may be imported, for the purpose not of introducing any additional element of

discrimination in its import licensing system but of enforcing permissible exchange controls.

This is not very helpful, as the two examples mentioned do not interpret the term "frustrate" in a manner that could shed light on currency manipulations as discussed here. It is clear, though, that the IMF has the authority to decide whether a currency is properly valued or not. Both Article XV of the GATT and the IMF-WTO agreement recognize as much.

GATT/WTO practice on this score has not always followed this interpretation. Ironically, the United States was the first to pay the price of GATT judicial activism in this respect: a GATT panel evaluating the import surcharge imposed by the U.S. administration in 1971, following its unilateral ending of the Bretton Woods system of fixed parities, rejected the IMF evaluation and found instead that the United States had inappropriately imposed the surcharge.[37] This remains an isolated instance, however.

The agreement signed between the WTO and the IMF in 1996 aimed to put to rest similar situations. Thereafter, WTO panels confronted with the issue of currency manipulation have always accepted the evaluation by the IMF.[38]

The IMF has been called upon on several occasions to evaluate whether the renminbi, the Chinese currency, is undervalued or not. One such instance took place in 2005, when a bipartisan bill introduced before Congress by Senators Charles Schumer and Lindsey Graham threatened to impose a 27.5 percent tariff on all Chinese products entering the United States unless the U.S. administration could convince China to revalue its currency. After much discussion, the IMF found that the renminbi was not significantly undervalued. Blustein provides an excellent account of this episode at the IMF (2019, 91ff.).

More recently, on August 5, 2019, under the auspices of President Trump, the secretary of the treasury determined that China is a currency manipulator and announced his intention to "engage with the International Monetary Fund to eliminate the unfair competitive advantage created by China's latest actions."[39] However, in its annual country report on China's economic policies published four days later, the IMF found no evidence of currency

37. Irwin (2013) provides an excellent account of this episode. Mavroidis cites the relevant parts of the GATT Working Party that discussed the Nixon surcharge (2016, 1:117ff.).

38. The panel reports on *India–Quantitative Restrictions* and *Dominican Republic–Import and Sale of Cigarettes* offer adequate illustrations to this effect.

39. https://home.treasury.gov/news/press-releases/sm751.

manipulation. As James Daniel, the IMF's mission chief for China, said, the renminbi's value in 2018 was "broadly in line with medium-term fundamentals and desirable policies, i.e. not significantly over- or undervalued."[40] This didn't stop Trump from imposing an additional tariff on $300 billion of imports from China due to what he perceived as currency manipulation.[41] The accusation stands, despite the IMF report on the matter.

We would be remiss if we concluded this discussion without mentioning the scholarly debate on this issue. Some in academia have called for action against China at the WTO on the grounds that they are engaged in currency manipulation, most notably Stiglitz and Charlton (2007) and Mattoo and Subramanian (2009). Whereas Mattoo and Subramanian's argument is largely aspirational, Stiglitz and Charlton argued that the United States should consider imposing countervailing duties against China.

This has not happened thus far, and we do not believe that it would be a legally sound option. We side with the persuasive arguments advanced by Staiger and Sykes (2010) and believe that nothing can be done about this concern at the WTO. In our view, it will be impossible to meet the specificity requirement embedded in Article 2 of the SCM Agreement, since currency undervaluations (or overvaluations) affect the entire economy, not just specific sectors.[42]

In May 2019, however, the U.S. Department of Commerce issued a notice of proposed rulemaking, whereby countervailing duties will be imposed against currency manipulators.[43] The new regulation became effective in April 2020, despite the conflict with WTO jurisprudence and criticism from the IMF.

Chinese FDI: Profit Oriented or Public Policy Oriented?
In the United States, Chinese FDI is scrutinized by the CFIUS. EU member states have also been examining Chinese FDI with increased intensity,

---

40. https://www.politico.com/story/2019/08/09/imf-report-trump-currency-manipulation-1653096.

41. Bown (2019) calculates that by that time, the average tariff on Chinese imports in the United States had increased by 24 percent. Bown also calculated the tariffs on Chinese autos, which increased from 12.6 to 42.6 percent by December 2019.

42. Goldstein and Lardy (2009) agree.

43. https://www.federalregister.gov/documents/2019/05/28/2019–11197/modification-of-regulations-regarding-benefit-and-specificity-in-countervailing-duty-proceedings. Paulson (2015) provides a detailed account of the negotiations between the United States and China on this score.

putting in place an EU-wide framework to assess such investments, although it is still far from an "EU CFIUS." In the meantime, China has acquired control over key infrastructure assets in a number of EU members, especially those in the southern and eastern periphery.[44]

Why are Western democracies paying close attention to Chinese FDI? Diamond and Schell (2018) provide some evidence that China often uses its companies to advance strategic objectives abroad (including, for example, gaining access to critical [physical or data] infrastructure and technology). They also claim that Chinese Chambers of Commerce in the United States appear to have ties to the Chinese government.

Chinese Services: A Closed Market?

Lardy (2019, 101ff.), among others, provides substantial evidence about the relative accessibility, or lack thereof, of Chinese services markets. China did make significant tariff reductions for various goods markets when acceding to the WTO. Even though China's average tariffs are higher than those imposed in the United States and the EU, they are a far cry from its own tariffs before accession to the WTO. In addition, China has recently made generous tariff commitments in the realm of environmental goods.[45]

This is decidedly not the case in markets for services. The commonplace view is that China has a long way to go to meet the openness practiced by, for example, the transatlantic partners. Paradoxically, this item does not figure high on anyone's agenda. China was not invited to participated in the TiSA (Trade in Services Agreement) negotiation, even though it did express its willingness to take a seat at the table. Although the WTO provides a platform (GATS) by which commitments to liberalize services markets can be agreed upon, in today's world, with the malaise surrounding a WTO hit by the dispute settlement crisis and handicapped by a malfunctioning legislative branch, there has been little or no movement in this direction. In the absence of a multilateral agreement, China's services markets remain relatively inaccessible to its trading partners.

China's Procurement Market

When negotiating its accession, China promised to join the WTO GPA. This promise has yet to materialize.

---

44. Holslag (2019) discusses this in considerable detail. As a side note, according to the World Bank, 40 percent of all the recent cases reviewed by the CFIUS have involved Chinese companies (2019b, 130ff.).

45. Mavroidis and Neven (2019) provide evidence to this effect.

The Chinese procurement market is vast. Chen and Whalley (2011) and Anderson et al. (2011) provided estimations of the size of the market ten years ago, when the accession of China was *ante portas*.

There was disappointment in some countries, especially in Europe, that during its preparation for WTO accession China turned to the U.S., not the EU, model for its procurement practices. The U.S. model contains a compulsory "Buy American" policy for federal and state agencies ("American" being defined by reference to the manufacturing place as well as the U.S. value added), with a possible waiver for companies originating in countries that are signatories to the GPA. It is suspected, however, that because of the transaction costs associated with obtaining the waiver, the level of success of foreign companies in the U.S. procurement market is lower than it would be otherwise.[46]

The China model did not go as far. China, as Weiss and Thurnbon (2006) explain, did not opt for a mandatory "Buy Chinese" policy but only for preferential treatment of goods originating in China.

STATE-OWNED ENTERPRISES

SOEs have been a thorny issue in the relations between WTO members and China and risk becoming even more of a problem in the future. President Xi, following years of consolidation and then reduction in the numbers of SOEs, has recently beefed up state involvement in SOEs, a provocative move that risks renewing the wrath of China's trade partners. Arguably, the move by President Xi violates the spirit of China's commitments when acceding to the WTO, but it is an uphill battle to demonstrate that they violate the letter as well. Here is why.

The WTO Agreement, like the original GATT Agreement (1947), is silent about state ownership and, more broadly, about state involvement in the trading regime. This reflected the fact that the GATT's main architects were Americans and British, the foremost market economies, and that all its original participants shared (or at least accepted) a liberal understanding of law and democracy.[47] State involvement in the workings of the economy

46. See some of the studies in Georgopoulos, Hoekman, and Mavroidis 2017 in support of this view.

47. Pollard (1985) provides a good deal of evidence to this effect. He refers, among other things, to the Clifford-Elsey report, prepared at the request of President Truman, a study on Soviet-American relations. This report concluded that American aid and trade were the mainstay in the battle against communism. Pollard (1985, 55ff.), Gaddis (2000), and Hook and Spanier

was confined to a few cases with special circumstances. As a result, there was no need to comprehensively discuss this issue particularly since these were capitalist regimes built around the protection of private property.

The only exception in the GATT legal framework, which confirms the rule, concerns STEs. Article XVII of the GATT permits contracting parties to maintain or establish STEs if they can ensure that their STEs "act in a manner consistent with the general principles of non-discriminatory treatment prescribed in [the GATT] Agreement for governmental measures affecting imports or exports by private traders." This rule was introduced in order to police milk and wheat marketing boards operated at the time (in 1947) by Australia, Canada, New Zealand, and the United Kingdom, four of the original twenty-three GATT signatories.[48]

The provision on STEs might sound oddly paradoxical when viewed against the liberal understanding of the GATT. However, it is quite intuitive. Some countries, and most prominently the four countries mentioned above, had introduced STEs to ensure adequate supply of staples in the period following the 1929 financial crisis and more so following World War II. There was a genuine concern to guarantee the supply of staples at affordable prices. STEs were thought of as the means to tame "animal spirits" in this context.

State involvement in the economy is also addressed, in a more general way, through the disciplines embedded in the SCM Agreement. This agreement was a product of successful negotiations during the Uruguay Round. Originally, the GATT contained only one provision aimed at taming subsidization, Article XVI. The rationale for its inclusion was to ensure that the exchange of tariff concessions, and the ensuing trade liberalization, would not be undone through state involvement. States, in other words, should not be allowed to take with one hand (the provision of subsidies) what they had granted with the other (tariff concessions). The SCM Agreement developed and strengthened the original discipline.

When negotiations with China were initiated, WTO members had already concluded the SCM Agreement. By that time, they were aware that the term "state-owned enterprise" did not even appear in the body of the SCM Agreement. Indeed, SOEs, an amplification of state involvement in the market when compared to STEs, were quite contrary to the GATT's

---

(2013) confirm this view. Pollard also provides evidence that the British shared this view of the world. He mentions a "threat" by Lord Keynes that "if the British swung to state trading they would have an important influence on many parts of the world," something no one in the U.S. administration at the time was prepared to entertain (1985, 69).

48. See Kostecki 1978.

liberal understanding. The starting point for the negotiation of the SCM Agreement was a GATT world where market economies participated, not a GATT world full of centrally planned economies. Thus the purpose of the SCM Agreement was to limit the occasional political economy-motivated state interference with the market and not to act as pushback against an overwhelming state presence in the economy.

Echoing the rationale for Article XVII of the GATT, where the idea was to limit the role of the occasional, narrowly mandated STEs, not to encourage and strengthen them, the negotiators of the SCM Agreement followed a comparable strategy and did not have to address SOEs as such. True, before China's accession, some states that had acceded to the GATT/WTO knew of SOEs. They were a marginal concern for international trade (ex-communist countries; some African and Arab states), however, and presented the world trading regime with no real issue, as the impact of African and Arab SOEs on international trade was, by any reasonable benchmark, marginal. In any case, they had signaled during their accession process that they had already embarked on a privatization process. China's accession, because of the size of its market and the omnipresence of SOEs in it, changed all this.[49]

There was widespread recognition during the Chinese accession negotiations of the potential incompatibility of SOEs with a liberal trading system. To cite just one author in this respect, Hufbauer (1998) reflected the commonplace view that the Chinese SOEs were presenting a clear and present danger for the multilateral trading system and that unless something was done to address this issue through the Protocol of Accession, the world trading system could suffer as a result.[50] Jackson went a step further. In his view, redrafting the WTO SCM Agreement had become imperative as a result of China's WTO accession:

> China's government-owned, or state-operated or owned, enterprises are a big challenge to the system, and it is hard to believe this will not shape some of the thinking about subsidies . . . one can predict that in a couple of years some of the definitions in the subsidies code will have to be revised, if that is manageable. (2003, 24)

49. Furthermore, China never really embarked on speedy privatization, or privatization for that matter. The Eastern European countries that joined the EU had to do so because of the legal constraints imposed by the EU. China, as we will see later, corporatized a lot and privatized a little; see Song 2018; and Zhou, Gao, and Bai 2019.

50. Forty-five percent of Chinese economies are run by SOEs, and 77 percent of Chinese companies appearing on the Forbes 500 list are SOEs (Lardy 2019).

Implicitly, this and similar views rested on the warranted assumption that the WTO multilateral regime, as it had been imagined by the time of China's accession, could not effectively deal with SOEs and the problems they would pose to the liberal trade order.

The WTO membership was unable to agree on a detailed list of its causes for concern as a result of the presence of SOEs in the Chinese market. The negotiating record, as reflected in the China accession documents, reveals various formal and informal statements about the role of SOEs, which capture the essence of complaints that individual WTO members had voiced during the negotiation process:

- SOEs have privileged access to financing,[51] often provided by state-owned commercial banks (SOCBs), because of the frequent intermingling between them.
- SOEs do not behave in accordance with commercial considerations, distorting conditions of competition in the Chinese market and thus hampering access to foreign goods and services.
- SOEs routinely subsidize and export-subsidize.

The negotiating process intended to address these issues, to the extent that they remained unaddressed by the existing multilateral obligations. The Protocol of Accession would, therefore, complement the obligations that China would assume upon entry to the WTO.

CHINA'S WTO OBLIGATIONS

China's obligations with respect to SOEs originate in the WTO agreements (especially the SCM, even though it does not address SOEs directly) and its Protocol of Accession (which does address SOEs explicitly).[52] With respect to the SCM Agreement, a Chinese SOE must not provide export or local content subsidies, which would violate its obligations under Article 3 of the SCM. Furthermore, assuming that it has subsidized (regardless of

51. Privileged access to financing could be a violation of the WTO, if it could be shown that beneficiaries received something they could not have received under normal market conditions ("private investor test"). Walter and Howie (2011) and McMahon (2018) make a strong case that SOCBs are not operating under commercial considerations, and this is the reason why the financial sector in China is, in their line of argument, quite fragile. Nevertheless, at the end of the day, a legal finding that financing does not correspond to commercial considerations can only take place against the framework that we discuss in the next subsections.

52. For a comprehensive discussion, see Qin 2004.

whether its subsidy is illegal, as per Article 3 of the SCM, or simply action-able, under Article 5 of the SCM), it runs the risk of having countervailing duties imposed against it.

For either of these two provisions to kick in with respect to SOEs, though, one thing is clear: SOEs must be acknowledged as "public bodies" in the sense of Article 1 of the SCM Agreement.[53] This article defines a subsidy as a financial contribution by a government or a "public body" that confers a benefit upon a recipient. Private actions that confer a benefit, in other words, can never be regarded as a "subsidy" in the SCM sense of the term.

If SOEs are not considered "public bodies," the only way to successfully lodge a complaint against their actions would be if complainants were to demonstrate that the Chinese government was using them as a conduit. Article 1 of the SCM Agreement states that a WTO member is liable under this Agreement even when it has "entrusted or directed" a private agent to provide a financial contribution that confers a benefit to a recipient. The amount of evidence required for this latter demonstration is, of course, higher than if SOEs were perceived to be public bodies. This is so because in the case of a demonstration that they have been used as "conduit," the party carrying the burden of proof must focus on the actual conduct of the agent at hand. Conversely, were SOEs to be judged to be "public bodies," it is the entity itself and its links to the government that matter, and there is no need to also discuss their actual conduct. An illustration here seems appropriate. Assume that a complainant wants to show that a private bank in China has been used as conduit for the state to offer preferential rates to certain customers. The fact that the bank offers such rates to some customers does not in and of itself suffice to show that it has been used as a conduit by the state. The bank could respond, for example, that the investment pros-pects were extraordinary. Absent detailed discussion of the facts, a claim that the bank was used as a conduit risks being baseless. Conversely, there is no need to review actual behavior in order to decide whether an SOE is a public body. In this realm, panels will typically check statutory language regarding institutional links and will also take into account elements such as owner-ship (which, as already discussed, is not in and of itself decisive as per case law), participation of state officials on the board, voting rights, and so forth.

---

53. SOEs can, of course, be the recipients of subsidies as well. This is not the question we ask here though, as, with respect to this issue, there is no need to go beyond the existing regime.

So much for the SCM. What about the Protocol of Accession? Mindful of the limits of the SCM Agreement to address SOEs head-on, WTO members insisted on the inclusion of various provisions, in different parts of China's protocol,[54] which deal specifically with this issue. For example, §10.2 (on subsidies) reads:

> For purposes of applying Articles 1.2 and 2 of the SCM Agreement, subsidies provided to state-owned enterprises will be viewed as specific if, inter alia, state-owned enterprises are the predominant recipients of such subsidies or state-owned enterprises receive disproportionately large amounts of such subsidies.

This is a China-specific obligation. No such presumption exists for SOEs operating in other WTO members.[55] Specificity is an additional requirement, and the complainant does not benefit from legal presumption if a subsidy is directed toward a particular addressee. Section 12.2 (in the section on agriculture), on the other hand, states:

> China shall, under the Transitional Review Mechanism, notify fiscal and other transfers between or among state-owned enterprises in the agricultural sector (whether national or sub-national) and other enterprises that operate as state trading enterprises in the agricultural sector.

This is also a China-only obligation. Other WTO members need to notify only financial contributions that are specific subsidies (Article 25.2 of the SCM), not any and all transfers as is required from China.

In addition, the report of the Working Party on the Accession of China contains an entire section not just on SOEs but also on state-invested enterprises (SIEs), economic agents where the state has some stake in the formation of the capital, even if the state's stake is not the controlling one.[56] It seems that, at the very least, WTO incumbents were aware of the limits of the multilateral legal arsenal and attempted to add to it in order to address this issue. Section 6 of Chapter II comprises seven paragraphs (§§43–49), some of which (§§46–47, 49) are explicitly mentioned in §342, the paragraph

---

54. WTO Doc. WT/L/432, November 23, 2001.

55. See Christiansen and Kim 2014 for an extensive discussion of the importance of SOEs in the world. See also Garcia-Herrero and Xu 2017 and Lardy 2019 for contrasting views on the role of SOEs in China and how trading partners should deal with them.

56. WTO Doc. WT/ACC/CHN/49, October 1, 2001. We explain what SIEs are in more detail in what follows.

of the report that includes all binding commitments entered into by China. Here we quote §§46–47 in full:[57]

> 46. The representative of China further confirmed that China would ensure that all state-owned and state-invested enterprises would make purchases and sales based solely on commercial considerations, e.g., price, quality, marketability and availability, and that the enterprises of other WTO Members would have an adequate opportunity to compete for sales to and purchases from these enterprises on non-discriminatory terms and conditions. In addition, the Government of China would not influence, directly or indirectly, commercial decisions on the part of state-owned or state-invested enterprises, including on the quantity, value or country of origin of any goods purchased or sold, except in a manner consistent with the WTO Agreement. The Working Party took note of these commitments.
>
> 47. The representative of China confirmed that, without prejudice to China's rights in future negotiations in the Government Procurement Agreement, all laws, regulations and measures relating to the procurement by state-owned and state-invested enterprises of goods and services for commercial sale, production of goods or supply of services for commercial sale, or for nongovernmental purposes would not be considered to be laws, regulations and measures relating to government procurement. Thus, such purchases or sales would be subject to the provisions of Articles II, XVI and XVII of the GATS and Article III of the GATT 1994. The Working Party took note of this commitment.

In fact, these provisions reproduce the obligations embedded in Article XVII of the GATT. Interestingly, §46 refers to the two obligations included in Article XVII of the GATT, without mentioning them as expressions of the nondiscrimination obligation. Nondiscrimination is separately mentioned in the same provision.

We should note, at this stage, the absence of case law on §46. Case law under Article XVII of the GATT has, in our view, improperly understood these two obligations—affording adequate opportunities to compete and

---

57. We will quote §49 later in the discussion on technology transfer. The report of the Working Party on the Accession of China contains various provisions. Some reflect binding commitments, some mention best-endeavors clauses, and others simply inform about the direction in which the acceding country is going. To avoid misunderstandings, the drafters of similar reports have included in one specific paragraph all the legally binding obligations that an acceding country has agreed to. Section 342 plays this role with respect to China.

acting in accordance with commercial considerations—as mere expressions of the obligation to not discriminate. This means that an STE that does not discriminate across foreign and domestic goods (sources of supply) is not violating Article XVII, even when not acting in accordance with commercial considerations. Thus, case law has eviscerated the bite of Article XVII of the GATT. By contrast, both the TPP and its successor agreement, the CPTPP, have distinguished nondiscrimination from these two obligations. This is the right approach and, as we will discuss later, the key issue is whether relevant entities have acted in accordance with commercial considerations. Problems emerge when the answer is no because they favor domestic producers and products.

For now, though, we need to explain in some detail the case law under Article XVII, since it is quite relevant to an understanding of the commitments embedded in §46.

It was a 1952 GATT panel on *Belgian Family Allowances* that established the independence of the "commercial considerations" criterion from the obligation not to discriminate, when, in an oft-quoted passage, it held (§4):

> As regards the exception contained in paragraph 2 of Article XVII, it would appear that it referred only to the principle set forth in paragraph 1 of that Article, i.e., the obligation to make purchases in accordance with commercial considerations and did not extend to matters dealt with in Article III.

In other words, this panel concluded that STEs must act in accordance with commercial considerations, irrespective of the obligation to not discriminate. Thus an STE that did not discriminate in its dealings with its transnational partners could still be found liable if it was acting under the orders of its government to the detriment of its own bottom line. What mattered was whether, in addition to avoiding discrimination, it had also acted in accordance with commercial considerations, that is, like a private agent.

But in 1983, the GATT panel on *Canada–FIRA* reached the opposite conclusion. It held that the obligations embedded in Article XVII.1(b) of the GATT (namely, the obligation to act in accordance with commercial considerations and to afford adequate opportunities to operators from other GATT members) are mere illustrations of the nondiscrimination obligation (§5.16). As a result, STEs did not incur any obligations in addition to the obligation not to discriminate.

This was not the end of the story, however, as the discussion regarding the ambit of the obligations imposed on STEs continued in the WTO era. The panel on *Korea–Various Measures on Beef* seemed to place the two obligations (nondiscrimination and acting in accordance with commercial considerations) on equal footing, as opposed to treating one as an illustration of the other (§7.57):

> A conclusion that the principle of non-discrimination was violated would suffice to prove a violation of Article XVII; similarly, a conclusion that a decision to purchase or buy was not based on "commercial considerations," would also suffice to show a violation of Article XVII.

Of course, acting on commercial considerations could result in discrimination. In this vein, one could, for example, understand why an import monopoly would like to favor goods originating in producers with whom it has entered into long-term contracts, for instance, by offering them better prices. Hence, this report was simply reflecting economic logic.

This opinion, nevertheless, did not win the day. The issue was finally resolved in the litigation on *Canada–Wheat Exports and Grain Imports*. The panel in this case (§6.60) disregarded the approach advanced in *Korea–Various Measures on Beef* and treated the obligation to act in accordance with commercial considerations as an illustration of the obligation not to discriminate, not as an additional obligation. On appeal, the Appellate Body confirmed the panel's approach, holding that not only the obligation to act in accordance with commercial considerations but also the obligation to afford "adequate opportunities to compete" discussed in Article XVII.1(b) of the GATT were mere illustrations of the obligation not to discriminate (§§89–106). As a result, the Appellate Body was unwilling to extend its review to any issues beyond claims of discriminatory behavior (§145):

> The disciplines of Article XVII:1 are aimed at preventing certain types of discriminatory behaviour. We see no basis for interpreting that provision as imposing comprehensive competition-law-type obligations on STEs, as the United States would have us do.

It is doubtful whether this understanding of the obligations on STEs captures the negotiating intent. It is, of course, equally doubtful whether it is at all reasonable to interpret this provision in this way. Let us use the facts of *Canada–Wheat Exports and Grain Imports* to illustrate this point. The panel dealt with claims by the United States to the effect that a Canadian STE, the Canadian Wheat Board, was not acting in accordance with commercial considerations in the trade of wheat and other grains. The Canadian Wheat Board was enjoying various privileges, namely:

- the exclusive right to purchase and sell western Canadian wheat for export and domestic human consumption
- the right to set, subject to government approval, the initial price payable for western Canadian wheat destined for export or domestic human consumption
- the government guarantee of the initial payment to producers of western Canadian wheat
- the government guarantee of lending it money, when necessary
- the government guarantee of extending credit sales to foreign buyers

The United States had advanced two claims. The first was that the Canadian Wheat Board was not fulfilling its obligation to operate in a way that only took into account commercial considerations. In the view of the United States, selling below market rates was not consonant with commercial considerations. Second, the United States had argued that the Canadian STE's behavior was GATT inconsistent, since it was seeking to maximize revenue and not profit and, hence, was not acting like a private grain trader.

The panel rejected all U.S. claims and arguments in this respect. It ruled that the Canadian STE could legitimately use its privilege to the disadvantage of commercial actors (§6.106), that selling below market prices was perfectly legitimate (§6.129), and that not selling to maximize profit should not be equated with acting without respecting commercial considerations (§6.133). In the words of the panel (§6.60):

> In our view, the circumstance that STEs are not inherently "commercial actors" does not necessarily lead to the conclusion that the "commercial considerations" requirement is intended to make STEs behave like "commercial" actors. Indeed, we think it should lead to a different conclusion, namely that the requirement in question is simply intended to prevent STEs from behaving like "political" actors.

And in a footnote it added:

> We use the term "political actors" here merely to contrast our understanding of the first clause with that of the United States. Non-commercial considerations include, but are not limited to, political considerations.

In the panel's eyes, thus, the obligation to act in accordance with commercial considerations was not necessarily captured by the obligation not to discriminate. It was, nevertheless, a very narrow obligation, since all that was required from WTO members was to avoid behaving like "political actors," as opposed to behaving like profit maximizers.

Following an appeal by the United States, the Appellate Body was presented with the opportunity to explain its own understanding of the term "commercial considerations." Stating first the panel's understanding of the term "commercial considerations" (§140), it went on to find that as long as STEs do not discriminate, they can be deemed to have acted in accordance with commercial considerations. The Appellate Body further held that STEs may legitimately use their privileges, which they do not have to undo in order to be deemed to be acting consistently with Article XVII of the GATT (§§146–51).

One can hardly find fault with the latter part of the Appellate Body's analysis, in the sense that it would be rather cavalier to read Article XVII of the GATT as requesting STEs to prepare their own demise. And yet something is missing in this picture. For example, using their privileges could enable STEs to engage in abusive behavior. In the absence of world competition law to punish monopolization, such behavior could undermine tariff negotiations. The only legal instrument that affected parties can lean on to address such concerns is nonviolation complaints (NVCs),[58] which are associated, nevertheless, with an important burden of persuasion for the complaining parties. Moreover, why is it that sales below cost, say, are necessary for an STE to continue to exist? Should we not have to inquire about the necessity of such actions? The Appellate Body did not have to go down this road, and yet by going halfway it raised dozens of questions that it left unanswered.

More to the key question that we are addressing here, the Appellate Body addressed in a definitive manner the relationship between the obligation to observe nondiscrimination and the obligation to act in accordance with commercial considerations. It held that the latter was an expression of the former, but it failed to explain the rationale behind its finding. Does it really make sense to understand the obligation to act in accordance with commercial considerations as a mere illustration of the obligation not to discriminate?

58. See the section titled "The Limits of Adjudication before the WTO" in chapter 4 for a brief explanation of NVCs.

In fact, following a U.S. proposal to this effect during the original GATT negotiations,[59] the following Interpretative Note was added to Article XVII.1 of the GATT:

> The charging by a state enterprise of different prices for its sales of a product in different markets, domestic or foreign, is not precluded by the provisions of this Article, provided that such different prices are charged for commercial reasons.

This note, which has the legal status of treaty language, makes two points: first, that differential pricing is perfectly legitimate as long as origin is not the reason behind it; and second, that differential pricing is also perfectly legitimate as long as it corresponds to commercial considerations. There is nothing wrong, in other words, with price discrimination if it does not hinge on the origin of imported goods. And yet, the Appellate Body totally disregarded this.

In this reading of the obligation embedded in Article XVII, there should also be nothing wrong with an import monopoly applying a lower duty on goods destined for industrial use and a higher one for like-used goods destined for final consumption. Such behavior would be considered discriminatory, and yet most people would agree that it is consonant with commercial considerations.

Alas, it is by now clear that, following the Appellate Body's ruling, a class of measures adopted by STEs that are not consonant with commercial considerations will be exonerated from liability under the GATT if they have been applied in a nondiscriminatory manner. This is so because the Appellate Body has understood nondiscrimination in a contextual manner. Nondiscrimination presupposes a benchmark, and the benchmark chosen by the GATT framers was origin. Through this case law, the Appellate Body indicated (as had some GATT panels before it) that anytime it faced a case where two goods of different origins had been treated in different ways, it presumed that the rationale for distinction was origin. It is, thus, less than clear that the Appellate Body's findings are in line with the negotiating intent, and perhaps even common sense.

Finally, we should also turn our attention to an unappealed finding of the same panel (*Canada–Wheat Exports and Grain Imports*) regarding the interpretation of the term "solely" that appears in the body of Article XVII of the

59. E/PC/T/C.6/27, January 30, 1947, p. 5.

GATT: STEs should not be simply acting in accordance with commercial considerations; they should be acting *solely* in accordance with commercial considerations. In the panel's view, an STE would not be acting solely in accordance with commercial considerations if it were to make purchases or sales based on any one or more of the following considerations (§6.88):

- the nationality of potential buyers or sellers
- the (wider) policies pursued
- the national, economic, or political interest of the member maintaining the STE

Thus the panel, through these criteria, accentuated the obligation to act with commercial considerations. Unfortunately, following the ruling of the Appellate Body in this case, all of this case law—very useful and quite pertinent as far as Chinese SOEs are concerned—has been relegated to oblivion.

It perhaps complicates matters that there is no statutory definition of the term "SOE" in the Protocol of Accession. It is unclear whether an economic agent must be owned 100 percent by the state to qualify as an SOE or whether a lower percentage would suffice. The term "SIE" similarly lacks a precise definition in the protocol. By context, and given our understanding of the term "SOE," the safe conclusion is that we are dealing with economic agents where state involvement is of a lesser degree than that of SOEs. Indeed, in *U.S.–Countervailing Measures (China)* (DS437), the panel noted the U.S. administration's definition of an SIE as an entity with a government ownership stake of any percentage, with no minimum threshold defined (footnote 100). Notably, China did not contest this definition.

However, the absence of definition does not affect the legal analysis. What matters is whether SOEs should be considered "public bodies" or private agents. Here neither the WTO (of course not, since SOEs are not even mentioned as such therein) nor the Protocol of Accession takes a stance. Indeed, the only obligations that China has accepted are:

- transparency requirements
- an obligation for SOEs to act in accordance with commercial considerations (but as we have seen, because of case law, this risks being understood as merely an obligation to not discriminate)
- an obligation to accept that subsidies to SOEs will be deemed specific

- an acknowledgment that purchases by SOEs/SIEs would not be considered government procurement

Taken together, do these obligations mean that Chinese SOEs should be defined as public bodies or, conversely, private agents? We start from the last point. On paper, purchases by SOEs/SIEs must observe the framework accepted by China (WTO multilateral obligations + Protocol of Accession). Implicitly, there is an acknowledgment that SOEs/SIEs are not state entities, even though this acknowledgment is in "hybrid" form, as it might change when China joins the GPA, the only meaningful WTO plurilateral agreement, where participation is optional.[60]

From a purely legal perspective, §47 does not amount to an acknowledgment by the WTO membership that SOEs are private agents. They are therefore not prevented from litigating the opposite, and practice confirms this point. The reference to the GPA in §47 is a unilateral statement by China, not by the WTO membership. It was deemed necessary since, from its accession days, China had promised to eventually join this agreement. This promise has yet to materialize. When it does, it could very well be the case that purchases by SOEs come under the disciplines of the GPA. This will be a matter for future negotiation, when and if it occurs.

Finally, subjecting SOEs to the disciplines of the GPA (eventually) will not ipso facto mean that they will then be acknowledged as public bodies. Georgopoulos, Hoekman, and Mavroidis (2017) explain why the legal framework allows WTO members to subject purchases by private entities to the GPA disciplines and provide empirical evidence to this effect. As far as the third point goes, it suffices to note that China has assumed a clear-cut obligation, which, as our discussion in the next subsection shows, has not resulted in any disagreements or litigation.

The second point is quite important. The Protocol of Accession distinguishes between distinct obligations imposed on SOEs, which must act in a nondiscriminatory manner, in accordance with commercial considerations, and afford adequate opportunities to compete to interested parties. As we have explained in detail, GATT/WTO case law has, in our view wrongly so, understood the latter two obligations as mere expressions of the obligation to not discriminate. This means that an STE that does not discriminate across foreign and domestic goods (sources of supply) is not violating Article XVII,

---

60. Georgopoulos, Hoekman, and Mavroidis (2017) discuss this point in detail.

even when not acting in accordance with commercial considerations. Thus, case law has eviscerated the bite of Article XVII of the GATT—and in our view has always done so. The transparency obligations assumed by China are similarly quite straightforward and leave no room for doubt as to what China has committed to do.

We are left still with the elephant in the room: Are SOEs private agents or public bodies? The Protocol of Accession did not take a stance on the innate nature of SOEs, but their characterization as one or the other is crucial for the disputes already brought against China. And this point has single-handedly dominated the discussions before the Dispute Settlement Body (DSB) where reports by WTO adjudicating bodies are routinely discussed. Like a stone in the shoe, this unanswered question is an irritant right at the point of closest contact between WTO members, and it has, more specifically, exacerbated trade disputes between the United States and China. The U.S. administration has been treating as "public bodies" (without defining them as either SOEs/SIEs) even entities where China had no ownership stake but over which, in the U.S. view at least, China has been de facto exercising meaningful control. It is this U.S. attitude that has brought China and the United States before WTO panels.

Complaints against SOEs before the WTO

This uncertainty around Chinese SOEs has played directly into bilateral trade disputes between the United States and China. Two disputes directly concerning Chinese SOEs have been brought to the WTO. China was the complainant rather than the defendant in both cases and, in each, China complained against U.S. measures that affected exports by Chinese SOEs, arguing that the U.S. authorities had been mischaracterizing their SOEs. The two disputes are *U.S.–Antidumping and Countervailing Duties (China)* (DS379), initiated in 2008, and *U.S.–Countervailing Measures (China)* (DS437), initiated in 2012.

The only provision of the Protocol of Accession cited in the two disputes was Article 15, which concerns price comparability in subsidies and dumping investigations. For the rest, the disputes concerned the question of whether practices implemented by China were consistent with the SCM Agreement. But the crux of the dispute was the disagreement over the ambit of the SCM Agreement: it is in this context that WTO panels (and the Appellate Body) had to decide whether SOEs (or, more particularly, the SOEs at hand) should be considered "public bodies" or not.

Who won or lost overall in these two disputes is immaterial for our purpose. What matters is how the WTO adjudicating bodies understood the term "public body" and, more precisely, whether SOEs qualify as such.

Article 1.1(a)(1) of the SCM Agreement specifies that a subsidy exists if "there is a financial contribution by a government or any public body within the territory of a Member." Since SOEs are not formally part of the Chinese government, one of the key questions before the WTO adjudicators was whether ownership, as such, suffices to qualify an entity as a "public body"— assuming, of course, that we are dealing with an entity owned by the state. If so, did a certain percentage—say, a controlling interest—suffice to consider an SOE a "public body"? If not, what additional evidence would be required for these entities to be treated as "public bodies"?

China lodged the complaint because the U.S. Department of Commerce (DOC), the domestic authority in charge of the investigation, had changed its parameters, and instead of asking whether an entity acts in accordance with commercial considerations (irrespective of eventual state ownership) was stating that ownership by the state defined an entity as a "public body." As a result, Chinese SOEs could potentially be considered public bodies, and hence, one of the two constituent elements of the subsidy definition under the SCM (the other being the conferral of a benefit) would always be present.

The response in the original litigation[61] was identical across the two disputes, and it was a flat "no."[62] The WTO Appellate Body refused to equate ownership with "public body." The Appellate Body found that for an entity to qualify as a public body, it must be pursuing policies mandated (or induced) by the government. This, in turn, would have required the U.S. DOC to inquire into the workings of the investigated SOEs. Having lost this point, the U.S. administration was asked to adopt corrective (implementing) action in order to bring its measures into compliance with the obligations that it had assumed under the WTO.

The U.S. administration, when implementing what it was asked to do in the adverse report, adopted a measure (a memorandum on public bodies), whereby it distinguished between three cases:

---

61. We will concentrate on the reports issued in the realm of the *U.S.–Countervailing Measures (China)* (DS437) litigation. This is the most recent pronouncement of the WTO Appellate Body on the issue of the definition of "public body," and for this reason alone, our choice is justified.

62. Cartland, Depayre, and Woznowski (2012) have criticized this approach as overly restrictive.

- SOEs fully owned by the state
- SOEs partially owned by the state[63]
- Companies in which the state is not a shareholder

It then added a series of relevant factors (the number and importance of which increase as we move from full to no ownership along the spectrum), which must also be considered when deciding whether an SOE is a public body. Consequently, ownership was not considered a sufficient condition in asserting whether an entity is a "public body." It could be a necessary, but never sufficient, condition.

Nevertheless, the U.S. measure did not adhere to the view that what mattered was whether China had effectively exercised control in practice over similar entities for them to be considered "public bodies." Whether this has been the case was a matter of circumstantial evidence and could be of interest only if China had used private agents as conduits. Various criteria have been employed in the relatively scarce case law so far, ranging from appointments in management positions (who has the right to do that?) to the question of whether the entity concerned has behaved as profit maximizer or, conversely, whether it has been pursuing public policy. In the U.S. view, it was the nature of the interaction between economic agents and the Chinese state that was dispositive, and even completely private agents could be considered "public bodies" because of the nature of the interaction. The U.S. administration thought that it had complied with its obligations, but China thought otherwise and requested the establishment of a compliance panel.

The panel report on *U.S.–Countervailing Measures (China)* (Article 21.5-China) found that the United States had complied with its obligation to implement the adverse panel report, at least with respect to its understanding of the term "public body." China appealed the report, and on July 16, 2019, the Appellate Body issued its final decision. The most pertinent part of the report is §5.99.

For China, a public body exists if the claimant has shown a clear and logical connection between an identified government function and conduct that constitutes a financial contribution. In other words, it is not sufficient for an investigating authority to establish that an entity has a close relationship with the government for the entity to be considered a "public body." It must also establish that it exercises government authority.

63. The U.S. administration adopted the term "SIEs," which allowed flexibility as to the amount of state investment necessary to qualify an economic entity as a "public body."

Conversely, for the United States, the qualification of an entity as a "public body" does not hinge on the qualification of its conduct. The qualification as a "public body" should depend solely on the identity of the entity: if it has a sufficiently close relationship with government, then it should be considered a public body. A private entity could still be considered a public body because of the possibility of government influence. This could be the case for several reasons: because state officials participate on the board of the company, because its own board members also participate in government committees, or because of the existence of institutional links that raise a presumption that the private entity will not be behaving as profit maximizer. What is important here is that, in the U.S. view, there is no need to show actual behavior. It suffices to show that, because of the links between the entity investigated and the state, there is the potential for the former to act in a manner that is not consonant with market behavior.

In the "conduct vs. entity" debate, the Appellate Body sided with the latter view (§5.100): the question of conduct matters only when an entirely private entity is involved, that is, when a WTO member government directs or entrusts a private agent with a mission. Thus, in principle, even private entities in close cahoots with their government can qualify as "public bodies." As per this case law, consequently, a complainant claiming that a private entity is an SOE will prevail even if it does not provide evidence regarding its actual conduct. It only has to provide evidence pointing to close links between the entity at hand and the state where it operates.[64]

This decision's importance for future cases that address similar claims requires us to unpack some of its details. Needless to say, the conditions under which a private entity will be considered a "public body" have a very important bearing on the subject matter of this volume: the higher the number of private entities considered public bodies, the higher the number of transactions that could qualify as subsidies (and thus be susceptible to countervailing tariffs). Indeed, the Appellate Body itself put it very aptly in §5.100 of its report:

Since it has been established that an entity is a public body, then "*all* conduct" of that entity shall be attributable to the Member concerned for the purposes of Article 1.1(a)(1). When that entity's conduct "falls within subparagraphs (i)–(iii) and the first clause of subparagraph (iv)", then

64. On this score, see Garcia-Herrero and Xu 2017.

it will be deemed to give rise to a financial contribution for purposes of Article 1.1(a)(1). (emphasis in the original)

So, what kind of evidence can a WTO member present in support of a claim that a private entity is a "public body"? In the Appellate Body's words (§5.100):

The *conduct* . . . is logically connected to an identified "government function" . . . the relevant enquiry hinges on the *entity* engaging in that conduct, its core characteristics, and its relationship with the government. (emphasis in the original)

It does not suffice to demonstrate the existence of a one-off action of this sort; the Appellate Body calls for providing evidence with respect to "sustained and systematic practice" (§5.101). The burden of persuasion, however, does not extend to cover instances of "meaningful control" that government exercises over a private entity. The Appellate Body explicitly refuted an attempt by China to push the evidentiary standard in that direction (§§5.102–3). If the complainant can make a convincing case that a private entity is intertwined with the government or has adopted sustained conduct akin to a governmental function, the private entity at hand will be deemed a "public body."

The report therefore seems to side with the approach favored by the United States in this respect and constitutes a departure from prior case law in the sense that the focus is now on the entity, rather than its conduct. In other words, investigating authorities dealing with SOEs will not have to assign government function to specific actions by economic agents in order to treat them as "public bodies."

The report is still unclear as to the probative value of an entity-based finding: Is it the last word, or simply a presumption? Assume, for example, that China can demonstrate that an SOE still acts in accordance with commercial considerations even with party members on the entity's executive board. Would that be sufficient to reverse the prima facie finding of "public body"? The answer to this question is yet to be determined and is crucial to any solution to the "China problem." We advance our own proposals in chapter 6.

The finding that an entity is a "public body" is not the end of the road. The next two questions are whether the public body has conferred a benefit to a recipient, and whether the benefit has been confined to specific recipients only. After all, the SCM Agreement does not allow action against financial contributions that confer no benefit, or that confer benefit but are not specific.

The Appellate Body did not manage to put forth a unanimous decision on these issues. The majority held that when calculating the benefit, recourse to out-of-country prices is legitimate when there is evidence of price distortion resulting from government intervention. It further held that this scenario is not limited to cases where government sets prices administratively. In other words, a country could be found liable even in a case where a distorted price level was not necessarily traced to a company or companies acting directly on government orders. In the Appellate Body's view, the U.S. DOC had done enough to show that the prices in China were not market prices. As a result, the U.S. DOC could legitimately have had recourse to out-of-country benchmarks, as indeed the U.S. DOC did in this case.

The United States still lost its claim, however, because it had not managed to show how distortions in China made recourse to out-of-country prices necessary in the case under investigation (§§5.141ff.). The minority view (§§5.252ff.) held that such a requirement was superfluous. If the U.S. DOC had demonstrated that Chinese domestic prices had been distorted, then of course it had the right to use out-of-country benchmarks without further ado. This seems quite sensible, and yet this view did not manage to convince two of the judges on the Appellate Body division that adjudicated this dispute. As a result, besides demonstrating that in-country benchmarks are inappropriate (because distorted), a WTO member imposing countervailing duties must now also demonstrate why recourse to out-of-country benchmarks is necessary. Most likely, this is a procedural requirement with little, if any, substantive content. Future practice in this context will reveal whether this is the case.

A similar divergence of views occurred with respect to the specificity analysis. In §§5.214ff., the majority view held that the U.S. DOC should have identified the subsidy program, explained its length, and so forth, otherwise it could not have reached the conclusion that it was facing a specific subsidy. The minority view (§§5.265ff.) held that the existence of a program is evidence that a financial contribution had been paid, and not evidence that the paid contribution was specific. The divergence here was not that important, since it concerns where, not whether, this analysis should take place.

As a result, this report made no one happy: the USTR was particularly unhappy and issued a statement to this effect, even though it seems to have scored a victory with respect to the understanding of the term "public body."[65] China was unhappy because even though it prevailed on specificity, it realized that it had lost a very important point when the Appellate Body had ruled that even private entities could be considered public bodies if they are in close cahoots with their government. This was probably the most important finding in this dispute.

A third dispute referred to Chinese SOEs tangentially. In *China–TRQs* (DS517), initiated in 2016, the United States requested consultations with China because, in its view, China had been violating obligations it had assumed with respect to the administration of tariff-rate quotas (TRQs) of various staples, like corn, rice, and wheat. More specifically, the U.S. request concerned the consistency of various Chinese administrative measures with various GATT provisions, as well as §116 of China's Protocol of Accession, which reads as follows:

> The representative of China stated that upon accession, China would ensure that TRQs were administered on a transparent, predictable, uniform, fair and non-discriminatory basis using clearly specified timeframes, administrative procedures and requirements that would provide effective import opportunities; that would reflect consumer preferences and end-user demand; and that would not inhibit the filling of each TRQ.[66]

This paragraph thus requested that China avoid measures that could jeopardize filling the quota that benefited from the lower rate. In 2003 a Chinese law distinguished between STE and non-STE portions for imports of grains. The only STE importing grains was China National Cereals, Oils and Foodstuffs Import and Export Corporation (COFCO). Non-STE portions would be imported by private parties and entities with trading rights to this effect. The National Development and Reform Commission (NDRC) of China was the entity entrusted with the authority to perform the distinction between STE and non-STE portions. It did not explain ex ante how it divided the two portions.

Furthermore, it imposed a series of restrictions on non-STEs, making it very difficult for them to use STE portions that had remained unsold. On top of that, non-STEs would be fined, and their quota (in tariff) would be

65. https://ustr.gov/about-us/policy-offices/press-office/press-releases/2019/july/statement-wto-appellate-report-china.

66. The Protocol of Accession makes it clear in §342 that this paragraph constitutes a legally binding obligation imposed on China, and the panel accepted as much in §7.5 of its report.

reduced if they could not absorb their allocated quota in a certain year. For all these reasons, the panel, in its report, which was adopted in May 2019 and not appealed, found (§7.115):

> In our view, the restrictions imposed on the possibilities for non-STE recipients to utilize STE portions of their TRQ allocations, and the implications on their ability to participate in reallocation and to receive the full amount of TRQ allocations in future years, violate China's obligation to administer its TRQs in a manner that would not inhibit the filling of each TRQ.

This is the first clear change in the way STEs exercise their discretion, even though it concerns a very narrow issue of economic activity. At the time of writing, the WTO had not been notified of the implementing activity by China. The quoted paragraph and the preceding analysis suggest, though, that China should ensure that in-tariff quotas be allocated and administered in a manner that would allow traders to make full use of them, instead of leaving this as an unused option (which would mean that Chinese competing products would profit).[67]

As we have seen, the development of case law has led to a rather broad view of the term "public bodies," subjecting even private agents to being categorized in this way. Assuming that this liberalization is a permanent trend, not a temporary idiosyncrasy, dozens of important Chinese economic agents will come under the purview of the SCM Agreement. However, there is still a lack of clarity (and indeed disagreements among the members of the Appellate Body) as to what is required to have recourse to out-of-country benchmarks.

Finally, currently when SOEs act as traders they must abide by a rather easily met standard: namely, to not discriminate across sources of supply. This understanding of the legal discipline embedded in Article XVII of the GATT flies against the negotiating intent, as we have seen. Case law has put in place an incoherent legal test, as it is not consonant with the rationale for the legal discipline: discriminatory behavior might be warranted, indeed it might be necessary, for an agent to act in accordance with commercial considerations, the obligation explicitly stipulated in Article XVII of the GATT. Hence, in chapter 6, we will recommend a return to orthodoxy.

---

67. In *China–Agricultural Products* (DS511), the role of SOEs was tangential in the finding that China had violated its commitments under the Agreement on Agriculture.

FORCED TRANSFER OF TECHNOLOGY

To begin with, it is necessary to distinguish between TT and forced TT. Vernon (1996) has already adequately explained the positive implications of TT beyond both firm and national boundaries. In TT, the right-holder retains some control over its patented product. In forced TT, it does not, and thus it might be unwilling to invest abroad in the first place.[68]

Transfer of technology was the pinnacle of Deng's agenda from the outset. Deng firmly believed that unless China was on the technology frontier, the whole transformation endeavor would end up in failure. Perhaps the following anecdote, mentioned by Vogel (2019), best explains Deng's pursuit of technology transfer and the response he initially faced. In 1978, during his visit to Japan, Deng met with Matsushita Konosuke, the founder of Panasonic and an icon in the Japanese business community. As Vogel describes the interaction:

> When Deng requested that Matsushita pass on his most recent technology, Matsushita explained that private businesses spend a great deal of resources inventing and developing new products, that this requires considerable time, trouble, and money, and that companies depend on using that technology to produce income to continue investing in new technology. Matsushita wanted to help China to develop low-cost consumer electronics to supply to Chinese consumers, he said, but like entrepreneurs elsewhere, he understood that his company's survival in the marketplace depended on it keeping its advanced technology to itself. (2019, 341)

Matsushita was taking Deng through IP 101, in effect, and it definitely did not suit Deng's interests. The China he had dreamed of was a country that would be producing cutting-edge technology.[69] To get there, the Chinese bureaucracy would employ both legal and illegal measures. Unwilling to fundamentally change China's planned economy, Deng tried to find shortcuts.

As China has implemented its plans, several WTO members, in particular the EU and the United States, have complained about China's various measures that ultimately have led to forced transfer of technology from their

---

68. Branstetter and Saggi (2011) and Branstetter et al. (2011) discuss this issue.

69. Vogel goes so far as to state that when Deng opened China to the United States, he made it clear that his priority was not trade or investment but science (2011, 321ff.).

firms operating in China to Chinese (private) firms.[70] In a nutshell, these complaints can be described as follows. China, through administrative guidance[71] and licensing procedures, obliges foreign firms to transfer technology to Chinese firms as a prerequisite for accessing the Chinese market. China can credibly do that because, in the absence of a bilateral investment treaty (BIT) protecting foreign investment, foreign companies can face any sort of (foreign) ownership restrictions.

This is how it works in more detail. China is requiring foreign companies to enter into joint ventures with Chinese companies in order to obtain similar credit conditions as Chinese companies. Chinese companies thus become the bottleneck for access to the Chinese market. When they receive requests to enter into a joint venture, they routinely agree to do so, but only under the condition that the foreign company agrees to transfer technology to them.[72]

The claim is that private agents are being used as conduits by the Chinese state. The Chinese state, which has been focused single-mindedly on obtaining technological advantages since the Deng reforms, has the power—so the argument goes—to impose its policy on private agents, with or without their approval.

This behavior has acted as a deterrent to access to Chinese markets. What is equally troubling, as far as complainants are concerned, is the fact that private agents (whose behavior liberal governments cannot fully control or dictate) might be willing to transfer technology in order to access the lucrative Chinese market. To the extent that the transfer of technology is in an area considered "strategic," this behavior could be a cause of concern for

70. Update Concerning China's Acts, Policies and Practices Related to Technology Transfer, Intellectual Property, and Innovation, office of the USTR, Executive Office of the President, November 20, 2018 (hereafter USTR 2018). USTR provides some numbers to substantiate the point that this practice is widespread and not necessarily targeted against U.S. companies; see USTR 2018, 23ff. The names of companies like DuPont, General Electric, and Advanced Micro Devices are explicitly mentioned.

71. The term "administrative guidance" made its first appearance in GATT-speak in *Japan–Trade in Semiconductors*, a dispute between the EU and Japan. The EU claimed that Japan, by entering into the Semiconductor Accord with the United States in 1986, had restrained its exports, including to the EU, and that, as a result, export prices of semiconductors had gone up. Japan had not imposed an export quota. Through a series of measures coming under the scope of the term "administrative guidance," Japan had incentivized its producers to behave accordingly. Since then, this term is used as a synonym for governmental measures that, even though not legally binding for their addressees, still manage to produce the intended effect because of the links between private sector and government institutions.

72. Blustein cites some anecdotal evidence that in a poll conducted by the U.S.-China Business Council, 36 percent of the respondents had been asked to make a technology transfer as a condition for getting an investment approval (2019, 134ff.).

those exporting it, even apart from the potential geopolitical consequences envisioned by complainants. But even cases where nonstrategic technology is transferred are a concern for exporters, who fear losses in market share and jobs, as well as all the other deleterious effects of losing their technological edge. The question, of course, is what can be done about it? This is a borderline area between trade and investment, and the latter does not come under the purview of the WTO as far as goods are concerned.

China's WTO Obligations

To understand whether complaints about forced technology transfer imposed on foreign companies that want to operate in China come under the scope of the WTO legal framework, we need to examine China's WTO obligations with respect to

- FDI in goods;
- FDI in services; and
- forced transfer of technology.

In principle, forced transfer of technology could be addressed through any one of these three.

With respect to FDI in goods, there is no multilateral discipline, neither within nor outside the WTO Agreement. There are only bilateral international investment agreements, typically BITs. China has BITs with Japan and many individual EU member states, but they contain no specific obligations regarding the issues we discuss here. The EU and the United States are both negotiating BITs with China that they hope will include obligations regarding transfer of technology, but the negotiations are not progressing well. At the time of writing, China has not assumed obligations under a BIT to this effect. Recently, free-trade area (FTA) agreements have included chapters on protection of FDI. China, nevertheless, has not assumed similar obligations in this context either, at least not with respect to the EU, Japan, or the United States (the Trilateral) or similar countries like Canada.

China has assumed obligations with respect to FDI in services under Mode 3 in its schedule of concessions under the General Agreement on Trade in Services (GATS). Mode 3 covers the supply of services in a foreign jurisdiction through commercial presence. It is in essence the only genuine multilateral agreement (albeit with a limited scope) on investment—that is, supply of services. Furthermore, assumption of commitments is voluntary, since there is no obligation imposed on China or anyone else to open its market to foreign FDI. Liberalization is thus a matter of negotiation.

We have already referred to Lardy's (2019) conclusion that various lucrative services markets in China remain closed to foreign suppliers. China has assumed obligations under Mode 3 with respect to various services sectors, and its obligations are asymmetric. Sometimes national treatment has been afforded to foreign services suppliers, and sometimes not. Sometimes recourse to the measures included in Article XVI of the GATS, relating to specific commitments on market access, has been made (or at least to some of the six measures included in this provision), and sometimes not.

Of interest here is the fact that a platform is available for China to commit on FDI and afford national treatment to foreign suppliers. Thus, in the realm of services, assuming reciprocity-related issues have been resolved, trading nations can in principle obtain assurances from China that their suppliers will be afforded competitive conditions in the Chinese market equal to those afforded to their Chinese counterparts. Even though it is difficult to conclude that this is sufficient—that by granting national treatment the concerns of foreigners will disappear—such an arrangement would certainly go some way toward addressing their concerns, since Chinese companies will not be in a position to act as "bottlenecks" anymore.

But even if national treatment has not been granted, foreign suppliers will see their situation improved—substantially improved, we might add— if China introduces market access commitments under Article XVI of the GATS. What matters to us for the purposes of our analysis is the imperative of Article XVI.2(e) of the GATS, which reads as follows:

> In sectors where market-access commitments are undertaken, the measures which a Member shall not maintain or adopt either based on a regional subdivision or on the basis of its entire territory, unless otherwise specified in its Schedule, are defined as:
>
> (e) measures which restrict or require specific types of legal entity or joint venture through which a service supplier may supply a service.

This means that China cannot subject the foreign commercial presence in its market to a prior establishment of joint venture. Hence, for China to behave in the realm of services trade in the same manner it allegedly does in the realm of trade in goods, it will have to indicate its willingness to do so in its schedule of concessions. In the opposite scenario, foreign companies can establish commercial presence on their own in China (assuming, of course, that China has made commitments to this effect).

Thus even in the realm of trade in services, there is a risk that China can have recourse to measures akin to transfer of technology, assuming it has agreed to a proviso to this effect in the relevant part of its schedule of concessions.

To conclude on this point, while disciplines regarding FDI are outside the coverage of the multilateral trading system with respect to trade in goods, they do come under the aegis of the GATS agreement. Nevertheless, WTO members are free to decide whether they will open up to investment by foreign services suppliers. If they do, unless there is specific indication to the contrary in their schedule of concessions, they cannot require that foreign investors operate in their market through a joint venture. Requiring the establishment of a joint venture is, of course, not tantamount to imposing technology transfer. In practice, however, it seems to be the quid pro quo often requested by Chinese companies for conceding to the joint venture in the first place.

With respect to the regulation of technology transfer per se in the TRIPS Agreement, the situation is more complicated. In a way the entire TRIPS Agreement is about counteracting forced transfer of technology, and various provisions are directly and/or indirectly relevant to our discussion.

For starters, forced transfer can only occur under the restrictive conditions of Article 31 of the TRIPS Agreement, which allows compulsory licensing but only with "adequate remuneration" of patent holders. Furthermore, by virtue of their accession to the WTO, trading nations must put in place an effective system of enforcement. They must, under Article 40, control anticompetitive practices in contractual licenses. Forced transfer of technology could be considered an anticompetitive practice.

With respect to the enforcement of obligations assumed under the TRIPS Agreement, Article 41.5 provides that parties do not have an obligation to establish a distinct judicial system for the enforcement of IP rights. There is thus no need to establish specialized courts, since the assumption is that the existing judicial system within each WTO member's sovereignty could be put into good use to this effect.[73]

---

73. There was some discussion regarding the implementation of Article 41.5 in the panel report on *China–Intellectual Property Rights*, in §§7.591ff. The implementation of the China Transitional Review Mechanism (TRM), which lasted until 2009–10, is also relevant in this context. As Farah and Cima (2012) note, in light of worries concerning enforcement of WTO obligations, a special "precautionary" instrument, the TRM, was included in Section 18 of China's Protocol of Accession to the WTO, as requested by the United States and supported by the EU. Both the U.S. and the EU delegations were pinning a great part of their hopes and financial support on

There was, however, widespread concern regarding China's ability and commitment to administer laws and regulations pertaining to trade in goods, services, and IP rights. As a result, Part I of China's Protocol of Accession contains a number of specific requirements. It is worth quoting the three most important ones at length. First, Section 2(A) (uniform administration) provides that:

> China shall apply and administer in a uniform, impartial and reasonable manner all its laws, regulations and other measures of the central government as well as local regulations, rules and other measures issued or applied at the sub-national level (collectively referred to as "laws, regulations and other measures") pertaining to or affecting trade in goods, services, trade-related aspects of intellectual property rights ("TRIPS") or the control of foreign exchange.

Second, we read in Section 2(C) (transparency) that:

> China undertakes that only those laws, regulations and other measures pertaining to or affecting trade in goods, services, TRIPS or the control of foreign exchange that are published and readily available to other WTO Members, individuals and enterprises, shall be enforced. In addition, China shall make available to WTO Members, upon request, all laws, regulations and other measures pertaining to or affecting trade in goods, services, TRIPS or the control of foreign exchange before such measures are implemented or enforced. In emergency situations, laws, regulations and other measures shall be made available at the latest when they are implemented or enforced.

Third, Section 2(D) (judicial review) provides that:

> China shall establish, or designate, and maintain tribunals, contact points and procedures for the prompt review of all administrative actions relating to the implementation of laws, regulations, judicial decisions and

---

the good performance of the TRM. The TRM was viewed as a complement to, not a substitute for, the Trade Policy Review Mechanism (TPRM), to which China, like every WTO member, is subjected. The TRM was more comprehensive than the TPRM, and its objective was to monitor and ensure the implementation of WTO commitments (which TPRM does not) and to promote transparency and exchange of information in trade relations with China. It was implemented in the TRIPS Council through an annual special reporting session, a very extensive and tense session one might add, in which China reported on individual IP enforcement initiatives and statistics and responded to WTO members' questions (mostly those of the United States and the EU). The final review of the TRM was in 2010.

administrative rulings of general application referred to in Article X:1 of the GATT 1994, Article VI of the GATS and the relevant provisions of the TRIPS Agreement. Such tribunals shall be impartial and independent of the agency entrusted with administrative enforcement and shall not have any substantial interest in the outcome of the matter.

2. Review procedures shall include the opportunity for appeal, without penalty, by individuals or enterprises affected by any administrative action subject to review. If the initial right of appeal is to an administrative body, there shall in all cases be the opportunity to choose to appeal the decision to a judicial body. Notice of the decision on appeal shall be given to the appellant and the reasons for such decision shall be provided in writing. The appellant shall also be informed of any right to further appeal.

These requirements are not specific to IP rights; they apply to the entire WTO Agreement, including the TRIPS Agreement. They are meant to impose greater discipline on China than that imposed on other WTO members for reasons that are clearly spelled out in §§76–79 of the report of the Working Party on the Accession of China.[74]

Through these paragraphs, the members of the Working Party stated in unambiguous terms that China needed to strengthen its judicial arsenal to ensure that the rights of the whole WTO membership would be effectively upheld. China accepted their demands. We quote §78 in full:

The representative of China confirmed that it would revise its relevant laws and regulations so that its relevant domestic laws and regulations would be consistent with the requirements of the WTO Agreement and the Draft Protocol on procedures for judicial review of administrative actions. He further stated that the tribunals responsible for such reviews would be impartial and independent of the agency entrusted with administrative enforcement and would not have any substantial interest in the outcome of the matter. The Working Party took note of these commitments.

The WTO membership also addressed technology transfer head-on, since there was clear uneasiness in some quarters about China's administrative practices with respect to technology transfer. Paragraphs 48 and

---

74. Qin (2010) agrees that Section 2(D) of the Protocol of Accession imposes on China an obligation that other WTO members have not assumed.

49 of the Working Party on the Accession of China capture this point to perfection:

48. Certain members of the Working Party expressed concern about laws, regulations and measures in China affecting the transfer of technology, in particular in the context of investment decisions. Moreover, these members expressed concern about measures conditioning the receipt of benefits, including investment approvals, upon technology transfer. In their view, the terms and conditions of technology transfer, particularly in the context of an investment, should be agreed between the parties to the investment without government interference. The government should not, for example, condition investment approval upon technology transfer.

49. The representative of China confirmed that China would only impose, apply or enforce laws, regulations or measures relating to the transfer of technology, production processes, or other proprietary knowledge to an individual or enterprise in its territory that were not inconsistent with the WTO Agreement on Trade-Related Aspects of Intellectual Property Rights ("TRIPS Agreement") and the Agreement on Trade-Related Investment Measures ("TRIMs Agreement"). He confirmed that the terms and conditions of technology transfer, production processes or other proprietary knowledge, particularly in the context of an investment, would only require agreement between the parties to the investment. The Working Party took note of these commitments.

Section 48 (like §§46–47) is explicitly mentioned in §342 of the Protocol of Accession, the paragraph including all binding commitments, which China accepted. The conclusion is inescapable: China undertook a firm commitment to abstain from forcing technology transfers from foreign firms operating within its territory. We need to explain this point a bit further, though, in order to fully appreciate the scope of the obligation assumed and avoid any misunderstandings.

China would be, according to the Protocol of Accession, liable only if transfer of technology was attributed to government intervention. If a request for transfer of technology was from a private entity, China would incur no obligation at all to this effect. The test for attributing behavior to a state had been developed already in GATT case law, in *Japan–Trade in Semiconductors*. There the panel effectively endorsed a "but for" test, asking whether a private agent would have adopted the challenged behavior in the absence of state intervention.

A key point in this analysis is that the panel did not equate attribution to legal compulsion to behave in a certain way. It sufficed that the governmental authority provided private agents with sufficient incentives to behave in a certain way.[75] This raises an interesting question, especially following our discussion regarding the understanding of the term "public body" in case law. If an agent is considered a "public body," then there is no need to discuss attribution at all.

The criteria thus established in case law regarding the characterization of an entity as a "public body" could, in other words, hold the key to understanding the scope of the obligation assumed by China regarding transfer of technology. They would have a direct impact on the amount of evidence required to attribute the behavior of a Chinese agent, even a private one, to the Chinese government.

Given these stricter boundaries, attributing behavior to the Chinese government should be an easier task than doing the same with respect to behavior by private agents elsewhere. If case law does not change, it seems that China would be liable for various activities by private agents as well. Recall that, as per the case law cited earlier in this chapter, panels will not have to inquire into the conduct of similar agents but into their links to government. The "entity vs. conduct" debate could tilt the balance of attribution heavily toward state behavior.

Complaints against TT before the WTO

On June 1, 2018, the EU requested consultations with China concerning certain measures imposed by the latter pertaining to (forced) transfer of foreign technology. It was the first time that a WTO member launched a formal complaint against China about technology transfer. This request was replaced by a new request for consultations circulated on December 20, 2018. In the new request, the EU claimed that certain Chinese measures adversely affected the protection of the intellectual property rights of foreign companies transferring technology to China and that these measures appeared to be inconsistent with various WTO obligations that China had assumed, including:

- Several articles of the TRIPS Agreement
- Article X:3(a) of the GATT 1994, concerning the administration of trade regulations

---

75. In *Argentina–Hides and Leather*, a WTO panel added (since it did not contradict the findings cited here) that a successful complainant must show a nexus between government action and behavior by private agents. For a detailed analysis on this, see Mavroidis 2016, vol. 1, chap. 2.

- Paragraph 2(A)(2) of Part I of China's Protocol of Accession, which also relates to the administration of trade regulations

The EU claimed more specifically that:

> Through its domestic legislation, China restricts the access and operation of foreign investment in its territory, by conditioning the approval of foreign investments upon performance requirements, including requirements related to the transfer of technology and the conduct of research and development in China. In addition, China imposes measures that adversely affect the protection of intellectual property rights of foreign companies, which transfer technology into China, including in the context of joint ventures with Chinese companies. In this respect, China discriminates against foreign companies by imposing on them conditions, which are less favourable than those applicable to the transfer of technology between Chinese companies.[76]

It further claimed that:

> Pursuant to Paragraph 7.3 of its Accession Protocol, China committed to eliminate and cease to enforce performance requirements made effective through laws, regulations or other measures. Moreover, China committed not to enforce provisions of contracts imposing such requirements. China also committed to ensure that the means of approval by national and sub-national authorities of the right of investment would not be conditioned on performance requirements of any kind, such as local content, offsets, the transfer of technology, export performance or the conduct of research and development in China. Pursuant to Paragraph 203 of its Working Party Report, China committed that the allocation, permission or rights for importation and investment would not be conditional upon performance requirements set by national or sub-national authorities, or subject to secondary conditions covering, for example, the transfer of technology.[77]

Thus the EU claimed that China had imposed performance requirements as a precondition for allowing investments in its market although it had explicitly committed to avoid imposing such requirements through the obligations it had assumed in its Protocol of Accession. At this stage, we can only speculate about the outcome of this dispute. Assuming that the consultations with

---

76. WTO Doc. WT/DS549/1/Rev.1, G/L/1244/Rev.1, IP/D/39/Rev.1, January 8, 2019.
77. WTO Doc. WT/DS549/1/Rev.1, G/L/1244/Rev.1, IP/D/39/Rev.1, January 8, 2019.

China fail and the EU requests the establishment of a panel, the EU has, of course, the stronger arguments. Its reliance in particular on provisions embedded in the Protocol of Accession seems to us to be the most promising legal basis on which to attack China's practices in this respect.

The EU complaints are, for now, the only official ones regarding forced TT. For the rest, the Trilateral has made a great deal of noise about lodging a formal complaint, and it has increasingly been joined by an ever-growing chorus of other trading nations. But these voices are still coalescing; no other dispute has been formally lodged thus far. Perhaps the situation might change as a result of the very recent understanding of the term "public body" in case law.

Was the Chinese Protocol of Accession a Missed Opportunity?

The discussion so far leads to one inevitable conclusion: there is not much that can be done to address the two key complaints—SEOs and forced TT— under the current legal regime regulating international trade.

To be sure, there has been some progress. Carefully crafted obligations exist in various areas of China's protocol. Trading nations did express their concerns about China during the accession process and often managed to introduce language that addressed these issues. Recall, for example, that §48 of the report of the Working Party on the Accession of China includes an unambiguous promise by the government of China to stop any state-mandated WTO-inconsistent transfer of technology. The working assumption must have been that if state involvement were completely absent it would have been quite difficult for private operators to collude and request transfer of technology. The meaningfulness of this provision depends, of course, on the way China implements its obligations regarding state interference with respect to the State-Owned Assets Supervision and Administration Commission (SASAC). Nevertheless, China has accepted a firm commitment to avoid interfering to assist domestic producers.

The provisions on export taxes (Annex V of the protocol) are equally carefully crafted. The meticulous drafting was certainly a contributing factor in securing victories for those affected by China's export taxes (in contravention of obligations it had assumed through the conclusion of Annex V).

On the other hand, we cannot help but notice that the disciplines regarding treatment of SOEs leave a lot to be desired. As we have noted, China assumed obligations regarding transparency and specificity in this context, but the big issue has remained an open question: Are SOEs public bodies? The carefully crafted language extant in current provisions still leaves much open to interpretation. This lack of clarity would be immediately resolved by clear parameters regarding the public/private nature of SOEs.

And, recall that GATT/WTO case law has eviscerated the discipline embedded in Article XVII of the GATT, which is relevant to SOEs as well, exacerbating the difficulty for complainants hoping to pin China down on its implicit influence over ostensibly private entities. The Protocol of Accession did not undo this admittedly poor case law construction.

Why has this been the case? Why have China's trading partners not insisted on clarification or continued to bring complaints until the confusion over SOEs has been cleared up? We advance three reasons that, in our view at least, help explain why this has been the case: a lack of coordination among China's trading partners, hopes for actual and lasting economic reform within China, and specific legal concerns.

AN UNCOORDINATED RESPONSE

There is no evidence that there was any coordination among the incumbents during the negotiation with China. To the contrary, the negotiation was never even between China and the WTO, nor was it a negotiation between China and a group of like-minded players. Instead, the Trilateral, a group comprising the EU, Japan, and the United States and focusing on relations with China, formed only a few years after the accession of China to the WTO. The negotiating record suggests that, as in the past, these major players focused on a series of bilateral negotiations instead of pooling their resources and conducting negotiations as a united front.[78]

Paradoxically, the big two (the EU and the United States), along with Japan, established their Trilateral to face the challenges posed by China after the latter had acceded to the WTO (and probably after realizing the limits of their prior individual approaches). By that time, though, the cat was at least partly out of the bag. However, if the Trilateral were to act jointly at the WTO, it could be a powerful combination to advance our proposals detailed in chapter 6.

Still, this was no ordinary negotiation. China was not only a behemoth in terms of trade potential but a country controlled by an authoritarian regime that interfered in its economy and civil society, lacked an independent

---

78. See Stewart 1993 for a comprehensive account of the negotiations.

judiciary, and engaged in human rights abuses, among other things. Even though WTO-wide coordination might have been difficult, perhaps altogether impossible, in light of the membership's heterogeneity, the EU and the United States might now wish that they had better coordinated their bilateral negotiations with China.

It is, of course, impossible to construct the counterfactual. One can only wonder, though, how much more could have been achieved in terms of disciplining SOEs/SIEs had the EU and the United States managed to adopt a common line in this respect. Why, for example, did the United States push for a comprehensive regulation of SOEs during the TPP negotiations, and not during the China accession process? Perhaps one reason was China's successful diplomatic campaign touting a process of reform; the United States bought what China was selling.

EXUBERANCE ABOUT DENG'S REFORMS AND THEIR (LASTING?) LEGACY

WTO incumbents were probably overly optimistic about the Deng reforms and the promise they held. There is, however, some excuse for this. After all, China was developing fast, so it was in its interest to use WTO accession as an incentive to continue and intensify the process of reform it had already begun. The incumbents might also have been impressed by the Shanghai Forum (the liberal voices in China), whose members participated heavily in the negotiation process and represented China's pro-reform liberals (as opposed to the conservative, i.e., party-loyal, Beijing crowd).[79]

Inscribing 2016 as the date by which China would be transformed into a market economy is the best evidence of the exuberance prevailing at the time of negotiations for China's accession to the WTO and the belief that Deng's supposedly reformist legacy would not only last but also expand. Needless to say, negotiators have now been proved wrong about the pace and persistence of Chinese reform (not to mention the date).

Some Western leaders were so sure that China was changing that even when facing explicit pushback they would not back down. We quote the following telling anecdote from McGregor:

79. Long Yongtu was China's chief negotiator and later a member of the Shanghai Forum. Anecdotal evidence suggests that Premier Zhu Rongji had confided to WTO director-general Mike Moore that the accession process was dominated by disagreements between the Beijing (government) conservatives and the Shanghai (private sector) progressives. Patterson (2018) discusses the influence of Long Yongtu during the accession process in some detail.

Zhu Rongji . . . when asked by George Bush Snr. how China's "privatization" programme was proceeding . . . protested that China was corporatizing its large state assets, which was just another way of "realizing state ownership". Bush responded with a nudge and a wink, saying that no matter how Zhu described the process, "we know what is going on". Bush was not the only western leader to misread Zhu, widely seen in foreign circles as someone dismantling the very roots of the state economy. (2010, 43)

This passage illustrates how (some) influential Western leaders were so certain that China was changing: even when Rongji, a leading Chinese government official, openly professed the continuing importance of state control of its economy, President Bush did not believe him. In a way, the problem of SOEs was hiding in plain sight the entire time.

The West may have misunderstood what was going on in China. Patterson argues (2018, 16ff.) that, of course, there were some genuine reformers in the party's leadership. Zhao Ziyang and Hu Yaobang led the liberal-reformist camp, but Zhao was set aside, and Hu passed away. Qiao Shi and Tian Jiyan belong to this group of committed liberals, and they both saw their influence within the party decrease rapidly (133ff.). But not all reformers were liberals. Some, like Zhu Rongji, were committed reformers but not liberals. They believed that reforms were necessary to keep the system going and consolidate the primacy of the party in Chinese political life.

Against this background, we could describe the spectrum of forecasts by the West, or at least by the United States, about China's life in the WTO as follows. At one end of the spectrum stands not only President George W. Bush but also President Clinton, who was very optimistic:

By joining the WTO, China . . . is agreeing to import one of democracy's most cherished values: economic freedom. . . . And when individuals have the power, not just to dream but to realize their dreams, they will demand a greater say. . . . Now people are leaving those firms [the SOEs], and when China joins the WTO, they will leave them faster. The Chinese government no longer will be everyone's employer, landlord, shopkeeper and nanny all rolled into one. It will have fewer instruments, therefore, with which to control people's lives. And that may lead to very profound change. (Patterson 2018, 55–56)

Clinton has been criticized for naivete in believing that trade and growth would change China's politics, but he did take some precautions as well.

Most importantly, he upgraded the U.S.-Japan defense agreement, and, as Nye underscores (2020, 138ff.), the 1996 Clinton-Hashimoto declaration is the hallmark of this endeavor.

At the other end of the spectrum, we find people like Mike Jendrzejszky, the director of Human Rights Watch for Asia: "WTO membership will not itself lead to political changes" (quoted in Patterson 2018, 19). And somewhere in the middle we have former U.S. secretary of state Madeleine Albright: "China's entry into the WTO is not a human rights issue—but it can only help the human rights and the political situation in China" (quoted in Patterson 2018, 19).

There were, of course, those who thought that China would never rise enough to threaten U.S. economic supremacy and that its accession to the WTO was a good opportunity for the U.S. industry to conquer the vast Chinese market. Patterson expresses amazement about such opinions. In his view (2018, 29ff.), the economic benefits of trade openness to China between 1978 and 2000 were completely to China's benefit, and he saw no reason why this would change after China's accession to the WTO.

SOME LEGAL CONCERNS

Protocols of Accession cannot be turned into wish lists, where incumbents can request from the new kids on the block all sorts of commitments, whether they relate to the covered agreements or not.

In the past, GATT and WTO incumbents had had to confront requests by heterogeneous members as the organization admitted countries with different economic systems (e.g., the former Soviet bloc nations). In these processes, Protocols of Accession served as a means to specify the terms and conditions for accession into the multilateral trading system, but not as the vehicle to impose obligations not covered by the GATT/WTO legal regime. There are sound legal reasons why this is the case.

The GATT/WTO was designed to bring together countries that espouse its liberal understanding, but it has also accommodated countries that do not. For this latter group of countries, the GATT/WTO regime can serve to nudge them toward change, but it is by no means a legal catalyst to impose change. The GATT/WTO is not, in this sense, identical to the EU formula, which requires that acceding countries be liberal democracies. In this sense, the GATT/WTO walks a tightrope, and to perform the balancing act successfully, it must carefully maintain stability between its commitment to Western-style liberal economic systems and its desire to prompt adherence to those liberal ideals from countries not steeped in liberal democracy. Yes, the GATT was predicated on a liberal understanding, but it has never required new entrants to espouse that liberal understanding as a condition of accession. The various GATT/WTO obligations might induce change but cannot require it. However, just because the GATT/WTO regime must accommodate countries espousing different regimes, liberal economies and centrally planned economies alike, does not mean that nothing should be done vis-à-vis China.[80] We oppose that view and will return to our rationale in chapter 5.

80. We would like to add one final reason why accessions have not led to change in domestic policies. As Copelovitch and Ohls (2012) have shown in their comprehensive survey, dozens of countries have joined the GATT through Article XXVI.5c, which allows former colonies to join under terms negotiated by the (former) colonial powers. The process of accession under this regime was typically minimalistic, and acceding countries profited from generous transitional periods to adjust. Goldstein, Rivers, and Tomz (2007) also discuss this issue.

3

Dealing with Heterogeneity in the GATT/WTO

LESSONS FROM THE PAST FOR CHINA

> Evolution is definable as a change from an incoherent homogeneity to a coherent heterogeneity.
> —HERBERT SPENCER

The original GATT members were fairly homogeneous in terms of their economic systems, but, beginning in the 1950s, they managed to accommodate prospective new members that operated under different systems. This has not always been a smooth process. Having an understanding of the historical context of GATT/WTO accession is crucial for analyzing the current issues surrounding China's accession. We will examine several such cases, including the accession of former Soviet bloc countries, Arab countries, and—most significantly—Japan, including specific elements of accession in several policy areas. To begin with, however, we must understand how Protocols of Accession work as individual countries try to join the international trading community.

The Function of Protocols of Accession

Should countries joining the WTO (or earlier the GATT) be subject to more obligations than incumbents (the founding members)?[1] To respond to this question, we need to understand the statutory function of the Protocols of Accession.

Acceding countries must, of course, abide by the multilateral agreements included in the WTO (the "covered agreements," which include the GATT, the GATS, the TRIPS, and their annexes, as well as the Dispute Settlement Understanding [DSU] regulating dispute adjudication at the WTO level), and they must also observe the specific commitments embedded in their Protocol of Accession. They can, if they wish, accede to plurilateral agreements, where, as in the Tokyo Round "codes," participation is optional.[2]

What kind of commitments can countries enter into when negotiating their accession, and how are those commitments reflected in the protocol? Is it a case of "anything goes," or are there limits to what the Protocols of Accession can cover? The natural place to start our discussion is the relevant statutory provision. Article XXXIII of the GATT, the original accession clause, states:

> A government not party to this Agreement, or a government acting on behalf of a separate customs territory possessing full autonomy in the conduct of its external commercial relations and of the other matters provided for in this Agreement, may accede to this Agreement, on its own behalf or on behalf of that territory, on terms to be agreed between such government and the CONTRACTING PARTIES. Decisions of the CONTRACTING PARTIES under this paragraph shall be taken by a two-thirds majority.

Article XII of the Agreement Establishing the WTO, the successor provision, contains slightly different terms:

> Any State or separate customs territory possessing full autonomy in the conduct of its external commercial relations and of the other matters provided for in this Agreement and the Multilateral Trade Agreements may accede to this Agreement, on terms to be agreed between it and the

---

1. Charnovitz (2008) discusses cases where new members assumed fewer (hence the expression "GATT-minus") commitments than incumbents, but they are quite exceptional. The nature of the bargaining process is such that even behemoths like China had to pay a heavier price than incumbents in order to accede to the GATT/WTO.

2. China has not, as yet, entered into any plurilateral agreements.

WTO. Such accession shall apply to this Agreement and the Multilateral Trade Agreements annexed thereto.

The difference between the two provisions lies in the last sentence of the WTO provision. In the GATT era, there were no plurilateral agreements. Accession to the GATT entailed accession *only* to the GATT and to no other agreement. The Tokyo Round (1973–79) agreements included their own accession clauses. The WTO contains both multilateral and plurilateral agreements. Article XII makes it clear that WTO accession covers only accession to the multilateral agreements. Accession under this provision, in other words, does not automatically entail accession to the Annex 4 (plurilateral) agreements.[3]

Is there more to this provision than meets the eye? In other words, can incumbents request, as a condition for WTO accession, that applicant countries observe obligations in areas that incumbents did not have to observe when they became WTO members? If the answer is yes, then WTO incumbents would be in a position to request adherence to the Havana Charter, for example, which reflects the GATT liberal understanding, in order to admit a candidate to the WTO.

The intuitive response is negative: of course, incumbents should not be in a position to make such requests. Why would a matter not germane to the subject matter of the multilateral agreements become a condition for adhering to them? Protocols of Accession, in this reading of the provision, should be a substitute for negotiating rounds in which new members never participated. "Terms and conditions" of Protocols of Accession should be confined to a negotiation of tariff commitments and/or liberalization of the Agreement on Government Procurement (GPA), if the acceding country opts for accession to the GPA as well. Adherence to the regulatory component of the WTO edifice, the covered agreements, is not negotiable anyway.

And yet, our discussion on the liberal understanding suggests otherwise, at least initially. Since the GATT was predicated on the liberal understanding, and since this understanding was not shared by the entire world community, why not translate it into explicit conditions through the Protocols of Accession? After all, going down this road would not require a legislative amendment to the GATT. Some coordination would be necessary, but at the end of the day, incumbents would impose rules regulating minimum conduct on acceding countries and not on themselves.

---

3. In a separate paragraph, Article XII makes it clear that accession to plurilateral agreements is governed by specific accession provisions embedded therein.

The letter of Article XII of the WTO Agreement could be interpreted as suggesting that only matters coming under the purview of the multilateral (and, eventually, plurilateral) agreements could form part of the negotiation during the accession process. It does not put all doubts to rest, however. Review of the relevant practice regarding the scope and subject matter of accession negotiations is necessary. And practice confirms the intuitive understanding that incumbents did not, through Protocols of Accession, impose obligations on candidates that were outside the scope of the covered agreements.[4]

During the first trade negotiating rounds (that is, until the Kennedy Round, which lasted from 1962 to 1966), "terms to be agreed" was understood as a reference to the schedules of concessions, which list the specific tariff concessions and related commitments that members have agreed to in the context of GATT/WTO trade negotiations. All GATT/WTO members have signed a schedule of concessions, which is annexed either to the original GATT/WTO Agreement or to a Protocol of Accession. In the GATT, schedules usually consist of maximum most-favored-nation (MFN) tariff levels, often referred to as "bound tariffs" or "tariff bindings."[5] The 1955 Protocol of Accession for Japan, which we discuss in greater detail later in this chapter, is a good illustration of this type of agreement.

Over the years, the language used when detailing terms and conditions of accession went beyond tariff concessions. The reason for the change was the increasing heterogeneity of the membership. In particular, countries wishing to join the GATT that were state-trading countries (STCs), where

4. One can only speculate what the legal argument would have been in the counterfactual. Assume that incumbents request that a candidate liberalize FDI in goods as a condition for accession to the WTO. Assume further that the candidate, post-accession, challenges the consistency of this clause with Article XII of the Agreement Establishing the WTO. The panel would, by virtue of its *EC–Bananas III* case law, ask whether this clause is consistent with the WTO covered agreements: inclusion of a clause in a schedule, by virtue of this jurisprudence, does not ipso facto guarantee legality for the clause concerned. On the one hand, it could hide behind the legal maxim *venire contra factum proprium* (no one may set himself in contradiction to his previous conduct). In other words, by accepting this clause, the complainant has waived the right to challenge its consistency with the WTO. WTO panels have never refrained from exercising jurisdiction on similar grounds, as discussed in Matsushita et al. 2015, chap. 3. On the other hand, however, inspired by the case law on *Turkey–Textiles*, it could inquire into whether such clause(s) that evade the scope of the WTO are necessary for accession to occur in the first place. The response to this question should be in the negative. Otherwise, all BITs would have to be MFNed, which is not the case.

5. There are other entries where preferential tariffs, as well as non-tariff bindings, are recorded. Williams (2008) provides the most comprehensive discussion of the accession negotiation record. Those participating in preferential schemes will, of course, also include the preferential rate. As of 2016, all WTO members participate in at least one preferential trade arrangement.

their imports and exports were controlled by the state, had to accept commitments that incumbents did not have to observe. More specifically, they had to commit to importing well-specified trade volumes, a solution that arose in order to keep Czechoslovakia in the GATT after it became a non-market economy (NME) in the 1950s. Eventually, in the 1990s, commitments extended to other areas as well.[6] They never extended to areas not covered by the WTO, though, like the subject matter of BITs.

Czechoslovakia: The First Challenge to the Liberal Understanding

The transition of Czechoslovakia, an original GATT member, to the Soviet bloc in the early 1950s was a shock to the international trading system. The original GATT Agreement was silent on state-trading countries (STCs), containing only rules on state-trading enterprises (STEs; Article XVII), which, as we have already discussed, originated in market economies and not in STCs.[7] STEs were therefore operating in countries that respected property rights and were within the constraints of national antitrust laws (and, often, liberalized investment). STCs were a completely different situation. The Czech transition to a non-market economy posed a problem to the GATT liberal order. The GATT could have expelled Czechoslovakia, but GATT decisions were consensus based. This meant that, in principle at least, Czechoslovakia could have blocked any decision to this effect.

The membership decided to do nothing, initially, and accommodate Czechoslovakia, probably hoping that the GATT liberal system would, over time, undermine the centrally planned character of the Czech economy. Eventually, at Czechoslovakia's request,[8] the GATT membership decided to amend Article VI of the GATT in order to address concerns regarding

---

6. Charnovitz (2008) offers a very comprehensive survey of the evolution of the commitments in this respect.

7. The Suggested Charter for an International Trade Organisation of the United Nations, a document released by the U.S. government in September 1946, which served as the basis for the London draft of November 1946 of what became in March 1948 the Havana Charter for an ITO, contained rules on both STEs and STCs. Article 26 of the Suggested Charter deals with STEs and is similar to Article XVII of the final text of the GATT. Articles 27 and 28 deal with STCs but were not incorporated into the GATT when it became clear that the Soviet Union, for whom the two articles were designed, would not participate in the GATT. Zeiler notes that the Soviets viewed the GATT as an effort to avert an inevitable crisis by the industrialized states and were opposed, if not hostile, to the whole endeavor (1999, 84ff.). McKenzie (2008), drawing on the archival record, has suggested that Dana Wilgress, a key Canadian delegate, favored negotiation of the GATT across like-minded players only, in order to avoid having the Soviets sabotage it.

8. GATT Doc. L/334, March 1, 1955.

pricing policies implemented in countries that did not qualify as market economies. Article VI was augmented with Interpretative Note Ad Article VI to deal with the problem of finding comparable prices in antidumping and anti-subsidy investigations when trade is operated by a state monopoly. This was not much, by any reasonable standard, but at the very least would provide trading nations with an extra weapon in case they wanted to block imports from STCs.[9] Czechoslovakia remained a GATT member, and its trading partners were in a position to defend themselves more effectively against dumping.

Protocols of Accession in Practice

Because Czechoslovakia was an original member of the GATT, it did not have to sign a Protocol of Accession as per Article XXXV of the GATT. The countries that joined after January 1, 1948, the date of the advent of the original GATT, had to agree to the terms of their accession with the incumbents. The question that we are interested in here is, what was the content of the accession protocols?

In what follows, we will be discussing the content of Protocols of Accession for countries that represented a challenge to the GATT, in the sense that they did not share the political and economic structure of the original or early members. We will follow a chronological presentation, but before doing so a few introductory remarks are necessary.

In the GATT era, the Protocols of Accession signed were limited to the scope of rights and obligations embedded in the GATT. This is strong support for our argument that Article XXXIII of the GATT (the corresponding provision to Article XII of the Agreement Establishing the WTO) was understood as a scope provision as far as the substantive content of the Protocols of Accession were concerned. In the WTO era, this practice has not changed. Acceding members might have, on occasion, agreed to liberalize more than the average incumbent. They have not agreed to obligations in areas beyond the scope of covered agreements.

Indeed, even when members of the Soviet bloc joined the GATT, they were not asked to abandon their economic system and embrace a market economy. Indeed, no obligation for non-market economies to privatize was ever included in their Protocols of Accession. Privatization was certainly

---

9. Only one case was reported during the GATT era where measures against exports originating in Czechoslovakia led to a formal dispute. In *US–Fur Felt Hats*, the United States had imposed safeguard measures against fur hats originating in Czechoslovakia, and the latter contested the legality of this imposition.

discussed, however, in various Protocols of Accession—and an implicit expectation that acceding countries would engage in privatization is evident in various protocols. Nevertheless, in all cases where privatization is mentioned it is described as a process that acceding countries have embarked upon unilaterally, not as a matter of compulsion. It is never a precondition that, if not met, would bring the whole accession process to a halt. This is further proof that the GATT/WTO regime might gently endorse a liberal trade order but not legally compel it.

For example, §342 in the Protocol of Accession for Vietnam includes an exhaustive list of the commitments that Vietnam agreed to as preconditions for accession to the WTO. In other words, this paragraph is tantamount to the "terms and conditions" that Article XII of the Agreement Establishing the WTO refers to. In Vietnam's Protocol of Accession, §§81–98 include the discussion on privatization. And yet only §95 features in the list of §342, and this paragraph (95) includes a mere transparency obligation and nothing beyond that. This transparency obligation falls squarely within the scope of Article XI of the GATT.

In plain language, the only thing Vietnam agreed to in its Protocol of Accession was to keep the WTO notified of its progress toward privatization. It could, in theory, notify the WTO that no progress had been made at all and still be in compliance with this toothless stricture. Vietnam did not agree to observe a specific privatization process; this was instead an independent process, which could influence its "life" within the WTO (hence, its inclusion in the Protocol of Accession in the first place) and upon which Vietnam had embarked unilaterally anyway.

One might legitimately wonder how a centrally planned economy could faithfully implement GATT disciplines. How could, for example, a regime regulating the quantities sold in its market fulfill the obligation to ban quotas embedded in Article XI of the GATT? Shouldn't Protocols of Accession make privatization of the economy a precondition for accession? They simply did not. Protocols of Accession did not require acceding countries to do anything beyond respecting the GATT contract. We explain all this in what follows.

HUNGARY, POLAND, ROMANIA, AND YUGOSLAVIA

Following Czechoslovakia's regime change, the issue of state-trading countries in the GATT took on a new dimension in 1959 when Poland became the first socialist country (centrally planned economy) to apply for full accession to the GATT. Poland was a full-fledged member of the Soviet bloc at the time it filed its request for accession to the GATT.

It is unclear what prompted Poland to request accession to the GATT, especially since the dominant figure in the Soviet bloc, the Soviet Union, had not done so. The claim advanced by Kostecki (1979), though, seems quite persuasive to us: Poland requested accession in order to gain (some) independence from the Soviet Union and, of course, to increase its access to the lucrative Western markets.[10] The Soviet Union was, according to Kostecki's excellent account, opposed to the Polish initiative. It preferred not to hinder it, however, probably because it was anxious to see how the negotiations between Poland and GATT incumbents, which were expected to be protracted, would turn out. In particular, the Soviet Union was interested in seeing whether participation in the GATT was feasible for a centrally planned economy that was unwilling to modify its basic economic model.

It is easy to understand why incumbents, especially the most influential ones like the United States and a few Western European states, responded affirmatively to Poland's request. The thinking was that Poland could be lured into the Western bloc once it had realized gains from participating in the liberal trade order, thus opening a rift in the Soviet alliance. McKenzie (2008), in this vein, has argued that the United States wanted to shake up the Communist bloc by opening the door to the accession of Hungary, Poland, and Romania.

Additionally, as Davis and Wilf (2017) have argued, the Soviet Union did not oppose Poland's participation most likely because Poland was not as intimately linked to the Soviet Union as other Soviet satellites, such as Bulgaria and East Germany. Bulgaria had applied for accession to the GATT in 1986, but the incumbents did not take any action on this request until 1990 when, following the fall of the Berlin Wall, it was becoming increasingly clear that the Soviet bloc would be dismantled.

The GATT Secretariat had mixed feelings about admitting Poland to the GATT. McKenzie notes that Eric Wyndham-White, the director-general of the GATT, believed that the GATT would be an easy political target if it continued with selective membership (2008, 100ff.). It had to open up

10. The historical context matters here for various reasons. These are the pre-Solow years, when the convergence theory had been advanced by many, including Rostow. The idea was that centrally planned economies would eventually lapse because the United States had reached the highest level of production and consumption worldwide and other countries would attempt to emulate its example. For a concise introduction into convergence theory and the writings at the time, see Kneissel 1974.

to new members. Nevertheless, he advised Poland to avoid requesting full membership, cautioning GATT incumbents that the fundamental differences between their economic systems and Poland's would make accession a tough ride. Therefore, he recommended that Poland content itself with observer status.

The incumbents ignored Wyndham-White. Their solution was instead to include several obligations in Poland's Protocol of Accession that, as such, had not been part of the GATT itself, namely:[11]

- A minimum import commitment from GATT members[12]
- An agreed-upon annual increase for imports from GATT members (7 percent in the case of Poland)[13]
- A commitment to address discriminatory quantitative restrictions
- A dilution of the Interpretative Note Ad Article VI of the GATT so that not all prices had to be fixed by the state anymore for a GATT member to be treated as an NME
- The possibility for GATT members to adopt safeguard measures, and thus legally limit trade, while observing conditions that are less stringent than those embedded in Article XIX of the GATT

11. Yugoslavia was the first socialist country that joined the GATT (in 1966), but it acceded as a market rather than a non-market economy.

12. This idea has its origins in discussions inside the U.S. administration during the negotiation of the ITO. Pollard (1985), in his remarkable account of the origins of the Cold War, notes sharp divisions in the U.S. administration among the principals. William Clayton (then undersecretary of state for economic affairs) favored Russia's participation in the ITO, and Dean Acheson (then undersecretary of state) suggested that Russia agree to a minimum annual volume of imports. Averell Harriman (then secretary of commerce), however, thought that such proposals were inappropriate, as Russians needed U.S. products anyway. In his view, the problem was "to get them to contribute to the world economy something even halfway commensurate to what they expect to get out of it" (Pollard 1985, 52ff.). On this score, see also the discussion in part 3 in Irwin 2017. Of course, this logic did not apply to smaller economies like that of Hungary. There the issue was more establishing commercial ties, increasing interdependence, and, consequently, increasing the price of aggression. In this vein, American diplomats commonly understood Soviet abstention from the ITO as evidence not only of the Soviet determination to maintain independence (as opposed to interdependence) in foreign affairs but ultimately of their will to destroy these institutions; see FRUS 1946: 1:1, 355ff. Hook and Spanier 2013, 29ff. and Gaddis 2000, 198ff. provide further confirmation.

13. The notion that STCs should import, over a specified length of time, a minimum value of goods from GATT members, which would be adjusted periodically, finds its origin in Article 28 of the Suggested Charter, the document that the U.S. administration prepared following discussions with the United Kingdom and that served as a blueprint for the GATT. The GATT, of course, did not endorse outcomes-based trade. For the reasons explained in Krueger 1964 and Bhagwati 1965, it made much better sense to ban quotas and allow tariffs only as a transitional means to protect domestic markets.

The Protocols of Accession for Poland also included for the first time a discussion on trading rights since, to varying degrees, private companies were forbidden to act as international traders in all of these countries. Nevertheless, the protocols imposed no detailed obligations in this context. There were at least two reasons why GATT members took this route.

First, it was unrealistic to expect that Poland would agree to abandon central planning or the state monopoly of foreign trade. These institutions could undoubtedly negatively affect the implementation of various GATT rules. The commitments to import more or less fixed quantities of goods would engender reciprocity, which otherwise could have been completely undone.[14]

Second, the relatively small size of Poland's economy, coupled with the belief/hope that GATT membership would promote a change in the country's economic and political regime, helps explain the relatively soft strictures of the Protocol of Accession. Poland would participate in the future negotiating rounds along with the rest of the GATT membership. It would be called on then, if necessary, to make additional commitments. The same approach was used later for the accession of Yugoslavia (1966), Romania (1971), and Hungary (1973).[15]

No other non-Western country applied for accession during the GATT era. The four socialist countries that had joined during the GATT era did not make any waves. As a result, the membership did not have to rethink the appropriateness of amending the rules in order to address issues originating from the centrally planned character of their economies.

Following the advent of the WTO, several "non-Western" countries joined the WTO. We divide them into four categories:

- Central and Eastern European countries (CEECs)
- Russia and other former Soviet republics
- Arab countries
- Vietnam and China

The countries in each group are linked by key similarities. Although the first two groups of countries were all part of the Soviet bloc, CEECs were joining the EU and thus were forced to transform into market economies during that

14. Kostecki provides very persuasive arguments to support the thesis that reciprocity was factored in when deciding to introduce targets. He also explains how it was a Swedish diplomat, C. H. von Platen, who introduced the idea of targets as a means to accommodate regimes from the Eastern bloc; see Kostecki 1979, 91ff.

15. See Reuland 1975 and Grzybowski 1977.

process, while conversely Russia and the remaining former Soviet republics, since they were not becoming EU members, were not compelled to change their economic regimes (although they did to some extent, without becoming full-fledged Western economies like the CEECs).

Arab countries, on the other hand, exhibit characteristics of STCs but are typically ruled by royal families, and their actions distinguish them from communist countries. They are autocratic regimes where an elite (the royal family) has ample discretion to run the national economy as it wishes.

Vietnam and China were one-party communist countries. They had both traveled some distance from their hard-line pasts without, nevertheless, going through transformations like those experienced in Eastern European countries.[16]

CEECs

The accession of these countries was uncomplicated. Some of them joined the WTO as founding members (the Czech Republic, Hungary, Poland, Romania, the Slovak Republic, and Slovenia), others as acceding members (Bulgaria, Croatia, Estonia, Latvia, and Lithuania). All of them had already been negotiating (or had already decided to negotiate) their accession to the EU. It was clear that all of them would be eventually adhering to the EU schedule of concessions, since by virtue of Article 207 of the Treaty on the Functioning of the European Union (TFEU), trade policy is a common EU policy. Member states cannot sign international trade agreements or adopt trade policy measures on their own.[17]

Most important, to become EU members, CEECs had to completely change their legal regimes. They had to implement the GATT liberal understanding, and much more. The EU accession process specifies that only well-functioning democracies can apply to join, and acceding countries must also demonstrate liberalization of investment, respect for basic human rights (including property rights), the existence of well-functioning antitrust policies, and a commitment to the enforcement of intellectual property rights.

16. The level of commitment differs across groups, as Evenett and Braga (2006) show. This is not a concern for the purposes of this study.

17. Following the advent of the Lisbon Treaty (2009), the common EU trade policy comprises not only trade in goods but also trade in services, as well as FDI. Portfolio investment remains a national competence (that is, each member state is free to decide if and under what conditions portfolio investment in its jurisdiction will be open to foreign investors).

In short, the EU requires that its members be liberal market economies. Once they have acceded, new members thus incur several legal obligations in order to ensure that their market economy will be up to speed with those of the incumbents. Accession to the EU meant adherence to the GATT liberal understanding.

FORMER SOVIET REPUBLICS

Despite their previous political links with many CEECs, the former Soviet republics had very different economies—in fact, economies similar to China's—and thus different experiences with the WTO. Although several of the former Soviet republics applied to join the WTO, we focus on three that cover the whole spectrum of situations: Russia, by far the biggest country; Kazakhstan, a member of the Eurasian Economic Union (EAEU), and thus with continued close trade links to Russia; and Ukraine, which has recently distanced itself from Russia by signing a free-trade agreement (FTA) with the EU.

The Protocols of Accession for these three countries are terse and refer to specific paragraphs in the corresponding Working Party reports, where specific obligations have been assumed.[18] The structure of all these reports is quite similar. For the purposes of our study, there are four themes permeating them:

- SOEs and privatization
- Pricing policies
- Trading rights
- Investment

Each of these economic themes sheds light on the issues at hand.

SOEs and Privatization

Russia, Kazakhstan, and Ukraine have all embarked on privatization programs. Privatization was not done at the request of the WTO. In fact, as Working Party reports make clear, all three had embarked on a privatization program even before they initiated their accession proceedings, probably

18. Kazakhstan's Protocol of Accession is reflected in WTO Doc. WT/L/357, July 30, 2015, and the Working Party report for its accession, in WTO Doc. WT/ACC/KAZ/93, June 23, 2015; the corresponding documents for Russia are WT/L/39, December 17, 2011, and WT/ACC/RUS/70, November 17, 2011, and for Ukraine, WT/L/718, February 13, 2008, and WT/ACC/UKR/152, January 25, 2008.

anticipating accession to the WTO. These programs covered vast swaths of each country's economy, including farm, manufacturing, and services industries. At the same time, all three left aside key strategic (in the view of the three countries) sectors. These omissions do not overlap, but it is clear that each country's leaders wanted to maintain state control over certain sectors.

The number of SOEs has been reduced as a result of privatization, of course. Still, in all three countries, the extent of the economy controlled by SOEs was substantial at the time of accession.[19] The three countries began to implement their commitment to ensure that their SOEs would behave in a WTO-compliant manner, which in practice means that they will observe the obligations assumed under the SCM Agreement and, to the extent that they act as traders as well, the discipline embedded in Article XVII of the GATT.

In our view, their Protocols of Accession are characterized by a number of significant omissions regarding SOEs and privatization. WTO members welcomed the three countries' efforts to privatize, but since these efforts were taking place outside the process of WTO accession no one could guarantee that they would be done in a competitive manner. In other words, it was unclear whether—or which—interested buyers (domestic and/or foreign) could bid for state property. Foreigners cannot bid for state property under the current WTO rules. As we have seen, there is no multilateral agreement in this respect, and acceding countries did not accept any WTO obligations regarding investment commitments during the accession process.

The problem is, of course, that state property could simply be transferred to cronies of the regime, and thus state control could continue to exist under the guise of privatization. This is an issue in the case of Russian privatization in particular; many observers have expressed concerns that the Kremlin is simply handing control of state industries to oligarchs under the thumb of the Putin regime. The absence of meaningful competition laws just exacerbates the problems caused by phony privatization. However, because the WTO regime does not prejudge the status of ownership, the incumbents could not request that privatization be restricted to mere corporatization.

SOEs must observe the SCM Agreement, but the problem is, as we know by now, that the SCM Agreement does not even mention the term "SOE." Thus, there is no presumption that SOEs (for example) have access to money markets at preferential rates. There is, in addition, no presumption that their actions result in subsidies. Under the circumstances, our conclusions

19. For instance, according to statistics supplied by the Ukrainian delegation during the accession negotiations, in 2006, 19.5 percent of the Ukrainian economy was controlled by the state.

regarding the necessity of bringing the disciplines embedded in the Trans-Pacific Partnership (TPP) into the WTO become all the more relevant.

With respect to STEs, and/or SOEs that operate as STEs as well, observing Article XVII of the GATT is of limited use. Case law has managed to eviscerate the intended content of this provision. It understood that the obligations to act on commercial considerations, and afford adequate opportunity to all interested parties, are mere expressions of the nondiscrimination obligation and not, as they should be, self-standing obligations.

As a result, to the extent that a WTO member (Russia, China, or any other country) does not discriminate across foreign suppliers, it can be presumed to act in accordance with commercial considerations (even if this is manifestly not the case).[20]

Pricing Policies

In all three countries, prices are regulated in specific markets, typically, in energy, alcoholic beverages, some farm products like fertilizers, and so forth. A state entity, such as, for example, the Ukrainian State Inspectorate on Price Control, is responsible for ensuring that minimum prices are being respected.[21]

The membership of the WTO expressed its discontent with such policies carried out by prospective members. Nevertheless, to the extent that they observe the legislative framework of Articles III and XX of the GATT, there is not much that can be done about them within the current WTO regime. And, not surprisingly, nothing much was done in this context in the relevant part of the Protocols of Accession either. This issue underscores the discrepancy between the kind of obligations that CEECs acceding to the EU had to accept and the way the three countries examined here pursue their pricing policies. While CEECs were carrying out the potentially wrenching process of fundamentally overhauling their economies to conform with market-based principles, Russia, Kazakhstan, and Ukraine were able to maintain state control over prices.

20. All relevant case law on this score is discussed in Mavroidis 2016, 1:399ff.

21. Minimum prices have routinely been judged inconsistent with the GATT. All three countries nevertheless argued that an eventual inconsistency with Article XI of the GATT (on the elimination of quantitative restrictions) could be justified through recourse to Article XX of the GATT (which provides for exceptions to GATT obligations). Ukraine, for example, argued that its minimum prices were meant to fight illegal production and trade of alcoholic beverages. Some aspects of this law have been disputed. In particular, Moldova has initiated a dispute to this effect, and, at the moment of writing, the dispute is still at the stage of consultations (*Ukraine–Taxes on Distilled Spirits* [DS423]).

Pricing policies are an issue that has not been adequately explored in GATT/WTO law, most likely because it was not an issue among the original members, since all of them came to the table as Western-style market economies. Minimum import prices have since been sanctioned for both farm and non-farm goods. The Agreement on Agriculture, in Article 4.2, leaves us in no doubt that minimum import prices are inconsistent with the agreement. Consistent case law has also outlawed minimum import prices for non-farm goods, which violates Article XI of the GATT. In this case, defense of similar policies by the regulating state would necessitate recourse to Article XX of the GATT.

What about minimum sale prices, a pricing policy that is a behind-the-border measure? In this case, assuming the question were brought before a panel, we believe that similar measures, when concerning imported goods, would have to be found inconsistent with Article III of the GATT if they afford protection to domestic production. For example, assume that an imported good, following the relevant customs valuation procedures and the payment of customs duties, enters the market of Home at price x. Assume further that Home has a domestic law obliging this good to be sold at price 2x. The complainant would have to show that the seemingly nondiscriminatory price violates national treatment. This would be the case if, for example, the cost of production of the domestic good were to be anywhere in the continuum between x and 2x. In this case, the measure would de facto impose a higher burden on imported goods.

There is no case law on this score, and maybe justification for similar measures could be sought through recourse to Article XX of the GATT (even though we fail to see how this could be the case). At any rate, perhaps the incumbents did not insist very much on this point, thinking that they could enforce their rights through subsequent adjudication claiming that the relevant GATT provisions had been violated. In the end, the three countries did not, in this respect, accept obligations that escape the ambit of the covered agreements.

Trading Rights

Trading rights is an amorphous concept. It refers in principle to the right to engage in international trade transactions. Such rights are as yet undefined in the GATT/WTO and potentially ramify into much more significant issues than the simple definition implies. It is only when reading the Protocols of Accession that one can grasp the scope of the term.

There was no need to define this term any further in the GATT, since the restriction of trading rights, in the form of STEs, was a narrow exception across the signatories. But what was unproblematic among the original members has become an issue as the WTO continues to expand. Restrictions on trading rights, an exception in most members, is conversely the rule in centrally planned economies.

Russia, Kazakhstan, and Ukraine all agreed to increase the number of individuals (physical or legal persons) who would hold trading rights but subjected them to various bureaucratic requirements. Note, nevertheless, that governments frequently adopt laws and regulations requiring traders to register with domestic authorities, otherwise they cannot engage in importing and exporting. Still, such conditions attached to the right to trade in goods may be inconsistent with GATT rules. This is probably the most genuine borderline case when it comes to classifying it as falling under the ambit or evading the purview of the GATT. For there is no doubt that trading rights can come under various GATS services sectors.

The GATT does not address this issue head-on. Nevertheless, the requirement to behave in a nondiscriminatory manner embedded in Article VII applies irrespective of whether an STE is dealing with state or private enterprises. Article X of the GATT, on the other hand, requires that GATT signatories ensure that dissemination of confidential information would not run counter to the interests of particular enterprises, public or private.[22]

As per our discussion about the liberal understanding, the existence of private trading rights was assumed by the framers of the GATT. Indeed, how can Article X of the GATT (which requires signatories to establish tribunals/forums where traders could complain about administration of national laws) ever have any meaning if the existence of private rights had not been assumed?

The GATT assumes that private agents acting as importers and exporters had trading rights to import and export and, consequently, imposed on its signatories the obligation to establish forums and tribunals where private agents could complain about import- and export-related laws and regulations. If it was only states trading through state monopolies, then the GATT

22. The term "private" appears only in these two provisions in the GATT text, even though all signatories were market economies. This is not unusual, since the GATT was strictly addressing state behavior. It is also further evidence of the liberal understanding: no one deemed it necessary to delve into this issue any further.

system would not have needed to add anything beyond Articles XXII and XXIII, the dispute adjudication provisions.

Viewed from this perspective, the sections on private trading rights simply discuss what has to happen for an important GATT institution (Article X) to function properly. Allocation of private rights, however, could also be seen as an obligation to divest. Private parties will move in where the state was or where the state could have invested. If, for example, only the state had the right to import/export, then it would have to abide by the discipline embedded in Article XVII of the GATT dealing with state trading. To the extent that the state is giving up its import/export monopoly, private agents move in to occupy this space. Since no similar obligation has been imposed on incumbents, the regulation of trading rights in the Protocols of Accession could be seen as evading the ambit of the covered agreements.

Nevertheless, we are inclined to reject this view. Unless we understand private trading rights as inherent in the GATT system, we would have to accept that the candidate countries would end up negotiating GATT-minus clauses, since Article X of the GATT would become inoperative. Permanent deviation from Article X of the GATT is not in the cards, however. At best, a waiver can be sought to this effect, for a limited time. Furthermore, Charnovitz (2008) mentions some rare GATT-minus clauses in Protocols of Accession. They are all of transitional value and hence irrelevant for our discussion here.

In the context of provisions on trading rights in the Protocols of Accession we discuss here, there are some glaring omissions as well. There is not enough detail about the conditions that must be satisfied regarding the way trading rights will be allocated. Arguably, some of the concerns can be addressed within the four corners of the existing regime (national treatment, that is, the obligation to treat domestic and imported goods equally). The recent Appellate Body report on *Brazil–Taxation* could offer some help here. But restrictions could be justified under Article XX of the GATT, and one would have expected negotiators to insist on this latter point.

The problem is that if trading rights are allocated to cronies of the regime, and with the de facto absence of competition law (and, more fundamentally, a culture of competition), the trade outcome could be manipulated in favor of domestic production. Nevertheless, other than an obligation to consult in the realm of trade in services (Articles VIII and IX of the GATS), the world trading system contains no provision on competition laws. No country has ever sought the enactment of competition laws during the accession process.

Investment

All three countries maintain restrictions on investment. During their accession process, they explained their preferences for investment in new technologies and in areas of strategic interest to them. WTO rules contain no obligations as far as investment in goods is concerned, so WTO members are free to act as they wish in this area. No obligation was imposed on the acceding countries to enact their investment laws in a particular way. On the other hand, WTO members may be bound by obligations with respect to FDI in the realm of services (Mode 3), although, as we have explained, there is no obligation to do so.

There are some omissions here too. Because (at least in some sectors) foreign ownership is capped and joint venture with local firms is compulsory (in the realm of trade in goods, where no discipline à la Article XVI of the GATS exists), forced transfer of technology becomes a possible outcome of foreign direct investment. Once again, no obligation was imposed in order to avert this (likely) scenario.

ARAB COUNTRIES

These countries presented only minor issues with respect to SOEs. In any case, because of their size and limited impact on international (import and export) trade, incumbents did not push for detailed binding commitments. Soft-law measures by and large took care of any issues.

The report of the Working Party on the accession of Saudi Arabia reflects disagreements between incumbents and the acceding country on the extent of obligations that the latter would assume. Incumbents requested that SOEs be subjected to the notification requirements applicable to STEs, which Saudi Arabia opposed. Saudi Arabia's promise to eventually privatize and reduce the size of state-owned enterprises sufficed to defuse the attention on this issue.[23] Other countries, like Oman, made similar promises. Similar promises are, of course, hardly challengeable before a WTO panel. Then again, this is proof that SOEs were not a high-priority issue with respect to these countries. Furthermore, these countries have already signed numerous BITs and have addressed various investment-related issues within this context.[24] As a result,

---

23. WTO Doc. WT/ACC/SAU/61, January 1, 2005, at §§38ff.

24. https://investmentpolicy.unctad.org/international-investment-agreements/countries /223/united-states-of-america.

it should come as no surprise that no complaint has been raised against them before a WTO panel thus far.

VIETNAM

Vietnam, along with China, joined the WTO as a non-market economy (NME). It accepted various obligations, as a result of its accession process, precisely because it was not undergoing a transformation into a market economy. We highlight what are in our view the two most important ones.

First, Vietnam agreed that foreigners as well as Vietnamese nationals could enjoy trading rights in its territory; this will be the default scenario. For goods listed in Table 8(c) of the Working Party report, though,[25] the default scenario will not apply. Access by foreign traders thus will be limited to the list of goods in Table 8(c).

Second, Vietnam agreed to ban all state-mandated transfers of technology.[26] Once again, the ban covers behavior attributed to government, not private, behavior. To the extent that private Vietnamese companies request and/or impose technology transfers from foreigners, they will only be liable under domestic laws. Because the state dominates the Vietnamese company, the contractual promise entered into by Vietnam matters.

THE VERY SPECIAL CASE OF JAPAN

There were few roadblocks to WTO accession for these smaller countries, despite, in varying degrees, the remnants of state control over their economies. The GATT regime, however, faced a greater challenge when Japan requested accession. Although not a centrally planned economy, the Japanese state had a heavy hand in the workings of the national economy, and this was a red flag for several incumbents where it had not been with other countries eager to join.

The complaints against China are quite reminiscent of the complaints trading nations first formulated against Japan in the 1950s, when Japan knocked on the door of the GATT and requested accession. As in the case of China, Japan had also been excoriated for the disproportionate involvement

---

25. WTO Doc. WT/L/662, November 11, 2006 (Protocol of Accession for Vietnam); the Working Party report has been published as WT/ACC/VNM/48, October 27, 2006. Table 8(c) is reflected in pp. 161ff. of the report and contains items such as cigarettes and tobacco, oil, and newspapers. The relevant discussion concerning trading rights is included in §§137ff.

26. WT/ACC/VNM/48, §§125ff.

of the state in the economy. The similarity was great enough that the title of Wu's (2016) excellent article, "China Inc.," recalls Japan Inc., the name with which some trading nations, especially the United States, christened Japan after its joining the multilateral trading regime.

The attitudes of the incumbents are also quite telling. The United States went full circle: it was the staunchest supporter of Japan's accession at the beginning, then became its fiercest critic, and then was a loyal ally once again. Most European states were opposed to Japan's accession to the GATT but warmed up to it years later. The China narrative might well follow a similar pattern. But beyond the pattern of support or resistance from trading partners, the question here is, what can be learned from Japan's experience in the world trading system that we can use to address the specific issues with which China has presented the WTO regime?

We are not the first to draw a parallel between the Chinese and the Japanese accessions, but our analysis has the benefit of fuller information and a much more detailed focus on trade itself. Forsberg (1998), for example, has investigated the same question. However, his detailed analysis, insightful as it is, was completed before China acceded. We are looking into the same question with the benefit of hindsight, almost twenty years after China became a WTO member. Vogel (2019), in his excellent account of the Japan-China relationship, also focuses on the same question but from a wider perspective. Trade is but a second-order concern in his analysis. It is, of course, the main focus in this volume.

Japan and the World Trading System

As early as the Annecy Round (1949), the United States tried to force the Japanese accession on its partners, insisting on the importance of this endeavor in the context of early Cold War tensions. For the United States, what mattered most was the geopolitical question. Japan in the GATT meant Japan away from the influence of its neighboring partners. At the time, Japan was just a few years removed from the regimes of militaristic hard-liners who had joined the Axis and brutalized their neighbors one after another. The United States, which had assumed the tutelage of Japan in the post–World War II era (1945–52), was keen to bring Japan into the liberal order.

All historical accounts unanimously conclude that accession occurred when it did only because of the strong U.S. push behind it.[27] President Eisenhower adopted an unflinching attitude in this respect. He ignored even his

---

27. See, for instance, Johnson 1982; Kaufman 1982; Forsberg 1996, 1998; and Irwin 2017.

own cabinet and important statesmen, like Daniel Reed, the chairman of the House Ways and Means Committee, who was urging for the establishment of a tariff wall to protect the U.S. market from Japanese exported goods.[28]

The primary reason the United States supported Japan's accession was a geopolitical one.[29] The United States was the occupying force in Japan in the years after the war. Because General Marshall had failed in his China mission, as Kurtz-Phelan (2018) has persuasively argued, Japan became even more important for U.S. interests in that region. The U.S. administration felt that it could not run the risk that Japan might veer toward the Communist bloc. It would do anything in its power to resist such a situation. George Kennan, a U.S. statesman of Olympian stature, was probably the architect of this policy.

> The strategic rationale for this "reverse course" in Occupation Policy was spelled out by George Kennan, America's leading Cold War strategist, who was dispatched to Japan in March 1948 to evaluate US policy on Japan. Kennan wrote a forty-two-page report based on his investigation, and his policy proposals for Japan were approved by President Truman in October 1948. Kennan believed that if the people of Western Europe and Japan continued to suffer from poverty, they could become prey to Communist advances. By the time his proposals were approved, the Communists had already taken over Czechoslovakia and blockaded Berlin, and the Chinese Communists were poised to win the Civil War in China. The central goal of Kennan's Japan policy was to create a strong stable economy. He concluded that the Occupation policy of destroying Japanese businesses should be reversed. With strong economies, he believed, Japan and Europe would become pillars in a global free-market economy. When Kennan was later asked to reflect on his career years, he said that along with his part in launching the Marshall Plan for Europe's recovery, his role in supporting the reverse course in Japan was "the most significant contribution" he had made in his service to the US government. (Vogel 2019, 302)

Accession to the GATT was thus a key step in realizing Kennan's vision. Free trade and national security concerns were intertwined. Through its military occupation, the U.S. administration was promoting national security

28. See Forsberg 1998, 187ff.

29. Eckes (1995) provides substantial evidence to this effect. Miller (2019) adds a very detailed account explaining how the United States aimed to use its involvement in Japan as a platform to inspire an Asia-wide endorsement of a Western democracy model of governance. Davis and Wilf (2017) also discuss and analyze the role of geopolitics in GATT/WTO accessions.

concerns[30] and strengthening the Japanese economy. U.S. military dominance over Japan was probably the reason why Europeans did not have to view Japan as an aggressor. They could thus safely approach the issue of Japanese accession in the GATT on purely commercial terms.

There were economic interests involved as well. According to Pollard:

> Both before and after the war, American economic interests in Japan greatly exceeded those in China despite the widespread and enduring popular belief in the fabled China market. During the 1930s the United States registered about three times more trade and investment in Japan than in China. American exports to Japan, for instance, averaged about 7.6 percent of all overseas sales during the pre-war decade compared with 2.3 percent for China. Neither China nor Japan offered strategic raw materials that the United States could not obtain elsewhere. Interestingly, the bulk of American exports to Asia (more than $1.4 billion out of $1.8 billion in 1947) went to countries—notably, the Philippines, Southeast Asia, and British India—that received little attention in Washington during the late forties. (1985, 169)

There was also some optimism, an exuberance one might say, that Japan, following its integration in the multilateral institutions (the GATT being a key step in this endeavor), would resemble and eventually emulate the U.S. economic paradigm, and quite quickly. Japan's accession to the OECD in 1964, to which we will turn later, proved them right.[31]

---

30. Vogel notes that Truman firmly refused a Soviet request to divide Japan into two zones, as had been the case with Germany (2019, 303). By that time, there was evidence that, in the inimitable words of Churchill, the Iron Curtain was casting its shadow over that part of Europe.

31. Not that the United States left everything to Japanese discretion. The Supreme Commander of Allied Powers (SCAP) forced the economic reform program in Japan, first focusing on dissolving the zaibatsu. These were highly concentrated industrial and financial combines, which enjoyed the advantages of tightly knit relationships among affiliated firms. The U.S. deconcentration policy aimed to restore prewar conditions by reversing the mergers that the Japanese government had initiated during the war to boost its war effort. The big four zaibatsu (Mitsui, Mitsubishi, Sumitomo, and Yasuda) had increased their share of paid-in Japanese capital from 10.4 percent in 1937 to 24.5 percent in 1946. The SCAP managed to push these reforms thanks to the help of Japanese conservatives, who shared his belief that Japan was a "Western" society and feared that absent such reforms, the communist threat would gain pace; see Pollard 1985, 175ff. Following disagreements within the U.S. administration, which led to the so-called "reverse course" in 1948–50, the U.S. government issued NSC 13/2, based on George Kennan's containment policy. In it, the economic reforms discussed here remained intact. Importantly, however, Japan signed a peace treaty in San Francisco in 1951 and a bilateral security pact with the United States that incorporated Japan into the U.S. defense perimeter. See Pollard 1985, 185ff.

Still, the United States failed to persuade its GATT partners. The potential economic threat is what mattered most for Western Europe, as Zeiler explains (1999, 173ff.). Since Japan did not pose a military threat to them thanks to the U.S. defense umbrella, they had the luxury to reason in terms of narrower, trade interests. Without the support of European states, the early U.S. efforts to get Japan in the GATT would have been in vain. But even when it finally succeeded in persuading its partners to accept Japan in the GATT, the United States was unable to solve all the problems surrounding Japan's participation.

For three decades, Japan had a difficult economic relationship with some of its main trading partners. In the 1950s, it had problems becoming a member of the GATT in the first place. After this first hurdle was overcome, it had to wait until the mid-1960s to enjoy the full rights of membership, which (mainly) European countries had been withholding. Peace, though, did not last for long.

As Japan became a full-fledged GATT member, started modernizing, and adopted an export-led growth model, it was increasingly perceived as a threat by many Western governments. The irony is that, in the 1970s and 1980s, after becoming an economic powerhouse, Japan's primary (but not only) critic was its original benefactor, the United States. The U.S. government accused Japan of unfair trade practices, and, as a result, Japan found itself on the receiving end of various trade sanctions.

Today's reality is a far cry from the belligerent, almost pugilistic relationship that Japan and its major trading partners had once had. Japan, the United States, and the EU are the best of trade partners and are holding trilateral meetings on how to deal with the new economic powerhouse, China.

Japan's Accession Process to the GATT

By any reasonable benchmark, Japan's accession to the GATT is a unique episode in the history of the trade body. Japan is the only acceding member that had to wait two years before joining the GATT. Several members spent time first as observers; Japan went through a sort of GATT purgatory instead. It first had to apply as a provisional member of the GATT. This amounted to a probationary period of sorts, during which it sought to persuade incumbents that its economic model could fit into the GATT system. No other GATT/WTO member has undergone a similar experience before or since.[32] Japan's probation period was the expression of the doubts various

---

32. China did not experience anything like this. Nevertheless, since it had not participated in any of the previous rounds, it was asked to initiate tariff reductions before the initiation of the

members had regarding its participation in the GATT—perhaps remembering Japan's militaristic past. It was also the expression of the fear that Japan might, following its accession, dump cheap manufactured goods at cut-rate prices.

In 1953, the GATT had 33 members, 23 of which agreed to provisionally apply the GATT to Japan during its probation period. The other ten refused to do so. This probation period lasted for two years, and Japan joined the GATT in 1955.

After its formal accession on September 10, 1955, only 19 members agreed to continue applying the GATT to Japan. The other 14 members, fearing that Japan would not accept the GATT liberal understanding and/or the export potential of Japan, invoked Article XXXV of the GATT, the non-application clause.[33] This is an idiosyncratic GATT provision, aimed to facilitate accession to the GATT, even though, temporarily at least, some incumbents might be opposed to it. When invoking it against an acceding country, an incumbent does not prevent it from acceding but refuses to abide by the GATT obligations in its bilateral relations with that country. The GATT thus applies to all as is, except for the dyads comprising the acceding country and each of the countries invoking non-application.

The fourteen members who invoked non-application were the following: Australia, Austria, Belgium, Brazil, Cuba, France, Haiti, India, Luxembourg, the Netherlands, New Zealand, Rhodesia, South Africa, and the United Kingdom.[34] To add insult to injury, some of these fourteen countries were applying MFN status to non-members but refused to do so to Japan, a full member of the GATT.

In contrast, when China acceded to the WTO, only one WTO member invoked Article XIII of the Agreement Establishing the WTO, the successor provision to Article XXXV of the GATT, vis-à-vis China: El Salvador.[35] This is probably due to the great success that the GATT/WTO regime has had in depoliticizing trade and bringing old enemies to the negotiating table. Japan did not benefit from similar good fortune, most likely owing to the timing of its accession.

---

negotiation process. From an average statutory rate of 43 percent in 1985, it reduced its duties to 15 percent by 1986 when the accession process was officially under way; see Lardy 2019, 83ff.

33. GATT Doc. L/420, October 11, 1955.

34. GATT Doc. L/405, September 13, 1955. Furthermore, some countries that joined the GATT after Japan also invoked non-application.

35. WTO Doc. WT/L/429, November 5, 2001.

It was to be expected that Japanese officials would eventually be outraged with the GATT incumbents.[36] What did accession mean if practically all of Europe refused to grant MFN status to Japanese exports? Japan did not stay idle. It retaliated by refusing to apply the GATT to those who had invoked non-application against it.

Japan tried the carrot as well as the stick. Aware that its (European) trading partners were worried about its focus on export-led growth and mindful of their critique of the statist nature of its economy, Japanese officials repeatedly argued that the GATT should be in a position to fit countries with different economic structures under its umbrella. Japan also promised to reduce the volume of its exports to levels viewed as more acceptable by its trading partners. And Japan, time and again, made a plea to those who had invoked non-application to stop doing so.

Japan's requests to this effect fell on deaf ears for years. Its trading partners took their time to change their view. For a considerable period, Brazil was the only GATT trade partner of Japan that had agreed to withdraw its invocation of the non-application clause.[37] Not all its remaining partners, though, were prepared to stick to their invocation of non-application permanently. At one end of the spectrum, the United Kingdom definitely was not prepared to warm up to Japan. The rest of the (European) GATT membership, however, was prepared to make concessions.

Belgium, the Netherlands, and Luxembourg (the Benelux countries) went on record stating that their non-application was temporary and justified by the lack of adequate safeguards in the GATT to deal with Japanese competition. At that time, no detailed antidumping/countervailing/safeguards agreement had been concluded. The imposition of contingent protection measures was far more infrequent than it is today. Furthermore, these countries started applying MFN to Japan first with respect to a few goods only and eventually across all traded goods.

France and Austria, echoing the attitude of the Benelux countries, blamed the lack of safeguards as the justification for their invocation of the non-application clause. France in particular claimed that it was doing what was necessary to protect its textiles industry.[38] Outside Europe, India, most notably, insisted that it was not acting the way it did because it had

36. See, for example, the angry reaction of Minister Takaseki. Press Release, GATT/247, October 28, 1955.

37. GATT Doc. L/670, August 28, 1957.

38. Press Release, GATT/249, November 1, 1955. On the hostile UK attitude, see Forsberg 1998, 186ff.

coordinated with others but simply in order to address Japanese competition. In November 1964 the representative of Japan drew attention to the fact that through the invocation of Article XXXV, nearly half of the contracting parties were not applying the General Agreement to Japan.[39]

The year 1964 was a turning point. That year, Japan became the first country outside Europe and North America to join the Organisation for Economic Cooperation and Development (OECD), a group of "advanced nations" committed to the liberal understanding. Following this milestone, nearly all European countries progressively withdrew their letters of non-application. It is not that the accession to the OECD, in and of itself, led them to do so, although as we shall see it certainly helped.

In fact, Japan did espouse the liberal understanding in the years following its accession to the OECD. The decisive change happened between 1967 and 1973. In 1950, Japan had enacted the Act on Foreign Capital (Act No. 163), which prohibited foreign direct investment (FDI), in principle. By joining the OECD in 1964, Japan was required to liberalize FDI pursuant to the "OECD Code of Liberalisation of Capital Movements and of Current Invisible Operations."

At first, Japan procrastinated. Citing the country's precarious economic situation, Japan did not immediately liberalize FDI across the board. Instead, as per the OECD recommendation, issued in 1966, Japan liberalized FDI step by step. Eventually, by 1973, Japan had liberalized FDI in almost all business sectors. Only FDI in very specific areas would be subjected to individual review, and, depending on the outcome of the process, an authorization could be granted.

Total de facto liberalization soon became de jure as well. Japan abolished the Act on Foreign Capital and amended the Foreign Exchange and Foreign Trade Control Act (Act No. 228 of 1949) in 1979 to formally liberalize FDI (which had been de facto liberalized since 1973).

Internal stability in Japan helped immensely in this vein. The key business federation, Keidanren, under the robust leadership of Ishizaka Taizo, developed strong ties with the ruling Liberal Democratic Party (LDP). The government's Economic Planning Commission, established in 1955, was a public-private partnership aiming to guide Japan into the future. Later, following the Structural Impediments Initiative (SII), a bilateral negotiation with the United States, Japan moved from an obligation to notify prospective

---

39. GATT Doc. 2SS/SR.2, p. 7. The countries that continued to invoke Article XXXV after 1964 were mainly developing countries, which had acceded to the GATT in the early 1960s.

FDI to a transparency obligation regarding the volume and number of FDI in Japan, which could occur at a later stage. This was not a dramatic change, though, in its FDI policy. The main changes thus, with respect to its investment laws, are not due to the SII talks, as is sometimes erroneously reported. They were the product of the accession to the OECD.

As a result, because of these legislative initiatives, transfer of technology, a thorny issue in the relations between China and many trading nations, as we have already seen, was a non-issue as far as the relations between Japan and the world were concerned. In fact, it had never been an issue. The aforementioned Act on Foreign Capital stated that FDI would be allowed only when it would contribute to the independence and development of Japan's economy and to the improvement of Japan's balance of payments. Nevertheless, the statutory language did not specifically refer to transfer of technology as a requirement for approval of FDI. Consequently, and since this statute was abolished, as we have seen, by more liberal statutes, no subsequent laws required transfer of technology as a precondition for FDI.

We are certainly not arguing that Japan became "Western" after World War II. It was Emperor Meiji (1867–1912) who had introduced a Western-style bureaucracy, as well as a capitalist economy. It was Meiji, after all, who conceived the Iwakura Mission, a turning point in the economic history of Japan. Led by Iwakura Tomomi, a member of the Japanese nobility and of the Meiji government, fifty-one Meiji government leaders visited fifteen foreign countries that might serve as an example for the transformation of the Japanese economy. Inspired by what they saw, they returned to Japan to plant the seeds of transformation.[40]

As Vogel notes (2019, 205ff.), this transformation survived Emperor Meiji. The Allied Occupation of Japan (1945–52) did, of course, reorient Japan away from militarism and toward democratic institutions. On the purely economic front, though, Japan already had a market-oriented economy in place, even though it formally did not qualify as a typical Western economy at the time it knocked on the GATT's door.

Adherence to the liberal paradigm, however, turned out to be both a blessing and a curse. Japan transformed its economy quickly and proved the original critics—those who denied Japan its rights under the GATT—correct when predicting an influx of Japanese imports of unprecedented

---

40. Vogel (2011, 217ff.) draws a parallel between the Iwakura Mission and the scientific and technical visits and exchanges of personnel that Deng organized during his first years in power, as we saw in chapter 1.

proportions into their national markets, even though they were proved right for the wrong reasons.[41]

Johnson (1982) is right in noting that no one in the 1950s had foreseen the future Japanese miracle. And yet, nothing short of a miracle is what happened.

Japanese export-led growth at the time of Japan's accession in 1955 was more of an issue for the European countries than it was for the United States, which was guided primarily by geopolitical concerns. The tables turned later. When export-led growth became more of an issue for the United States, it did not hesitate to look for solutions outside the GATT to try to solve its problems with Japan. Worse, the U.S. actions created problems for others, like the European Union, which had to pay the price (literally) for the U.S.-Japan Semiconductor Pact of 1985.[42]

Complaints and Measures against Japan

For fifteen years after joining the GATT, Japan enjoyed exceptional economic growth. During this time, which is often referred to as the period of the "Japanese miracle," its average annual GDP growth was nearly 10 percent. During the same period, U.S. GDP growth averaged "only" 4 percent. As a result, the size of the Japanese economy significantly increased relative to the U.S. economy. In 1955, Japan's GDP amounted to roughly 5 percent of the U.S. GDP. By 1970, this ratio had reached 20 percent.

During the 1970s and 1980s, Japan's economic growth slowed down significantly, but it still averaged nearly 5 percent anually. Consequently, the Japanese economy made up a continuously higher percentage of the U.S. GDP. Eventually, it reached an all-time high of 71 percent in 1995.

The rapid increase of Japanese production and exports caused a backlash in other countries, especially in the United States, which first reacted by adopting defensive trade measures. The U.S. authorities imposed antidumping and countervailing duties on various imports from Japan. These instruments were quite transparent and provoked negative reactions. In 1970s and 1980s, the United States and to some extent the EU convinced Japan

---

41. Forsberg provides evidence to this effect (1998, 187ff.).

42. The U.S. and Japanese administrations negotiated this pact, which obliged Japan to raise its export prices. The EU complained and won the case before the GATT. The pact ended up increasing the profits of Japanese producers and reducing those of the U.S. industry, which was slowly reduced to a few players. Barfield (2003), Dallmeyer (1989), and Parsons (2005), among others, have criticized this ill-conceived initiative. The U.S. administration enjoyed better luck in its efforts to tame Japan through other initiatives, like the Plaza accords, which we discuss later.

to "voluntarily" restrain its exports of various products. In the 1980s, Japan agreed to voluntary export restraints (VERs) that the United States had requested from it, on a range of products, including steel, color television sets, automobiles, and, of course, semiconductors, as already discussed.[43]

Eventually, Japan's partners also grew increasingly irritated with the difficulty of penetrating the Japanese market. Grievances in this respect focused on two issues:

- The lengthy approval procedures to accept only investment that was deemed profitable to Japan, where, for example, technology could be transferred to Japanese companies, as described by Mason (1992, 151ff.)
- The omnipresent administrative guidance, whereby the Japanese government would dictate behavior to Japanese economic agents

Japan Inc. became Japan's de facto name in trade circles. Through this sobriquet (or nom de guerre, depending on the perspective), its trading partners wanted to denote that private agents played second fiddle to idiosyncratic (if not whimsical, echoing *folie de grandeur*) aspirations of the Japanese government to dominate international economic relations. Japan's trading partners adopted both multilateral and bilateral measures to try to change Japan's practices.

Multilateral Measures

The United States, Canada, and the EU litigated what was allowed under the GATT multilateral rules. Japan was a defendant in nine cases that reached formal adjudication between the time of its accession in 1955 and 1994, before the advent of the WTO. The cases (listed in chronological order) are: *Japan–Silk Yarn* (United States, 10/25/1977), *Japan–Leather I (US)* (United States, 7/19/1978), *Japan–Leather (Canada)* (Canada, 10/26/1979), *Japan–Tobacco* (United States, 11/7/1979), *Japan–Leather II (US)* (United States, 2/24/1983), *Japan–Agricultural Products* (United States, 8/12/1986), *Japan–Alcoholic Beverages* (European Community, 10/31/1986), *Japan–Semi-Conductors* (European Community, 2/19/1987), and *Japan–SPF Dimension*

---

43. It was not difficult to convince Japan to adopt VERs. Smith and Venables (1991) have shown that, under realistic assumptions, VERs can be a very acceptable second-best instrument (especially when switching costs, e.g., the costs associated with changing export destination are low). We will examine this later.

Lumber (Canada, 3/19/1988).[44] Japan prevailed only once (*SPF Dimension Lumber*) and implemented all reports where its measures were found to be inconsistent with the GATT. Actually, it formally adopted only six reports, since twice (in *Silk Yarn* and *Tobacco*) it settled with the complainant (the United States) before the report was issued. The two instances where Japan settled concerned state-trading enterprises having a monopoly over the import of silk yarn and tobacco. Note also that seven of the eight cases lost by Japan concerned its import regime. The other case concerned its export prices for semiconductors, where the European Community (EC), as the European Union was then called, acted as complainant.

The complaints about Japan, as is the case with complaints against China, also demonstrated the limits of what can be done against countries with heavy state involvement in the economy within the four corners of the world trading regime. In a communication to the GATT membership in 1983, the EC complained about what it viewed as "a serious problem: the difficulty of penetrating the Japanese market." It requested the establishment of a Working Party under Article XXIII:2 of the GATT (Nullification and Impairment), on the basis that "benefits of successive GATT negotiations with Japan have not been realized owing to a series of factors peculiar to the Japanese economy which have resulted in a lower level of imports, especially of manufactured products, as compared with other industrial countries."[45] While acknowledging that Japan had recently taken some measures to alleviate the situation, the EC noted that "the impact of these measures as a whole is limited and not commensurate with the magnitude of the problem." Consequently, the EC demanded

> a solution . . . which requires a co-ordinated series of general and specific measures, which go beyond the formal barriers at the border, and which are designed to bring about a definitive and substantial improvement in the present situation. In this context, the European Community reiterates that it is not seeking a fundamental change in the Japanese socio-economic system. It is interested in results: a situation in future where Japan offers equal opportunities of trade expansion to its trading partners, in conformity with the overall objectives of the General Agreement.
>
> The European Community is of the view that the present situation constitutes a nullification or impairment by Japan, of the benefits

44. The information in parentheses refers to the complainant and the date of its request for adjudication.

45. GATT Doc. L/5479, April 8, 1983.

otherwise accruing to the European Community under the GATT, and an impediment to the attainment of GATT's objectives. In particular the general GATT objective of "reciprocal and mutually advantageous arrangements" has not been achieved.[46]

The complainant was arguing that because of a series of measures adopted by the Japanese government, the ratio of consumption to savings was unfavorable. If consumption was diminutive, then international trade would, by definition, suffer as well.

Under the GATT rules, however, there was not much that could be done to curb the Japanese. Unsurprisingly, the complaint was thus ultimately not pursued beyond the original communication cited above. This complaint, however, is indicative of the kind of issues that the Japanese accession to the GATT had raised, as it is illustrative of the GATT's limits in dealing with it.[47]

Unilateral Measures

We can't be certain of the degree to which Japan's trading partners were directly influenced by incidents like the ones cited above, as they veered toward unilateral measures. They were likely a contributing factor to the strategy that a few trading partners adopted vis-à-vis Japan as a means to halt its conquering of one international market after another.

The United States overwhelmingly opted to deal unilaterally with Japan, using Section 301 of the Trade Act of 1974 and the threat of trade sanctions in order to enlarge the scope of obligations that Japan should accept, given its newly acquired status as an economic giant. From this perspective, one could view the 1980s negotiations between the United States and Japan, called the Structural Impediments Initiative (SII), as the accession negotiation of Japan that the United States had not wanted to conduct thirty years earlier due to geopolitical circumstances. Section 301 authorized, and in some instances required, the U.S. government to act against foreign countries that violate trade agreements or engage in unfair trade practices. It was originally adopted by Congress in 1974 but has been amended on several occasions.[48]

The U.S. government's negotiating leverage with its trading partners was significantly increased when Congress amended Section 301 in the Omnibus Trade and Competitiveness Act of 1988. The new "Super 301" provision

---

46. GATT Doc. L/5479, April 8, 1983, p. 3.
47. See GATT Analytical Index, p. 671.
48. See Bhagwati and Patrick 1990 for an extensive discussion of Section 301.

required the U.S. government to implement trade retaliations when a country was named an unfair trading partner and negotiations about specific products failed to produce satisfactory results.

The enactment of "Super 301" was motivated by congressional concern "that certain foreign countries, most notably Japan, engage in broad and consistent patterns of unfair practices that serve to keep their home markets free of significant competition from US and other foreign firms."[49] The new provision was passed in a broader environment of what some in Washington were referring to as "Japan bashing."[50] As Hugh Patrick, the famous American economist specialist of Japan, noted at the time, the U.S. attitude was not surprising:

> After all, Japan had emerged in the 1980's as the most important economic and technological challenge (some would say threat) to the United States. Japan is by far the world's second largest economy . . . [and] with the United States, is at the frontier of a far wider range of civilian goods technologies than any of the Western European countries. It has demonstrated immense competitive strength in a number of industries important to the United States—including automobiles, steel, consumer electronics, office equipment, semiconductors. (1990, 3)

Even in academia, many Americans perceived Japan to be on the heels of the United States—an existential threat, perhaps. Meanwhile the future EU was in third place and economically struggling. China, of course, was nowhere in the picture.

In 1989, Japan was named an unfair trading nation, and negotiations began with the United States on liberalizing trade in three areas: supercomputers, telecommunications satellites, and wood products.[51] In all three, the government of Japan made commitments to remove the relevant barriers and the U.S. government dropped its threat of sanctions.

For Japan, it was of course preferable to negotiate instead of facing unilateral measures every now and then. It suited U.S. interests as well. That same year (1989), President George H. W. Bush and Prime Minister Sōsuke Uno initiated the SII talks, which focused on structural impediments that hindered Japanese imports, though the talks also addressed a number of U.S. problems. The final report of the SII, issued in June 1990, urged the Japanese

49. Senate Finance Committee Report on Omnibus Trade Act of 1987, S. Rep. No. 71, 100th Cong., 1st Sess., 77 (1987), cited by Grier (1992, 6).

50. See, for instance, Tolchin 1988.

51. See Grier 1992.

government to rectify the situation in six different areas: saving and investment patterns, land policy, the system of production distribution, exclusionary business practices, keiretsu relationships, and pricing mechanisms.

Some issues raised in the SII were closely related to the GATT mandate, though not actually covered by it except in an oblique and minimalist way: distribution of goods and the treatment of restrictive business practices (RBPs) belong to this category. All that the GATT requires is that the same distribution channels be available to both domestic and foreign goods and that competition law, no matter whether efficient or inefficient, be applied in a nondiscriminatory manner. The U.S. administration wanted to go further than that. Other issues, although quite remote from the GATT mandate, nonetheless played an important role in the outcome of trade talks: public expenditure, land-use policy, and the notoriously close intercorporate relationship across Japanese behemoths.[52]

In the early 1990s, at a time when Japan was at the peak of its economic success and had emerged as the primary threat to U.S. economic supremacy, it was difficult to predict how the U.S.-Japan relationship would evolve as a result of the SII agreement. Quoting from Hugh Patrick once again:

> How the United States and Japan move from where they are today is unclear. The path certainly is difficult. Indeed, the United States–Japan economic relationship is fraught with danger. Both nations lack vision; both are beclouded by emotionalism and misperceptions. But beyond that, both nations have severe problems both in managing the relationship and in managing themselves. The great challenge in the relationship for the United States is whether it can learn how to share power as well as burdens with Japan. The respective national interests overlap but will not be identical; compromise will be necessary but will be difficult for the United States. For Japan the crucial issue is what sort of vision it will develop of itself and the world; and how it will exercise power responsibly. (1990, 12)

What was lacking was a framework to enable this relationship, with its sometimes contradictory goals, to foster cooperation across the two nations. The

---

52. Japan made a few concessions in each one of them. See, for instance, Matsushita 1991 and Saxonhouse 1991. Matsushita mentions both parties' dissatisfaction with the SII agreement: "Not surprisingly, the SII was criticized both in the United States and Japan. Japanese critics felt that the U.S. government was trying to interfere with Japanese domestic matters. In the United States, some critics believed that the SII would have a minimal effect, if any, on the trade imbalance" (1991, 436).

issue, of course, was ensuring that whatever bilateral cooperation emerged would not contravene the GATT commitments of the two partners.

How effective was SII? It was negotiated a few years after the Plaza agreement (1985),[53] which had led to a rapid appreciation of the yen after 1985, the consequence of which was that imports were more attractive in Japan, and had also slowed down Japanese exports. So by the time the SII talks were concluded in June 1990, trade frictions between Japan and the United States had already started to decline. Nonetheless, frictions continued for a while in some areas, especially high-technology sectors, as discussed in Laura d'Andrea Tyson's *Who's Bashing Whom?* (1991). Tyson also served as chair of President Clinton's Council of Economic Advisors and then as director of his National Economic Council during his first term in office (1993–96). Obviously, influential policymakers remained suspicious of Japan's commitment to openness in trade.

However, the collapse of the Japanese asset price bubble in the early 1990s and the ensuing "Lost Decade" reduced trade tensions even further. During the period between 1990 and 2018, Japan's economic growth averaged less than 2 percent, a full percentage point lower than that of the United States. As a result, according to data from the IMF, the ratio of Japanese GDP to U.S. GDP continuously declined from its peak of 71 percent in 1995 to 24 percent in 2018.[54] Similarly, Japan's share of international trade never recovered to its peak level in 1990. Japan was not a threat anymore. Various contributions in the work by Hamada, Kashyap, and Weinstein (2010) lend ample support to the view that trade frictions disappeared after the burst of the asset price bubble. Still, the SII had an appreciable impact on trade relations, even apart from the underlying effect of the burst of the bubble. For instance, Japan did change its large-scale retail law. As a result, conditions for opening up large stores in Japan were relaxed, though the subsequent emergence of e-commerce lessened the importance of this change.

The lesson we draw from our brief review of Japan's experience in the GATT/WTO is threefold:

- Japan, like China, provoked the wrath of its trading partners, but unlike China, it managed to do so from day one, and not a few years after its accession process had been completed.

---

53. Appelbaum discusses the background of this agreement, paying particular attention to U.S. pressure (2019, 241ff.). Aliber and Kindleberger discuss the Japanese crisis following the Plaza agreement (2015, 138ff., 231ff.).

54. https://www.imf.org/external/pubs/ft/weo/2019/02/weodata/index.aspx.

- Japan embraced to a large extent the GATT "liberal understanding" through a combination of factors, ranging from unilateral Japanese decisions, to pressure by the U.S. occupying forces, to its accession to the OECD. What matters for our discussion is that it moved closer to the Western world not because of GATT compulsion.
- A key reason why Japan was prepared to bow to various demands by its Western counterparts was its military dependency on the United States.

COMPARING CHINA TO JAPAN

Our discussion so far points to the conclusion that, for drastically divergent reasons, the GATT/WTO in the past managed to "absorb" the shock created by the accession of either small centrally planned economies (à la Hungary) or big players with substantial state involvement in the workings of the economy (e.g., Japan).

It bears repeating that we are not arguing that the GATT/WTO is a safe, which can "lock in" a transformation of national economies to make them compatible with the implicit liberal understanding of the world trade order. The GATT and even the WTO are not structured in such a way as to achieve that goal, nor do they have the disciplinary power or institutional will to do so.[55]

Transformation occurred for reasons exogenous to the GATT/WTO. Many ex–Soviet bloc countries joined the EU and thus were obliged to change their domestic policies. Japan, on the other hand, espoused the liberal understanding on its own, through its participation in the OECD and similar international forums. Participation in the GATT/WTO helped bring about but did not cause Japan's transformation.

China is different. It is both big and statist—it combines, that is, the features of both "problematic" groups of countries that the multilateral trading system has had to accommodate. It is also nowhere near acceding to the OECD, and it can never join the EU. To make matters worse, there is no sign at all that China is undergoing a regime change on its own—in fact (as we will see), it seems rather to be going backward. There is substantial evidence that President Xi is beefing up the involvement of the Communist Party in SOEs.

55. This is why, in our view, proponents of the commitment theory to explain trade agreements have a hard time being persuasive.

Some of the current trade complaints and measures against China are very similar to those lodged against Japan earlier, but others are quite different. This is because China and Japan have both similarities and differences, and because the current WTO system is similar in some ways to the GATT system that existed earlier but different in others. We begin by examining the similarities and differences between China and Japan and then look at how they have translated into differences and similarities between the complaints and trade measures against each country by their trading partners.

Both countries shared at the time of their accession the belief that export-led growth was the way forward. This was the outcome of strategic policy decisions: the domestic market would remain closed to foreigners, and through a mix of the ensuing gains from economies of scale and generous government help, domestic companies would be in a position to conquer export markets.

Japan, like China, was not living in an idealized world, where winners are the outcome of international competition.[56] It was all about strategic policy. The success of such strategies depends in part on global demand and on the willingness of foreign partners to play the game. Japan was practicing it at just the right moment. When it joined the GATT in 1955 and for the next fifteen to twenty years, the U.S. economy was booming, and many European economies were enjoying *les trentes glorieuses*, the thirty years after World War II when everything went right, with exceptionally high growth and low unemployment. Moreover, the integration of the EU market provided Japanese exporters with fewer barriers to implement their export-led growth strategy.

Negotiations with China regarding its entry to the WTO were initiated at the apex of the liberal triumph, following the dismantling of communism in Russia and the symbolic fall of the Berlin Wall. However, the global environment especially in the Trilateral countries (the EU, Japan, and the United States) has been less favorable during the period after China joined the WTO in December 2001.

Did it make sense, therefore, for China to pursue an export-led strategy like Japan's despite the changed global conditions? Yes, respond Haddad and Shepherd (2011), quite persuasively. Writing after the 2008 crisis, unprecedented worldwide at least in the post–World War II era, they explain why, because of the resilience that some key features of the WTO regime have

56. See Melitz 2003.

exhibited, export-led growth could still pay off in today's world. Bown (2018) has provided sufficient evidence to this effect.

Notwithstanding the difference in the global environment between then and now, the two Asian countries adopted export-led growth strategies and have enjoyed a similar export-led economic miracle during the first fifteen years after their accession the GATT/WTO, with their GDP growing at an average annual rate of close to 10 percent during this period. There are, however, three important economic differences between China and Japan that have a bearing on their main trading partners' reactions to their highly successful export-led growth strategy.

The first is economic size. As we already mentioned, Japan's GDP was barely around 5 percent of the U.S. GDP in 1955 and, although it grew rapidly during the next fifteen years, it was equivalent to only 20 percent of the U.S. GDP in 1970. By contrast, China's GDP was already equal to 13 percent of the U.S. GDP in 2001 and had surpassed 60 percent of the U.S. GDP fifteen years later.

The second difference is per capita income. In 1955, Japan's per capita income (measured at PPP) was equal to only 22 percent of the U.S. level; in 1970, it had reached 56 percent. And it continued growing. In fact, Thurow (1992), an MIT economist, thought that Japan would soon rival the EU and the United States. China is much poorer. In 2001, its per capita income was barely 10 percent of the U.S. level. Fifteen years later, it was still at only 24 percent.

The third difference is the role of the state in the economy and the extent of the rule of law. China joined the WTO as an NME and, although there are discussions as to whether it is still an NME today, China certainly considers itself to be a "socialist market economy," thus acknowledging the importance of the state in the functioning of the economy. In addition, China has been a country where the rule of law has been, over the years, an uncertain prospect.

By contrast Japan was never an NME, never mind a socialist economy, and has great respect for the rule of law. The Japanese domestic legal regime was never a cause for concern in terms of international trade. Private rights were acknowledged in the Japanese constitution, and enforcement was quite meticulous. As a result, the country integrated into the "Western club" quite rapidly after joining the GATT. It even became a certified member of the club in 1964, when it joined the OECD.

There is, finally, a geopolitical difference between the two countries, which is crucial as it pertains to their trade relationship with the United

States in particular. Since World War II, Japan has been dependent on the United States for its security; there is a large presence of U.S. military personnel and weapons on its soil. China, conversely, has never depended on the United States for its national security. To the contrary, it is increasingly becoming a military rival to the United States, especially in the South China Sea.[57] As a result, while both Japan and China have at times been labeled "economic rivals" by the United States, the Trump administration has also labeled China a "strategic competitor."[58] Indeed, as Kroeber correctly notes, by staying outside the U.S. alliance structure, China, unlike Japan, Korea, and/or Taiwan, did not benefit from programs of technical assistance, from educational exchanges, and, in more general terms, from unfettered access to the very lucrative U.S. market (2016, 15ff.). This is probably the single most important reason why Japan was willing to change a host of its domestic policies, while China has pushed back on challenges to its domestic policies. While Japan conformed relatively readily to the liberal economic understanding and Western rule-of-law standards, China has remained committed to an economy led by the state and at least a measure of authoritarian control.

The highly successful Japanese and Chinese export-led growth strategies were both met with a backlash from their leading trading partners. In part, this is because the GATT/WTO contains an extensive arsenal of rules that permit countries to adopt trade defense measures such as antidumping, anti-subsidy, and safeguard duties.

In the case of Japan, as we have already seen, its exports were initially limited by the fact that European and other countries invoked non-application for about ten years after it joined the GATT. Nonetheless, Japan's share of world merchandise exports grew rapidly. From 1.5 percent in 1955, it increased to 6 percent in 1970 and reached a peak of 10 percent around 1990. The result, as we have seen, was the imposition of other more drastic measures to limit Japan's exports by its trading partners, including VERs that were clearly in violation of GATT rules but were nonetheless tolerated by the

---

57. Ross (2018) mentions a very persuasive argument to this effect. The United States had encouraged the Philippines to challenge China's maritime claims before the United Nations Permanent Court of Arbitration (PCA). The PCA issued a decision (2016) in favor of the Philippines, which China disregarded. The new Filipino president, Rodrigo Duterte, not only avoided enforcing the favorable award to his country but instead sought rapprochement with China. China rewarded him for his actions with infrastructure and military aid, and eased restrictions on Filipino fishermen working in disputed waters. It exhibited even less restraint when drilling for oil in disputed waters in the South China Sea as of 2014.

58. Trump 2017.

GATT membership.[59] The WTO Agreement on Safeguards (SG Agreement) banned the use of VERs and similar other "gray area" measures (such as orderly market arrangements) that had become widespread in some GATT members to limit imports from Japan and other countries.

In the case of China, non-application was probably not a realistic option. Only one WTO member, El Salvador, which was not one of the leading trading nations, invoked Article XIII of the Agreement Establishing the WTO (the successor provision to Article XXXV of the GATT) vis-à-vis China.[60] The others were divided into three distinct groups, some of them inhabiting more than one of the three. Some wanted to avoid a clash with the most populous country in the world at a time when it was regaining its seat in the multilateral trading system. Some saw huge trading opportunities for their companies in the Chinese market. And some, as we have seen, genuinely believed that China would transform quickly—perhaps thinking of the Japanese experience.

The GATT/WTO contains adequate disciplinary measures to address the rise of Chinese exports with trade defense measures. Furthermore, until 2016, because of a clause inserted to this effect in the Protocol of Accession, WTO members could presume that China was an NME and use surrogate countries or constructed costs when imposing antidumping duties.

WTO members can further impose countervailing duties if they can show that Chinese SOEs (or private companies) have been receiving subsidies from the state. Case law might have made it more difficult to impose duties on imports originating in SOEs, but this is a matter of interpretation. Similar issues can be avoided in the future by preempting judicial discretion (as we suggest in our recommendations). Safeguards can always be imposed against an influx of imports, assuming the statutory conditions have been met.

The fact that trade remedies in the WTO are de facto prospective (the losing party in a panel simply has to stop the illegal behavior from the end of the compliance period, roughly four years from the initiation of the dispute, assuming an appeal has been launched) means that importers have a

---

59. Japan had little reason to complain. Certainly VERs were second-best, but an acceptable second-best. Smith and Venables (1991) have explained how, through such measures, Japan managed to pocket monopoly rents. Only once was a VER litigated before the GATT. It was in the aforementioned semiconductor case, where the EU (and other importing countries) suffered from the rise in the prices of Japanese exports as a result of the VER Japan had concluded with the United States.

60. WTO Doc. WT/L/429, November 5, 2001.

comprehensive arsenal at their disposal to address unfair (dumped, subsidized) or even fair trade to the extent that it has caused damage to their domestic industry (injury to competitors, not to competition). As had been done earlier with Japan, China's main trading partners are, therefore, quite able to deal with its exports in a satisfactory manner using the WTO arsenal.

The situation is different with regard to China's domestic market, as it was at the time with Japan's domestic market, because GATT/WTO disciplines are not very effective when it comes to opening import markets beyond border measures. In essence WTO members, say, the EU and the United States, can always prevent the entry of foreign products into their markets by putting up antidumping, anti-subsidy, or safeguard tariffs against these products, even though in the case of a large country, like China, they will have to worry about possible retaliation.

On the other hand, WTO members cannot simply force access to a foreign market if that market does not comply with unilaterally set, behind-the-border laws and regulations. Similar measures are usually prima facie nondiscriminatory but could de facto be affording an advantage to domestic producers and products. The standard for demonstrating de facto discrimination is, on paper at least, quite high.

Moving to positive integration, and thus eliminating the possibility of unilaterally deciding on conditions for market access, is not a realistic option for a heterogeneous group like the WTO. Leaving it as is (negative integration) means that market access might be inhibited by what appear to be on the surface neutral but de facto discriminatory measures. That was the problem GATT members faced with Japan in the 1980s, which led the EU to threaten nullification and impairment and the United States to use Section 301 to impose the SII bilateral negotiations. And, to an extent, it is the problem that WTO members face today with China.

WTO disciplines on behind-the-border measures are stricter than earlier GATT disciplines. Hence, in principle, China (like any other WTO member) should have less opportunity to restrict access to its market than did Japan (or any other GATT member at the time). Moreover, the Protocol of Accession for China contains binding obligations to respect China-specific commitments, whereas no similar specific obligations had been included in the Protocol of Accession for Japan.

The counterbalancing factor is, of course, that the involvement of the state in the Chinese economy and the extent to which China abides by the rule of law make it more difficult to enforce WTO commitments in China. This is especially the case when it comes to behind-the-border measures that are intrinsically difficult to enforce for a member-driven organization like the WTO, which has no investigative, let alone enforcement, power on its own initiative.

This largely explains why China's trading partners have grown frustrated with its import policy in recent years and have employed a host of measures to try to remedy the situation.

4

Unilateral Responses
Do Not Work

Unilateralism is not internationalism. It is national egotism gone mad.
—HUGH DALTON

In August 2019, Donald Trump's comment that "somebody had to take China on"[1] made headlines. It is unclear what he meant by this oddly half-hearted boast. On its face, this sounds like an attempt to tame China. De facto, though, President Trump has been focusing on reducing the trade deficit with China. This does not make much economic sense, as we will explain, but another way of putting it is, as Campbell and Sullivan (2019) have argued, that the structural imbalance between the U.S. and Chinese markets, because of the many formal and informal barriers in the latter, has pushed President Trump to his current policies. Assuming China is willing to abide by the law, there are ways to correct this imbalance, as we have seen. A more forceful response would require the adoption of extra-WTO measures, even if a fairness claim with the WTO regarding China's practices accompanied them. In either case, the confrontation has been and remains a tense standoff.

1. https://www.reuters.com/article/us-usa-trade-china-trump/trump-says-he-had-to-take -china-on-regardless-of-short-term-impact-on-us-economy-idUSKCN1VA21B.

It could easily get worse. Bown and Irwin argue that the current show-down could present the world community with a scenario that will be difficult to undo. In their words:

> This is not protectionism in the sense of trying to help a domestic industry in its struggle against imports. The goal is much broader and more significant: the economic decoupling of the United States and China. That would mark a historic fragmentation of the world economy. It would represent in the words of former Treasury Secretary Henry Paulson, the falling of an "economic iron curtain" between the world's two largest economies. Such a separation would have foreign policy and national security implications well beyond the economic consequences. (2019, 134)

Is this an exaggeration? Hardly. The possibility recalls the nascent tensions between East and West in 1946 when George Kennan, the chargé d'affaires in the U.S. embassy in Moscow, published a version of his notorious "Long Telegram" in *Foreign Affairs* (under the byline "X"). In "The Sources of Soviet Conduct," Kennan forcefully argued in favor of Soviet containment. The Soviet system, in his view, threatened the very existence of the prevailing liberal system and its ideals. Westad (2019) mentions that Kiron Skinner, the director of policy planning at the State Department, has explicitly called for a new "X" article—this time concerning the containment of China. Such a worst-case scenario cannot be ruled out.

Even short of a new Cold War, though, the basic message of the Trump administration remains: the solution to the China problem is unilateral. In our view, this simply cannot be, and indeed, events have put the lie to such a binary solution. China has not kowtowed to U.S. pressures and is quite unlikely to do so going forward. More significantly, the damage from Trump's blithe, ignorant unilateralism affects not only the United States and China but innocent bystanders as well. From the declines in stock prices, to seasonal job losses, to a host of other short-term effects, President Trump's policies have added to the problems, not solved them.

What is more, the U.S. administration's recourse to unilateralism has eviscerated the credibility and relevance of the WTO. If the United States can impose tariffs because it runs a trade deficit, why can't other countries that can afford to disregard their multilateral obligations exit the WTO contract whenever it suits them?

However, it is not enough to demonstrate, whether through economic analysis or using relevant historical examples, that the Trump administration has drawn the wrong lessons from history (if it has drawn any lesson at all). Trump's unilateral bluster is not, unfortunately, easily balanced by a readily available multilateral solution—yet. The current WTO regime, as we have seen, has difficulty dealing with complaints about SOEs and forced TT. These limits extend to the argument that recourse to nonviolation complaints (NVCs) can be of help. We will show why even this quite imaginative proposal falls short of addressing these two key concerns of the world trade community. One thing is certain, however: unilateralism has not worked and will not work.

Inefficient Unilateralism

Amiti, Redding, and Weinstein (2019) have provided the data and Bown and Irwin (2019) the reasons showing why, in the case of China, unilateralism cannot work. In a nutshell, the U.S. tariffs entail negative welfare implications for

- U.S. consumers, who have to switch to other products, costlier than the Chinese goods that are now burdened with higher tariffs;
- the U.S. industry that was using cheap Chinese imports as inputs for the production of U.S. goods and now has to switch to other, costlier inputs; and
- the employees of concerned U.S. industries, who will risk losing their jobs as the rise in the cost of production might (will) be accompanied by a restructuring (downsizing) of the production units.[2]

Because China has retaliated and continues to do so every time President Trump announces a return to his cherished tariff wars, U.S. producers of goods burdened with the new, higher Chinese tariffs suffer losses resulting from the inability to access the Chinese market.

Both from a U.S.-centered and from a cosmopolitan perspective, the hike in tariffs does not help. It has not helped thus far, and there is no reason to believe that things will change in the future. To be sure, we are not saying that only the U.S. economy has suffered; the Chinese economy has suffered as well. Our point is that because China can continue to suffer while inflicting comparable damage on the U.S. economy, this is not the way to resolve the

---

2. Lovely and Liang (2018) have argued that, ultimately, these measures will affect U.S. technological competitiveness, as other countries will be in a position to procure cheaper inputs in China.

China issues. Trade wars, contrary to President Trump's prediction,[3] are not that easy to win when they are fought against behemoths of comparable size as the United States. Worse, the damage is not limited to the two belligerents. Because of their size, it affects many other players as well.

The trading community and the WTO have been observing the unfolding trade war between the United States and China without taking any initiative to get in the way or broker a compromise. But the WTO was instituted at least in part with the express purpose of preventing such disputes. In 1995, the world trading community had hailed its establishment as an edifice with strong, dissuasive powers that could put an end to the unilateral trade wars that had harmed everyone in the past. Twenty-five years later, the promise of 1995 looks like a long-forgotten mirage.

The real problem, though, is that confidence in the WTO edifice, in the world trading system that is, is waning and waxing all the time. At present, the WTO membership knows that any time a big player is unhappy with the state of affairs, irrespective of whether the source of unhappiness is legitimate or not, it can simply step out of the system until it has worked out a solution to its liking.

The thrust of the game thus could be interpreted as the search not for cooperative solutions that will benefit some today and others tomorrow but for solutions that will always make the same people happy. What is the incentive of third parties to invest in such an endeavor, unless their interests are aligned with those of the major trading powers? The whole idea of a rules-based system was to establish a framework that would apply to all, irrespective of size and bargaining power.

Super 301 2.0, or, Creating a "Good" WTO

During the mid- to late 1980s, the United States embarked on a series of unilateral actions aimed at curbing the reactions of those opposing the expansion of the mandate of the GATT. The incentives of the business community and the U.S. government were aligned. The former wanted to access services markets abroad and to bring about an international regime that adequately protected IP rights. The latter wanted to reduce the trade deficit.

Finding that persuasion did not work, the United States had recourse to unilateral measures. Invoking Special 301 and Super 301 procedures, the United States asked Brazil and India (its main targets) to open up their

---

3. https://www.cnbc.com/2018/03/02/trump-trade-wars-are-good-and-easy-to-win.html.

services markets (telecoms, financial industry, etc.) and beef up their regime for protecting IP rights. For the most part, this strategy paid off. It is widely acknowledged that the U.S. push contributed substantially toward the expansion of the GATT competence. The GATS and the TRIPS Agreements are the fruits of this endeavor.

This episode might seem to offer a potential solution to the present difficulties with China. In reality, there are important differences that preclude such an outcome.

For starters, the U.S. unilateralism of the 1980s was not oriented toward a particular result. It was meant to persuade its trading partners to take their seats at the negotiating table and start bargaining to open up the services markets and improve IP rights protections. The outcome would be co-defined by the entire GATT membership, and the United States had only one vote throughout the process. In other words, this was a unilateral effort only in the sense of getting the ball rolling; the final deal was multilateral.

Second, the United States enjoyed the implicit support of almost the entire industrialized world. All OECD members, predominantly services economies, were in favor from the start or became supporters of the expansion of the GATT to services and intellectual property protection. Today, although many of these countries may well want to see the Chinese export-led growth model curtailed, so far none of them subscribes to the manner in which the United States is pursuing this agenda.

What do we mean by this? The EU and Japan would, of course, be delighted if the U.S. actions could lead to a WTO agreement with China. President Trump, however, is doing what no U.S. president has ever done. President Reagan's actions and extensive use of all possible 301s against India and Brazil are a far cry from what is happening today. President Trump has been gambling with the system itself. He seems to be willing to sacrifice the WTO system for a win against China, even though his preference might be a win within a reformed system. That seems to best capture President Trump's (and his administration's) method.

The Trump administration's attitude toward global trade is mirrored by their alarmingly dismissive attitude toward the Paris Agreement to combat climate change, an existential issue worldwide. They exhibited the same dismissiveness when abolishing President Obama's initiatives with respect to an eventual agreement to forestall Iran's nuclear weapons program. For President Trump, it is better to have no deal at all than a "bad" deal—which means, for him, one that might carry negative consequences for the United States in the short term or even just cause the United States to lose face (as he perceives it). In this logic, it is better to have no WTO than a "bad" WTO. This is the point of departure for the U.S. allies; the EU and Japan are by no means willing to pursue the same line. They seem to prefer, when the world is viewed from Trump's perspective, a "bad" WTO to no WTO at all.

Our argument, at its core, is to create a good WTO. We disagree with President Trump, as we believe that the WTO as it stands is a far better option than having no WTO. We further disagree with his preferred way to move forward. We believe that calling all the parties to the negotiating table at this stage should be the way forward. This avenue, alas, has not even been contemplated by the U.S. administration, never mind attempted.

The United States' main partner, the EU, is torn. It cannot afford to weaken its current relationship with China, even though its participation in the Trilateral is evidence that it adheres to the view that some Chinese policies are suspect.[4] And of course, as Smith and Taussig (2019) correctly observe, it cannot abandon its long-standing ties with the United States, its disapproval of unilateralism notwithstanding.

Thus far, the very measured EU response has been to screen, more carefully than before, Chinese investment in the EU. This is not a China-only policy. The new EU legislative framework enhances cooperation between member states and the European Commission and provides a platform to discuss in detail upcoming FDI with a security dimension. As China emerges as a major capital-exporting country, its investment decisions will be increasingly scrutinized at the EU level rather than at the member-state level.[5] Smith and Taussig (2019) note that the EU has undertaken a bilateral initiative with China, while participating in the Trilateral, and has multiplied the number of discussions aiming to strengthen disciplinary measures on subsidies at the WTO level.

Recall that the targets in the 1980s were Brazil and India. Neither of these countries, their relative size notwithstanding, can compare to the China of today. As we have stated in this chapter, China does not kowtow to the demands of the United States, and it is shortsighted folly to expect otherwise.

---

4. Smith and Taussig (2019) recount a very telling episode. In 2013, Chancellor Angela Merkel fought EU plans to impose tariffs on China for dumping solar panels on the EU market for fear that similar measures would entail a reaction by China. As many German industries either traded heavily or had invested large sums in the Chinese market, Merkel's action corresponded perfectly to protecting German interests, irrespective of the wider implications of dumping solar panels in the EU market. In Smith and Taussig's view, this initiative paid off, as Germany became China's leading trade partner in Europe, even running a trade surplus with China. On EU-China trade relations, see Pelkmans 2018.

5. Regulation 2019/2012 has been supplemented by COM (2017) 487 of September 13, 2017.

Furthermore, the Trump administration has veered wildly away from prior attempts by the United States to tame China. When it realized that the Protocol of Accession would not in itself do the job of transforming China into a market economy (or, more realistically, bring it closer to "Western" habits), the Obama administration opted for putting pressure on China to change its economic system by creating a grouping of Pacific countries led by the United States and excluding China. This led to the establishment of the TPP.

The TPP did not contain dramatic solutions. It laid down a framework that China could live by, but at the same time it was a framework that would tilt the balance toward market-like behavior. Wu (2016) has elegantly argued in favor of this option. In Wu's account, solutions must be incremental and implementable, as one should not underestimate China's ability to avoid the bite of agreed-upon contractual obligations. The late, lamented TPP represented a real-world approach, an attempt to find a workable solution to an intractable problem even if it wasn't ideal for all sides. The Trump administration's approach is, comparatively, the fantasy of a unilateralist.

Phase One

On January 15, 2020, as our manuscript was going to the publisher, the United States and China signed Phase One[6] of the Economic and Trade Agreement between the two countries, hailed by President Trump as the means of "righting the wrongs of the past and delivering a future of economic justice and security for American workers, farmers and families."[7] Unsurprisingly, Phase One deals with the two high-priority issues we have identified in this volume. Equally unsurprisingly it confirms our claim that bilateral solutions will not help redress the current unsatisfactory situation.

Chapter 2 of the agreement, for example, is titled "Technology Transfer." Articles 2.1 and 2.3 of this chapter contain clear-cut prohibitions of technology transfer mandated through administrative acts. But such solutions will only get us so far. The key issue is what to do with private behavior, which leads to similar outcomes. We are back to square one, in other words. And for

6. Economic and Trade Agreement between the United States of America and the People's Republic of China, Phase One, January 15, 2020, https://ustr.gov/sites/default/files/files/agreements/phase%20one%20agreement/Economic_And_Trade_Agreement_Between_The_United_States_And_China_Text.pdf.

7. https://www.cnbc.com/2020/01/15/trump-and-china-sign-phase-one-trade-agreement.html.

the rest? The agreement does contain provisions on exchange rates (Chapter 5) and trade in food and agricultural products (Chapter 3), but the main provision (Chapter 6) lists specific targets for increased Chinese imports of U.S. goods and services, amounting to $200 billion over 2020 and 2021, using 2017 as the benchmark year. If this is not trade discrimination, then what is it? It would be a miracle (for the Trump administration), and a victory for managed trade, if litigation by third countries does not strike this clause down, as it violates the cornerstone provision of the GATT (Article I, the MFN clause), as well as another key GATT provision (Article XI, calling for elimination of quantitative restrictions).[8]

The Phase One deal is the best demonstration of our claim that the political economy in the United States will induce U.S.-centered solutions. When we divide the content of Phase One into systemic (e.g., treatment of SOEs and transfer of technology) and narrower (e.g., U.S. export interests to China) issues, we see that it is definitely tilted toward the latter. How could it have been otherwise, one might ask? Here we are facing a classic collective action problem. Why would the U.S. government incur the full cost of negotiating elaborate disciplines on SOEs and transfer and technology with China when it would have to share the benefits of the deal with China with the remaining 162 members of the WTO?

President Trump announced in January 2020 that he would be going back to China soon to sign Phase Two. If it is anything like Phase One, and there is no reason to believe that it will be any different, it will suffer from the same shortcomings: it will not only be WTO inconsistent; it will also, and crucially, fail to address the key concerns that we have identified in this volume.

As a matter of fact, the Trump administration seems to recognize that bilateral deals with China cannot substitute for multilateral agreements when it comes to issues such as SOEs and forced TT, which are at the heart of the Chinese economic system. In a surprising and unprecedented move, on February 20, 2020, the U.S. delegation to the WTO submitted a communication to WTO members, tellingly titled "The Importance of Market-Oriented Conditions to the World Trading System,"[9] calling on the WTO

8. Chowdhry and Felbermayr (2020) find that the U.S.-China trade deal will impose huge losses on China's major trading partners. As far as goods trade is concerned, the main losers are expected to be Australia, Brazil, the EU, Japan, and Russia.

9. WTO Doc. WT/GC/W/796.

General Council (the WTO's highest-level decision-making body) to adopt a formal decision, the operative part of which reads as follows:

> The General Council *affirms* Members' citizens and businesses should operate under market-oriented conditions and notes the following elements indicate and are important so that market-oriented conditions exist for market participants:
>
> i. decisions of enterprises on prices, costs, inputs, purchases, and sales are freely determined and made in response to market signals;
> ii. decisions of enterprises on investments are freely determined and made in response to market signals;
> iii. prices of capital, labor, technology, and other factors are market-determined;
> iv. capital allocation decisions of or affecting enterprises are freely determined and made in response to market signals;
> v. enterprises are subject to internationally recognized accounting standards, including independent accounting;
> vi. enterprises are subject to market-oriented and effective corporation law, bankruptcy law, competition law, and private property law, and may enforce their rights through impartial legal processes, such as an independent judicial system;
> vii. enterprises are able to freely access relevant information on which to base their business decisions; and
> viii. there is no significant government interference in enterprise business decisions described above.
>
> The General Council *agrees* to reaffirm Members' commitment to open, market-oriented policies in order to achieve market-oriented conditions that are critical to ensure a level playing field for workers and businesses and a fairer and more open world trading system that benefits their peoples.

At the moment of writing it is unclear whether this communication will be endorsed by the WTO membership, and even less so whether it will be used to redraft key WTO rules. But it does underscore the U.S. view that the "liberal understanding" of the GATT, which has been hitherto implicit also in the WTO Agreement, should become explicit. We agree.

The Limits of Adjudication before the WTO

We discussed in chapter 2 whether current WTO rules are able to adjudicate complaints regarding Chinese practices with respect to SOEs and forced TT. Our conclusion was: not much.

In a recent article, Jennifer Hillmann (2018), a former member of the WTO's Appellate Body, proposed an alternate solution: those affected by China's practices could obtain a victory by lodging a nonviolation complaint (NVC) before the WTO.

Briefly, an NVC allows WTO members to request compensation even for legal measures, which nevertheless nullify or impair the benefits accruing to them. What matters is that benefits have been impaired, irrespective of whether the action described in the complaint is legal or not. To this effect, the WTO member has to show that its benefits have been impaired as a result of a measure by another WTO member that they could not have reasonably anticipated.[10] Hillmann does not discuss exhaustively the complaints that an aspiring complainant could bring under an NVC. We will, nevertheless, examine the potential of an NVC complainant to be successful when challenging the legality of Chinese SOEs and/or forced TT before a WTO panel. In our view, this option is not a recipe for success, if what we are looking for is a change in China's behavior with respect to its handling of SOEs and forced TT.

NVCs are associated with a high burden of proof. Following the ruling in the panel report on *Japan–Film*, the leading case on this score, the burden of persuasion varies depending on when the challenged measure occurred. Since NVCs are linked to tariff concessions, what we care about is the point in time when the challenged measure occurred, as compared to when a concession was negotiated.

In the case of China, the first (and last) tariff concessions were agreed to in 2001. In line with the allocation of the burden of proof as per the panel report on *Japan–Film*, if the challenged measure (any challenged measure) occurred before 2001 (when tariff concessions between China and its trading partners were exchanged), then the complainant must demonstrate that although it was aware of it, it could not have anticipated its impact.

For Chinese measures adopted after 2001, the presumption works in the opposite way. It will be incumbent on China to show that although unknown to the complainant at the moment when tariff concessions were

10. For a detailed discussion, see Bagwell and Staiger 2001.

being exchanged, the complainant should still have anticipated that the challenged measure would eventually occur. Therefore, one can easily understand that, with respect to the first category of measures, complainants will have an Everest to climb. They will have to demonstrate that although they were fully aware of the measures challenged, they could not have anticipated their eventual impact.

Keep in mind that this allocation of the burden of proof is not conditional on transparency-related concerns. It is a legal presumption. Incumbents must do their homework and find out what kind of measures exist in the Chinese market that might affect the outcome of their tariff negotiation with China. In order to prevail, they have to show why the impact of these measures, the eventual impact, that is, could not have been reasonably anticipated. The limits of reasonableness are quite elastic, which is why no WTO member has been successful so far in adjudicating similar measures.

Alas, even if they succeed, it will not be a panacea for the world trading system because NVCs do not lead to an obligation to remove the challenged measure, since the measure is not illegal in the first place. This is true for measures that occurred before as well as after the date when concessions had been negotiated. In other words, the allocation of proof is immaterial (we will assume that China has lost the argument). China has the option throughout the process to simply offer compensation to the complainant, without incurring the obligation to change its policies. It could also just settle before the judgment, thus avoiding condemnation of its practices in the first place.

If the objective is to reduce or remove state involvement in the Chinese internal market, then NVCs are not the way to go about it. Of course, NVCs could provide relief to individual trading nations, and much-needed compensation, but that is an argument for another time and a different venue.

5

Staying Idle Is No Solution

The problem with doing nothing is not knowing when you're finished.
—BENJAMIN FRANKLIN

A WTO, Good for All?

The U.S. administration's hubris regarding China is not limited to the expectation of winning an "easy" trade war. Its position, articulated by various officials in different forums, goes far beyond that. It was expressed in July 2018 by the U.S. ambassador to the WTO during a discussion concerning the review of China's trade policy in the realm of the WTO's Trade Policy Review Body. We quote §§4.105 and 4.112, the most characteristic passages, in full:

> 4.105. China's failure to fully embrace the open, market-oriented policies on which this institution is founded must be addressed, either within the WTO or outside the WTO. Given China's very large and growing role in international trade, and the serious harm that China's state-led, mercantilist approach to trade and investment causes to China's trading partners, this reckoning can no longer be put off. If the WTO is to remain relevant to the international trading system, change is necessary.
>
> 4.112. Going forward, the best solution is for China finally to take the initiative to fully and effectively embrace open, market-oriented policies.

China knows what needs to be done, and we urge China to take that route.[1]

The view of the U.S. government seems to be that China must accept a regime change and abandon its "state-led, mercantilist trade and investment regime"[2] or risk the demise of the WTO system and/or further trade retributions. The U.S. reaction is in response to the fact that nearly twenty years after its accession to the WTO, China has not become the type of market economy that the United States (and a few others, including the other members of the Trilateral) had envisaged back in 2001.

The confrontation between China and the United States is made worse by its timing. The world trading system is, overall, struggling. Unable to deliver on the Doha agenda, with no compass pointing to its future role, it must also address this thorny issue, which risks aggravating the overall situation even further.

Some who oppose the U.S. position have called for China to resist the pressure to become more "Western" in the way it manages its economy and for the WTO to accommodate a diversity of economic systems. A vocal proponent of this view is Dani Rodrik (2018), a Harvard economist, who recently approved of the "fact that many of China's policies violate WTO rules," arguing that "any sensible international trade regime must start from the recognition that it is neither feasible nor desirable to restrict the policy space countries have to design their own economic and social models."[3]

1. WTO Doc. WT/TPR/M/375.

2. WT/TPR/M/375 at §4.110.

3. We would also like to note, at this stage, the claims advanced by Segal (2011), who argues that the best response for the United States would be to do what it does best: continue to innovate. The author notes that China has developed the "hardware" (basic research, communications, infrastructure, etc.) but not the "software" (the web of relationships between researchers and government). He argues that the U.S. government should develop highly localized clusters of academia, business, and industry that serve as platforms to give birth to game-changing ideas. This is a noteworthy analysis, but it does not address the question we care about in this volume. If at all, this strategy, if pursued and successful, might address the U.S. worries in the medium to longer run but not the worries of other WTO members that might lack the means to put together a similar strategy as a response to China's growth.

In 2019 Rodrik, together with other scholars, established the U.S.-China Trade Policy Working Group, which has issued a call for a more nuanced approach toward U.S.-China trade disputes. The group suggests that harmful trade policies should be divided into "four buckets" depending on the level of cost these policies shift to foreign partners. The idea is to tolerate incidental harm and to address, instead, policies that cause the most harm to foreign parties. See https://rodrik.typepad.com/dani_rodriks_weblog/2019/10/announcing-the-us-china-trade-policy-working-group.html. As far as U.S.-China disputes are concerned, the group has said that the four buckets

Implicitly, Rodrik is criticizing the very framework upon which the WTO stands—the liberal understanding with its capitalist underpinnings.

We disagree with both views. We have already expressed our disagreement with the former view in chapter 2. The U.S. ambassador could not point to specific WTO language that would require China to change. As things stand, with respect to SOEs and forced TT, China can be accused of violating the spirit but not necessarily the letter of the WTO. Some of the liberal understanding will have to be translated into operational, contractual language for the United States to be able to make a legitimate request for such sweeping change from China, in the eyes of the world trading community. Looking at it from this perspective has profound consequences: to request a change from China, in other words, we need to first amend the WTO.

Of interest to us, in this chapter, is the second proposal. We do not agree that China should be allowed to violate WTO rules because it needs policy space. But more to the point, the GATT was not thought of or designed as a multipurpose institution, where both liberal markets and centrally planned economies could happily coexist. The GATT spirit is that of the liberal market order. This "liberal understanding" is at the very heart of the GATT order.

The GATT Liberal Understanding

The GATT, on its face, does not discipline domestic instruments (policies) beyond the requirement to apply them in a nondiscriminatory manner to both domestic and imported goods. Some domestic policies had been regulated in the International Trade Organization (ITO), the umbrella organization, under the aegis of which the GATT was originally meant to operate in order to regulate only state barriers to international trade. The GATT would become, in fact, one of the chapters of the ITO.

Dissociating the GATT from the wider ITO project during the London conference in 1946, and anticipating its advent by a few years, meant, among other things, that the disciplining of domestic policies would be reduced,

---

of policies fall into two categories: those that should be banned altogether, and those that should be pursued through bilateral negotiations between China and the United States, without enlisting the WTO or seeking to modify its rules. This contrasts drastically with our approach in this volume, which views the WTO as central, indeed essential, to resolving trade disputes between China and the United States and to prevent any bilateral agreement between the two countries that would result in harmful consequences for third countries. See Cerutti et al. 2019 for a quantitative evaluation of the spillover effects of a U.S.-China trade arrangement on third countries.

provisionally at least (since the ITO was supposed to enter into force a few months/years after the GATT), to an obligation to observe nondiscrimination when applying unilaterally defined domestic policies on domestic and imported goods. Thus GATT members could, for example, decide whether or not to adopt consumption taxes. Those who decided to levy a consumption tax on a particular product would have to apply the same levy on domestic and imported goods.

Importantly, this obligation became operative from day one and served as an insurance policy to safeguard the value of tariff concessions agreed to in the summer of 1947, which preceded the entry into force of the GATT. Jackson (1969) provides a very detailed discussion to this effect. The architects of the world trading system feared that the whole endeavor might have been imperiled if the advent of the GATT chapter was conditioned on the success of the wider ITO agenda. Since the GATT could in any case address many of the issues that they had identified as problematic, the framers decided to anticipate its advent while continuing to negotiate the ITO agenda.

Baldwin (1970), in his unparalleled account, argues persuasively that this decision was eminently sensible. In his "snags" parable, he explains that, logically, the priority should be to tame border protection first, the GATT content, that is. At any rate, the bite of behind-the-border instruments could not have been properly assessed, since high tariffs and import quotas would blur the issue. Following the disciplining of the GATT agenda, negotiators could work on behind-the-border protection—the ITO agenda. They would be in a better position to evaluate the bite of snags at this stage, since border protection would no longer blur the picture.

This provisional solution became a permanent one with the passage of time. The ITO never entered into force, and it was not until the creation of the WTO that a global trade organization was set up. The WTO did not distance itself from GATT-Think; rather, domestic policies continued to be unilaterally defined, and the only binding obligation imposed on WTO members with respect to them was nondiscrimination. The WTO maintained the quintessentially negative integration of the GATT, where domestic policies are unilaterally defined but must be applied in a nondiscriminatory manner across domestic and foreign goods.

There is one exception now to this rule. WTO members are not free to determine the level of protection as far as intellectual property rights are concerned. Because of the advent of the TRIPS Agreement, WTO members must ensure a minimum level of protection with respect to the rights embedded in the agreements protecting intellectual property rights that they had decided to include in the TRIPS Agreement. They are no longer free to decide whether to protect such rights. They must, at the very least, conform to the level of protection embedded in TRIPS. This agreement thus imposes a minimum level of protection that all WTO members must abide by.

THE GATT AND REGIME NEUTRALITY

Does this mean that the GATT was neutral toward its signatories' choice of economic system? Should we equate negative integration with Rodrik's thesis, to the effect that the metaphorical house of international trade should be large enough to accommodate all regimes? Was the GATT intended to be equally accessible to liberal market economies and to centrally planned economies?

The short answer is no. There is ample support for the argument that the GATT was predicated on an implicit liberal understanding.

First of all, the GATT was negotiated exclusively by like-minded, Western countries, following a proposal by Canada (probably echoing the U.S. view) to this effect.[4] There was no "clash of civilizations," in other words, at the negotiating table. At that early stage, there was an implicit assumption that signatories would abide by Western standards—and, perhaps, the further assumption that countries wanting to accede in the future would trend in that direction.

The WTO negotiation was not harmonious in this sense. The divide between developed and developing countries permeated the negotiation of both the General Agreement on Trade in Services (GATS) and the TRIPS Agreement. The inclusion of TRIPS in the multilateral order was a point of contention, and the inclusion of GATS was hanging in the balance even during the Ministerial Conference at Punta del Este, where the Uruguay Round was officially launched.[5]

4. Irwin, Mavroidis, and Sykes (2008) write that an invitation was issued to the Soviet Union to participate, which was refused, probably expectedly so. Pollard (1985) notes that the invitation to the Soviet Union was issued because the instigators wanted to avoid the problems posed by the non-participation of Russia following the Bolshevik Revolution in the Treaty of Versailles. As it turned out, the refusal by the Soviet Union to participate allowed them to negotiate a deal corresponding to their common understanding of liberal trade. Note also that the private sector made its presence known as it was quite vocal in the negotiation of the GATT. The participation of Russell Leffingwell, senior partner at the House of Morgan, is singled out by Hearden (2002, 39–40). Slobodian (2018) provides additional evidence to this effect, underscoring the liberal consensus on which the GATT was built.

5. Paemen and Bentsch 1995.

None of this echoes the original GATT negotiation. Even though detailed accounts of the negotiation reveal that the United Kingdom, the United States, and the other participants did not see eye to eye on all issues,[6] they all shared an adherence to the market economy. They also shared a firm opposition to the centrally planned economy, not only, or not primarily, because of economic reasons but also, and perhaps mainly, because of the threat to their political regime, and, ultimately, to their national security, that centrally planned countries represented. True, all original GATT participants acknowledged a role for the state in the organization of their market economies, and the degree of state intervention differed among them. But the basic premise for all participants was that the state should correct market failures rather than dictate market outcomes. The UK delegation, for example, inspired by James Meade's commercial union project, translated their ideas into a policy document that was named "The Overton Report" after the permanent secretary of the Board of Trade, Sir Arnold Overton. This report, which reflected the quintessential British negotiating position, included disciplines on subsidies, quotas, and export taxes that would significantly constrain the actions of governments so as to leave trade flows largely unaffected.[7]

In addition, the GATT disciplines themselves are the brainchild of the two most liberal countries at the time, the United Kingdom and the United States. In discussing the property rights in the GATT, Irwin, Mavroidis, and Sykes (2008) provide evidence that 75 of its 89 provisions were taken almost verbatim from the U.S. Suggested Charter.[8] Were we to move the discussion to a more disaggregated level, we could single out the discipline on STEs, the only GATT provision that addresses head-on the behavior of the state acting as an economic operator. This provision makes it clear that in such circumstances the state, when acting as a seller or distributor, must behave as any other market participant. Indeed, Article XVII of the

6. See, for example, Brown 1950; Irwin, Mavroidis, and Sykes 2008; Jackson 1969; Wilcox 1949; and Zeiler 1999.

7. Zeiler 1999, 28ff. The author mentions that the British aimed at building a "capitalist alliance" of America, the Commonwealth, and Western Europe (31). In a similar vein, the author refers to the efforts of the Truman administration and the president himself, who was prepared to go a long way in order to ensure that, as per John Ruggie's famous expression, liberalism would be embedded in the final text of the GATT (1982, 398ff.).

8. The GATT has of course only 38 articles, but Irwin, Mavroidis, and Sykes (2008) identify 89 provisions in light of the negotiating record. The U.S. Suggested Charter was based on the UK/U.S. Atlantic Charter. On this issue, see also Zeiler 1999.

GATT mandates that STEs act in accordance with commercial consider-ations.[9] Thus, while it acknowledges that state-owned companies can trade internationally (and, by inference, not be forced to privatize), this provision imposes on GATT signatories the obligation to ensure that, when engaging in international trade, STEs will act as if they were profit maximizers.

This is not to suggest that the GATT called for deregulation of any sort. To the contrary, the GATT was concerned with eliminating behav-ior that, under the guise of pursuing legitimate regulatory objectives, resulted in protection of the local producer. GATT (and WTO) members remained free to regulate or deregulate as they wished, as long as by doing so they would confer no advantage to domestic over foreign (imported) goods.

But the coup de grâce, in our view, is this. If by centrally planned econo-mies, we are referring to a regime where decisions regarding production, investment, and allocation of capital goods are entrusted to a bureaucracy (and not to the market), then similar regimes are incompatible with the GATT. The quintessential element of the GATT is protecting the equality of competitive conditions. While each member can unilaterally determine the regulatory regime in its jurisdiction, it cannot quantify the amount of goods traded (as import and export quotas are impermissible). It is the market that will decide this issue.

By this, we do not mean to suggest that the GATT explicitly contradicts regime neutrality. In principle, we should not care about the ownership of firms, private or public, as long as they behave according to commercial considerations. The benchmark for deciding whether an entity behaves in accordance with commercial considerations must be the market. There is no paradigm of totally uninhibited market behavior. Some intervention exists in all markets, and market behavior cannot be judged in clinical isolation from the overarching legal regime.

The degree of state intervention differs, of course, across jurisdictions. And incumbents have their fair share of state intervention in their national economies. No WTO member is an anarchy. The commonplace view, for example, is that the United States is more willing to question the rationale for regulating, whereas EU regulators are more trigger-happy. Regulatory diversity is quite consonant with the WTO, an institution that by and large aims to harmonize conditions of competition *within and not across* markets.

---

9. Case law, alas, has eviscerated the bite of this discipline by equating it to nondiscrimination.

What the liberal understanding amounts to is an acknowledgment that governments do not preempt the market mechanism.

Consider the following example. In the *Softwood Lumber* saga, a long-running dispute between Canada and the United States, the key question was whether Canada had been subsidizing the use of land from which timber was harvested and (eventually) exported to the U.S. market. The U.S. claim was that since Canada overwhelmingly owned the land, the lease price could not be taken into account to decide whether a subsidy had been granted. The market was so distorted that even if a small percentage of land were privatized (there was some private land leased for harvesting timber in Canada), the market price for leasing had irreparably been influenced by the prevailing fixed administrative price.

We believe an analogy can be drawn to serve the purposes of our discussion here. Regime neutrality is a question of degree. There is nothing wrong with employing STEs, if they are exceptional and if they operate in a predominantly private-enterprise regime. In this setting, one can judge whether the public enterprises are behaving like private operators in a commercial manner. Indeed, this is exactly the logic of the legal discipline reflected in Article XVII of the GATT. When the predominant system, conversely, is a centrally planned economy, then it becomes quite onerous, if not impossible altogether, to determine whether an operator has observed commercial considerations. Note that the EU regime, for example, addresses the question of regime neutrality head-on. Article 345 of the Treaty on the Functioning of the European Union (TFEU) reads: "the Treaties shall in no way prejudice the rules in Member States governing the system of property ownership."

Does this mean that centrally planned economies can be EU member states? Of course not. The Court of Justice of the European Union (CJEU) understood this provision very much along the lines that we have suggested. Early on, in *Costa* (6–64) it held that nationalization is not precluded. It provided the counterbalance, when holding that privatization is not precluded either (C-244/11, *Commission v. Greece*). More recently, in C-105, 106, and 107/12 (*Staat der Nederlanden v. Essent NV, Essent Nederland BV, Eneco Holding NV, and Delta NV*) the CJEU was called on to decide on the consistency of a Dutch measure prohibiting privatization of a distribution system in the realm of utilities.[10]

---

10. This jurisprudence has been confirmed in case law recently a few times; see, for example, C-563/17, C-305/17, and C-52/16.

The CJEU agreed that there was, in principle, nothing wrong with the Dutch measure, which, nevertheless, had to observe the prohibition of discrimination, as well as the freedoms of establishment and capital (FDI and portfolio investment) across EU member states. A measure banning privatization was, of course, putting a dent in these two freedoms. It would be tolerated, as long as the dent was justified on the grounds of public interest. This means that reasons of a purely economic nature cannot justify similar measures, unless they pursue a legitimate public interest objective.

This judgment thus permits that, only for reasons of serving the public interest, a refusal to privatization can find its place under EU law. To act in accordance with commercial considerations admittedly does not go that far. It presupposes a market benchmark. The EU regime, as understood by the CJEU, undeniably goes further than the corresponding GATT regime, but certainly in the same direction.

THE (INVISIBLE) CONTENT OF THE LIBERAL UNDERSTANDING

We have made a clear case that a liberal understanding permeates the GATT discipline. We have described, in other words, the spirit of the integration process that the GATT (and later the WTO) has put in place. The precise content, nevertheless, of the liberal understanding remains to be specified. Influential work by Tumlir (1984), Hudec (1975), Jackson (1969), and Jakobson and Oksenberg (1990) confirms the existence and, simultaneously, the lack of specification of the content.

Other than the discipline embedded in Article XVII of the GATT, we have not pointed so far to any provision that translates the liberal understanding into explicit, contractual language. It is, of course, the property regime, the degree of liberalization of investment, and the organization of competition policy that determine the degree of market friendliness of any national economy. Market access is in large part a function of these elements. What help is it, for example, to have a 0 percent tariff binding if all goods imported must be distributed through one state-owned distributor? How can we judge, in this extreme scenario, whether distributors operate under commercial considerations?

Recall our conclusion in the immediately preceding section where we stated that regime neutrality is a question of degree. STEs, if exceptional, and assuming that they operate in a predominantly private-enterprise regime, have their place in the GATT system.

The regulation of all these elements, though, has been omitted from the GATT-Think. All that GATT-Think does, in this respect, is request that behind-the-border policies be applied in a nondiscriminatory manner.

Consequently, a question naturally arises: Why did GATT signatories spend so much time designing mechanisms to protect their domestic market from excessive or unfair imports but not show the same zeal in addressing practices that might inhibit them from exporting even when they were exporting fairly or in moderate quantities? Why were the framers of the GATT convinced that they did not have to do much in order to ensure effective market access, especially when customs duties had been tamed and, eventually, eliminated? The answer lies in the negotiation of the GATT.

We have already noted that the GATT was one of the agreements that would come under the aegis of the ITO. The ITO Charter, an agreement that, on paper at least, would eventually be signed by the world community, contained specific provisions on various domestic policies, ranging from investment and competition policy to employment.

Article 12 of the Havana Charter for an International Trade Organization was the provision regulating international investment. Ten years before the first bilateral investment treaty (BIT) had been signed between Germany and Pakistan, the ITO signatories had paved the way toward treating foreign investors on a nondiscriminatory basis, vis-à-vis both all other foreign investors and their domestic counterparts. The importance of international investment, and its potential contribution to development, is highlighted in various other provisions of the Havana Charter (the Preamble, Article 11, Article 49). The ITO Charter, thus, already in the late 1940s, had adopted a liberal approach toward FDI by espousing nondiscrimination, the cornerstone of today's BITs.

Then there is, of course, Chapter V of the ITO, which addresses restrictive business practices (RBPs). It requests that ITO members address RBPs (Article 46 of the ITO Charter). Trade liberalization can, of course, be negatively affected by both state and private restraints. While the GATT addressed the former, Chapter V addressed the latter.

A host of provisions provide a framework for consultations in cases where RBPs have been tolerated and entailed transboundary negative externalities for foreign traders.

Even though the ITO Charter did not ultimately see the light of day, this provision survived, albeit in reduced form. There is a reminder in the GATT (Article XXIX) to the effect that signatories should endeavor to observe the principles of Chapter V of the ITO Charter. This provision does not contain a legally binding obligation of result—never mind of specific conduct. Nevertheless, it does, its lack of bindingness notwithstanding, denote what is in principle expected from GATT signatories.

Finally, Chapter IV of the ITO addresses state involvement in the national economy in an elaborate manner. Two sections are of particular importance to our discussion here: Section C, dealing with subsidies, and Section D, dealing with STEs. The GATT did not contain elaborate disciplines on subsidies, but the ITO Charter did. Article 12, Chapter IV, and Chapter V of the ITO epitomize the type of domestic policies that trading nations would be called to abide by, had the ITO seen the light of day. This never happened and the WTO, its eventual successor, did not reproduce these disciplines.[11] Does this mean that the decision to abandon the ITO meant the abandonment of the liberal understanding? And could, therefore, the GATT bring under its roof all countries, regardless of their economic system? We take these two questions in turn in what follows. We will show that the GATT did not undo the liberal understanding of the ITO and that its implicit rather than explicit nature did not prevent the GATT from having members with different economic systems.

LIBERAL UNDERSTANDING, NATIONAL SECURITY, AND GEOPOLITICS

Why was the ITO Charter not approved? More specifically, we are interested in asking whether the failure to enact the ITO was because of opposition to the embedded liberal understanding. It is clear that this was not the case. The ITO Charter was not even submitted for approval to the U.S. Congress, as Irwin, Mavroidis, and Sykes (2008) note, probably out of fear it might be voted down. One thing is clear, though. The ITO was not rejected by Congress because of its disciplines on competition, subsidies, or investment. Detailed historical accounts[12] point to the prioritization of other (than the ITO) issues at that time by the Truman administration and the uneasiness with the chapter regarding employment policies. There were no qualms about Article 12 of the ITO Charter, or the substantive content of

---

11. The GATS, of course, includes investment-related disciplines. It does not, however, request a general nondiscriminatory policy vis-à-vis foreign investors. Nondiscrimination in the services context (in the sense of national treatment, that is, treating foreign investors in the same manner as their domestic counterparts) is a voluntary specific commitment, not a compulsory general obligation that all WTO members must abide by.

12. See, for example, Brown 1950; Wilcox 1949; and Zeiler 1999.

Chapter IV, much of which found its way into the GATT text. Article XVI of the GATT reproduced a small part of the discipline on subsidies. And, of course, provisions like Article XVII of the GATT clearly requested that GATT members discipline their state entities participating in international trade, as it includes an inference, a presumption to use a legal term, that state agents do not base their decisions on commercial considerations.

Finally, there were no qualms with respect to the aforementioned Chapter V of the ITO Charter addressing RBPs. Indeed, what better proof that GATT signatories agreed to ensure that trade would not be inhibited by RBPs than the body of Article XXIX of the GATT? This provision kept the connection to Chapter V of the ITO Charter, which was designed to address RBPs: GATT members, even though not legally bound to observe the ITO Charter (which had not entered into force), accepted a clause (Article XXIX of the GATT) to endeavor to abide by its substantive content and, consequently, avoid beggar-thy-neighbor policies, like RBPs.

De facto, the GATT membership continued to observe the liberal understanding despite the abandonment of the ITO. Competition laws, independent competition authorities, and liberal investment regimes continued to flourish in all countries that were the original signatories of the GATT.

With the liberal understanding firmly in place, did the incumbents then impose it on newly acceding countries? In terms of legal conditions for joining the GATT (and eventually the WTO), the answer is no. Acceding countries did not have to adopt policies like those described in Article 12 or Chapters IV and V of the ITO Charter as a precondition for membership in either body. In fact, some Soviet bloc countries, as we have already seen, joined the GATT without undoing their centrally planned economic model.

The mystery, then, is why the original signatories did not require compliance with the liberal understanding as a precondition for access to the GATT (WTO). The GATT did not have to go as far as the EU and adopt some form of positive integration. Incumbents, nevertheless, could have produced a "light" version of the liberal understanding, incorporating elements from the parts of the ITO Charter that we mentioned above, and request observance as a quid pro quo for accession. After all, they were observing these rules anyway, so why not impose them on countries eager to reap the benefits of accession?

There are various reasons why this did not happen—in fact, was not even contemplated. It is true that the leading Communist nations (China and the Soviet Union) did not request accession to the GATT. Conversely, the size of the Soviet bloc countries that requested accession to the GATT was such that they posed no threat to the overwhelmingly liberal trading system. As we have seen, Japan, which was not a centrally planned economy but certainly more of a statist economy than the GATT incumbents, initially posed more of a threat.

It is logical to postulate that geopolitical considerations (undoing the alliance of the Soviet bloc) led the GATT incumbents to accept countries like Hungary and Poland. It is easy to see why some incumbents might have thought that these countries would realize the positive implications of interacting with liberal democracies and would unilaterally make changes to their economic system. It could also be that, because of their size, these countries represented no threat to the world trading system.

The link between trade liberalization and national security was clearly on the mind of the Western—especially U.S.—policymakers from the outset. There is ample proof of the U.S. negotiators' exasperation with the attitude of their more permissive UK counterparts during the GATT talks, as recounted by Irwin, Mavroidis, and Sykes (2008). Fearing that some of the "weaker" countries participating in the GATT negotiation would turn away from the liberal understanding, U.S. negotiators in particular were prepared, to a certain degree, to promote the unity of the "Western world" over their own economic interests. The writings of Steil (2018), Kurtz-Phelan (2018), McKenzie (2008), and Zeiler (1999) support the thesis that national security advisors were holding the pen during the last stages of the GATT negotiation and forced a deal even though economically it might not have been perceived as best for the ascendant economic power of the United States. They insisted because, they thought, it was best for America's geopolitical interest.

This attitude continued in subsequent years. Walker provides further confirmation that the U.S. administration continued to be worried that unless some concessions were made, peripheral countries might migrate to the Soviet bloc (2018, 81ff.). He describes the U.S. attitude toward Japan, which was running a large trade deficit in 1952 with its reserves steadily declining: "A stagnant economy, US officials feared, might hasten a turn toward China as a trading partner. Acting Secretary of State Walter Bedell Smith in April 1953 pledged that if conditions worsened 'we would want to sit down together with [the] Japanese to try [to] consider ways in which we could help'" (82). Prime Minister Yoshida, after visiting several European capitals, arrived in Washington, D.C., in November 1953. He asked for a "Marshall Plan" for Asia, which did not happen. Nonetheless, Yoshida did not turn to China in search of a strategic partner and instead chose to resign. President Eisenhower then became even more adamant about

Japan's importance during the Cold War and turned toward securing Japanese accession to the GATT. We saw in chapter 3 that Eisenhower was prepared to disappoint even his own people and close advisors in order to support the Japanese quest for accession to the GATT.

In a nutshell, the incumbents did not have to face the important dilemmas that would have been posed had (then) communist China and/or the Soviet Union requested admission to the GATT. Furthermore, they might have taken the view that opening the door to the smaller European members of the Soviet bloc would introduce cracks in the Soviet alliance because of the positive economic implications associated with trade liberalization. And they would have to agree among themselves on a common set of rules before asking others to observe them.

There was, in other words, no strong policy reason to impose the "liberal understanding" on those acceding to the GATT. There were further substantial (negotiating) costs that they would have had to incur in order to go down this path.

There was an additional, legal reason why the liberal understanding was not translated into concrete legal obligations à la Article 12 and/or Chapter V of the ITO Charter. Legally, it was impossible to impose on acceding countries obligations that lie beyond the scope of the GATT (and eventually the WTO covered agreements). This fundamentally affected the content of and rationale for Protocols of Accession.

Why There Is No Room for WTOx
in Protocols of Accession

Horn, Mavroidis, and Sapir (2010) examined the content of FTAs signed by the EU and the United States. They suggested a distinction between WTO+ and WTOx clauses, which helped advance our thesis as to why FTAs are being pursued when tariffs are at an all-time low and why tariffs are the only instrument that can legally segment markets and favor the domestic producer.

Horn, Mavroidis, and Sapir understood WTO+ as cases where trade partners liberalize further an area where WTO obligations already exist. For example, reducing the MFN tariff by x percent is considered a WTO+ provision. Conversely, WTOx covers areas where trade partners agree to take commitments in areas not covered in the WTO agreements currently in place. For example, protection of foreign private investors is an area that escapes the purview of the WTO; if such provision is included in an FTA, it is qualified as WTOx. There is, of course, nothing wrong with introducing WTOx clauses in an FTA, an instrument that allows deviations from the GATT/WTO contract, assuming that the statutory requirements have been met.

However, it is legally and logically impossible to introduce them in Protocols of Accession. We explained in chapter 3 why, even if Article XIII of the Agreement Establishing the WTO were not to be considered a scope provision, practice confirms that no WTOx clauses have been introduced through similar instruments. Reciprocity, the key GATT/WTO instrument upon which the multilateral edifice is built, would be ill served otherwise. Recall our point that, through a Protocol of Accession, acceding countries substitute for their lack of participation in negotiating rounds because they were not members of the body.

The subject matter, then, of a Protocol of Accession must replicate that of the (prior) negotiating rounds. It cannot extend beyond them—otherwise the acceding country would be overpaying for its entry ticket. The idea is as follows: when acceding to the GATT/WTO, countries can only be bound by the obligations in areas where GATT/WTO incumbents have already accepted commitments as a result of their GATT/WTO membership. However, in these areas, the acceding country may be asked, and may agree, to take on obligations that go beyond those already accepted by incumbents.

Our conclusion from the discussion in this chapter is thus twofold:

- The liberal understanding does permeate the GATT/WTO regime. It is the spirit of the GATT that China is violating through its policies with respect to SOEs and forced TT. Under the circumstances, the trading community could not stay idle. Sooner or later, the crisis had to knock on the door of the WTO house. It already did, in fact, when the trade war between the United States and China erupted, though no one attempted to defuse it. The world community is in search of a solution.
- What could the solution be? Since the liberal understanding cannot be imposed through a Protocol of Accession, the only means available to the world trade community is to negotiate agreements that will translate the spirit of the GATT, or at least the priority items (SOEs, forced TT), into contractual, legal language.

The next chapter includes our proposals to this effect. Before we conclude, however, we would like to add a few final words explaining why renegotiation at the WTO emerges as the most attractive solution, to us at least. The trading community cannot undo (without violating the WTO) its current legal relationship with China as expressed in the Protocol of Accession that China and incumbent WTO members signed. As of 2016, China cannot automatically be considered a "non-market economy." Yet it has not transformed into what is generally understood to be a "market economy" either. Unilaterally, then, China did not act upon its earlier promise to continue down the road of transformation, at least not at the anticipated pace. The nudge in this direction can only come from the leading trading nations of the WTO.

6

The Way Forward

The future has a way of arriving unannounced.
—GEORGE F. WILL

Dealing with China

The solution we advocate is, for all practical purposes, a translation of some of the GATT liberal understanding described in the previous chapter into legal, contractual language. In our view, the best way forward is to break with the recent past and renew the commitment to multilateralism.

The United States has been a key contributor toward establishing the (relatively) peaceful, post–World War II era by promoting the creation of multilateral institutions, including the WTO, to achieve these ends. Its commitment has been unparalleled, especially in the years during and immediately following the war, when towering figures like Cordell Hull and Dean Acheson led the push toward international cooperation.

However, the United States did not bring about this internationalist order on its own. It had to rely on willing fellow travelers. As far as international trade cooperation is concerned, the United Kingdom was the other pillar that helped build the GATT edifice. The EU picked up where the United Kingdom left off. In an ever-changing world, the United States has remained a constant and the number of participants willing to pull their weight has increased. The old Quad (Canada, the EU, Japan, and the United States) became the antechamber of the GATT negotiations in the 1980s, and the new Quad (Brazil, the EU, India, and the United States) took its place in the early years of the Uruguay Round.

China, the world's second largest economy, can now legitimately request a seat at the table, and it should have it. That seat, however, should have responsibilities attached to it. China must contribute toward preserving both the letter as well as the spirit of the GATT/WTO regime.

To be fair, China has been taking some unilateral measures in this direction. Unlike Japan, which joined the OECD as a full member within ten years of joining the GATT, China has been participating in the OECD as an observer for over twenty years now. It is quite active in the discussions on competition and financial policy, FDI, and corporate governance, and enjoys observer status in various relevant OECD committees. It does not, however, need to abide by the various OECD codes of conduct, since it still is not a formal member.

In a similar vein, China participates in the Asia-Pacific Economic Cooperation (APEC) side by side with various developed economies, as well as in the G20. As Lardy (2019) correctly observes, however, neither of these two institutions imposes sufficient constraints on China to commit to specific pro-market regulatory reforms.

Instead, China behaves as the rising hegemon, intent on creating its own system of international trade; it is not a leader in the larger collaborative effort. Admittedly, it has not been given much of a chance to play this role. This must change.

Our preferred option for addressing the grievances with respect to SOEs and forced TT is a WTO-wide solution, which would consist of reinforcing the WTO by amending it. Mindful that in heterogeneous settings, incrementalism has the best chance of increasing the likelihood of endorsement and subsequent implementation, we borrow (to the extent possible) from regulatory solutions that have been tried by the key WTO players.

Both the EU-Vietnam Free Trade Agreement (implemented in 2020) and the EU-Vietnam Investment Protection Agreement (signed in 2019 but still awaiting ratification), as well as the Comprehensive and Progressive Agreement for Trans-Pacific Partnership (CPTPP), the successor to the TPP Agreement, from which the United States withdrew in January 2017 a few days after President Trump's inauguration, contain chapters that address the issues we focus on in this volume. They could serve if not as a blueprint certainly as a source of inspiration for new WTO agreements on SOEs and forced TT.

We have attempted to demonstrate why the options advanced so far to resolve these two issues will do little to address the China problem, but there is one more element to keep in mind. A Protocol 2.0 is not only legally but also logically impossible. At this stage, the world simply cannot ask China to go back to the negotiating table and rework the terms of its accession to and participation in the WTO. In any event, the issues regarding SOEs and forced TT, as we have shown in this volume, are not China-specific. Our choice is clear: a WTO 2.0 is a far better solution than a Protocol 2.0. With this in mind, in what follows we outline our proposals with respect to a new regulatory framework that will address forced TT and SOEs.

First, it is important to consider the issue of enforcement. A lot has already been said in this respect, and doubts persist concerning independent and impartial enforcement before Chinese courts, especially when foreigners' interests are at stake. Nationalist behavior by the judiciary is not, of course, the exclusive privilege of Chinese courts. In different shades and colors, we observe similar behavior elsewhere as well. Because of the size of its market, however, the consequences of such behavior matter more in China. In any case, a detailed and innovative regulatory framework that can adequately address expressed concerns is pointless without adequate enforcement.

Second, we are mindful of the negotiating costs that are associated with the endeavor we propose. For this reason, we will explain why a plurilateral agreement, where participation can be limited to a few key players, could prove to be the most appropriate way forward.

The door, of course, will be open for others to join in the future as well. Since the trade community is pressed for time, it seems, the starting point could be a plurilateral agreement in which China and similarly situated countries (e.g., Vietnam, Russia, etc.) would agree to participate. With this in mind, we turn to our specific proposals.

Transfer of Technology

Chinese companies are able to force TT from foreign investors because, under Chinese laws, they can act as bottlenecks for foreign investment. Foreign investors cannot access the Chinese market unless they have first established a joint venture with a Chinese company. According to the complaints, it is the Chinese state that incites or even imposes this behavior. Its requests to private Chinese agents to act in this way leave the latter with no option other than to comply.

Recall that this is less of an issue as far as services are concerned since commitments under GATS Mode 3 must, in principle at least, be void of conditions to form a joint venture for establishment to take place. The GATS thus provides for a forum to negotiate this issue, which the GATT and the Annex 1A Agreements on trade in goods do not offer.

The WTO regime does not address this issue head-on. As we have explained, China undertook an obligation to abstain from forcing TT in its Protocol of Accession. Unless a complainant can attribute behavior of private agents to the Chinese state, it will never be successful before a court.

THINK CPTPP

The issue of forced technology transfer is better addressed in other trade agreements, for example, in Chapter 9, Article 9.10 of the CPTPP.[1] This provision reads as follows:

1. No Party shall, in connection with the establishment, acquisition, expansion, management, conduct, operation, or sale or other disposition of an investment of an investor of a Party or of a non-Party in its territory, impose or enforce any requirement, or enforce any commitment or undertaking:

   (f) to transfer a particular technology, a production process or other proprietary knowledge to a person in its territory.[2]

This carefully drafted provision includes an obligation not to impose or enforce forced TT. By outlawing imposition *and* enforcement, it kills two birds with one stone. States (parties to the CPTPP) cannot impose similar requirements in any event. That much is what China promised to do by signing its Protocol of Accession.

What is more, in the CPTPP setting this provision also outlaws enforcement of requirements for forced TT. It thus drastically reduces the incentive of private parties to request or insist on nonvoluntary transfer of technology. If no court will enforce similar requirements, what is the use in asking for them in the first place?

This provision could find its way into the WTO world as an amendment to the current TRIPS Agreement. Or, depending on the level of ambition of

1. This provision is titled "performance requirements," a designation not as dramatic as forced TT. De facto, though, it covers the same space.

2. The full text of the CPTPP is available at https://www.mfat.govt.nz/assets/Trans-Pacific -Partnership/Text/9.-Investment-Chapter.pdf.

the trade community, it could also be included in a new agreement on investment. As the WTO has already initiated discussions on investment facilitation, and the voices arguing for a comprehensive agreement on trade and investment multiply, this solution will become an even more elegant one.

TIER: THE FIRST, INADEQUATE STEPS THAT CHINA HAS ALREADY TAKEN

To be fair, China has already taken some steps in this direction by adopting a Technology Import Export Regulation (TIER). On its face, this law does not force technology transfer in the sense that "forced transfer of technology" is used in practice. This, of course, in and of itself does not amount to proof that transfer of technology does not happen at all. Complainants cannot base their arguments on TIER only when mounting such claims. They must also produce other (circumstantial) evidence to demonstrate a link between the behavior they challenge and a state authority in order to prevail, if they wish to pursue litigation.

TIER is no panacea for another reason: it contains two clauses that both the EU Regulation Technology Transfer Block and the U.S. Transfer Guidelines have included among the nine clauses that no enterprise or state should ever request or enforce. The two clauses are:

- The regulation mandates, irrespective of the willingness of licensors and licensees, that the foreign licensor surrenders ownership of any improvement, that is, there is no forced grant back to the licensor.
- Under the same circumstances, TIER prohibits licensing agreements that unreasonably restrict the export channels (marketing rights) of Chinese licensees.

These two conditions have been embedded in TIER, and the Chinese Ministry of Commerce aims to ensure that they are being observed in practice, but these clauses are problematic for several reasons. A licensor might never be willing, for example, to reduce royalty payments for licensees, absent some sharing of improvements on the original license. What is worse, the licensor is excluded from improvements on the IP right it has been ceding. Under the circumstances, it might be unwilling to conclude a deal with a Chinese company or be forced to accept deals for short-term gains, endangering its own mid- to long-term position in the market and, in any event, providing Chinese companies with a considerable advantage. Furthermore, assuming that there are challenges against the license, TIER requires that the licensor bears all responsibility, even if the challenge is directed against the way the licensee has been utilizing the license.

More specifically, with regard to marketing rights, absent flexibility, both licensor and licensee might have to forego their licensing agreement in the first place. In this respect, Article 40 of the TRIPS Agreement reads as follows:

1. Members agree that some licensing practices or conditions pertaining to intellectual property rights which restrain competition may have adverse effects on trade and may impede the transfer and dissemination of technology.

2. Nothing in this Agreement shall prevent Members from specifying in their legislation licensing practices or conditions that may in particular cases constitute an abuse of intellectual property rights having an adverse effect on competition in the relevant market. As provided above, a Member may adopt, consistently with the other provisions of this Agreement, appropriate measures to prevent or control such practices, which may include for example exclusive grantback conditions, conditions preventing challenges to validity and coercive package licensing, in the light of the relevant laws and regulations of that Member.

3. Each Member shall enter, upon request, into consultations with any other Member which has cause to believe that an intellectual property right owner that is a national or domiciliary of the Member to which the request for consultations has been addressed is undertaking practices in violation of the requesting Member's laws and regulations on the subject matter of this Section, and which wishes to secure compliance with such legislation, without prejudice to any action under the law and to the full freedom of an ultimate decision of either Member. The Member addressed shall accord full and sympathetic consideration to, and shall afford adequate opportunity for, consultations with the requesting Member, and shall cooperate through supply of publicly available non-confidential information of relevance to the matter in question and of other information available to the Member, subject to domestic law and to the conclusion of mutually satisfactory agreements concerning the safeguarding of its confidentiality by the requesting Member.

4. A Member whose nationals or domiciliaries are subject to proceedings in another Member concerning alleged violation of that other Member's laws and regulations on the subject matter of this Section shall, upon request, be granted an opportunity for consultations by the other Member under the same conditions as those foreseen in paragraph 3.

Grantback is negotiated when there is a concern that the licensee improves a license it lawfully acquired without compensating the licensor. Fearing this outcome, the licensor might be unwilling to license in the first place. To avoid this, grantback is concluded. Assignment and exclusive grantback lead to the same outcome (for all practical purposes): only the licensor and the licensee can use the improvements to the original patent. Nonexclusive grantback allows the licensee to sell improvements to others as well.

Exclusive grantback (licensing rights) might lead to greater innovation in competitive markets, while nonexclusive rights, as Gilbert (2006) has shown, lead to the opposite outcome, even though exceptions do exist. Nevertheless, exclusive grantback can lead to antitrust concerns, since, so the argument goes, they might be anticompetitive in that they inhibit innovation. Nonexclusive grantback does not suffer from similar vices.

Enforcement of competition law will take care of this and similar issues, but there is nothing comparable to world competition law. Chapter V of the ITO Charter, which was supposed to introduce multilateral disciplines on this score, never saw the light of day.

It follows that, for now, WTO members, China included, can allow their own national competition law to have a role in technology transfer agreements, if such agreements are injurious to competition and to future innovation. This seems, prima facie, like a promising avenue to us, but it is far from clear that complainants would be successful. In fact, the possibility of success is rather remote. For starters, there are good reasons why thus far no complaint has been raised that China has violated Article 40 of TRIPS through its practices regarding technology transfer.[3] In the absence of world competition law, it will be national (e.g., Chinese) law that will come into play. This means that China has the right, in accordance with the language of this provision, to exercise discretion as to whether it will intervene. Furthermore, it will also enjoy the margin of discretion embedded in its national law as to the way it will address the issue, assuming it decides to go

---

3. Recently, the WTO has embarked on a discussion (not formal negotiation) regarding transfer of technology; see https://www.wto.org/english/news_e/news19_e/trip_13feb19_e.htm.

forward. One cannot exclude a nonviolation complaint (NVC) here, even though, for the reasons explained earlier, it might be a long shot.

Assuming an NVC has been raised, it would be interesting to see whether it can lawfully be raised against a decision not to invoke competition law in this context. In this case, the question will be whether an NVC can successfully be invoked against an omission. In some jurisdictions, an omission takes the form of a legal act and is hence equated to a "measure" adopted by a WTO member. We believe[4] that this should be the case across the board, as omissions do have an impact on tariff concessions. Nevertheless, we have to acknowledge the lack of precedent on this score.

Recently, China undertook a legislative initiative aiming to placate foreign investors. It deleted a few provisions of the TIER legislation, namely those regarding liability for licensed technology, as well as a series of restrictive practices (bundling, licensing expired patents, restrictions on making improvements or licensing competing technologies, price fixing for products made with the technology, and limiting export channels).[5] Although there is still some way to go on this front, it is expected that these changes will provide some relief at least to companies with Chinese affiliates when setting up agreements regarding transfer of technology.

We should add here a remark to avoid misunderstandings. The EU's formal complaint against China about forced technology transfer discussed in chapter 2 concerns a very clear obligation assumed by China (in Paragraph 7.3 of its Protocol of Accession) to avoid enforcing performance requirements. Here, we discuss transfer of technology in other areas as well, where current rules (Article 40 of TRIPS) are far from imposing an unambiguous obligation (like that imposed through Paragraph 7.3). This is why we favor, in this respect, and in light of the fact that transfer of technology is a major concern for technology-exporting countries, a clarification of the rules.[6]

In 2015, China launched the Mass Entrepreneurship Initiative aimed at reducing market restrictions. The initiative included several major innovations:

4. In line with Hoekman and Mavroidis 1994.

5. https://www.lexology.com/library/detail.aspx?g=fba3ea7d-d53a-40d3-9bef-29962a0f8f7e.

6. Liang, Lovely, and Zhang (2019) provide evidence that it is foreign-invested companies in China that have gained the lion's share across China's total exports. This means that liberal FDI has supported China's export-led growth. This also explains, in part at least, why foreign investors in China lack the incentive to complain against some of China's restrictive policies.

- It increased damages and fines for IP infringements.
- It addressed local protectionism by moving cases relating to IP enforcement away from local courts and administrative tribunals to out-of-area instances, which were less prone to local interests.
- It established specialized IP courts.
- It increased transparency about courts' decisions.

But, according to the World Bank (2019b), enforcement remains a problem. Maskus (2004) was right when he claimed that the many legislative changes China went through as a result of its accession to the WTO would not amount to much if it did not manage to address its biggest challenge, namely, enforcement.

China has become a capital exporter and should therefore participate in formulating international rules for FDI protection. Its new foreign investment law (FIL), which went into effect on January 1, 2020, explicitly prohibits forced technology transfers through administrative measures, but it stops short of addressing private behavior. A successful conclusion of the long-running BIT negotiations between China and, separately, the EU and the United States would be an important step forward since it would mean that China and its two biggest economic partners have finally agreed on provisions regarding private behavior.[7]

SOEs

Recall that the current SCM Agreement does not even mention SOEs and the Protocol of Accession does not go far enough, in our view at least. SOEs, SIEs, and SOCBs (state-owned commercial banks) in China pose a series of problems,[8] essentially by not acting in accordance with commercial considerations. Access to financing is facilitated for SOEs/SIEs, which are often in close cahoots with SOCBs, since they all fall under the same roof, the SASAC. As to STEs, WTO case law is a source of problems, as we explain in what follows.

7. The U.S.-China BIT negotiations started in 2008, and those between the EU and China in 2013.

8. Lardy provides evidence of the growing performance gap between private firms in China and SOEs, even though (or perhaps because) the latter have benefited from borrowing rates lower than those of the former (2019, 50ff., especially 63ff.). Corruption and poor management explain largely, in his view, the reasons for this growing gap. Reform of SOEs was initiated in the 1980s under the reformist Zhu Rongji, but problems, in Lardy's account at least, persist. On Zhu Rongji's personality and background, see Gewirtz 2017, 239ff.

CASE LAW FIRST CREATED PROBLEMS,
THEN TRIED TO SOLVE THEM

We believe that some progress can be achieved through a less formalistic understanding of the SCM Agreement: that is, the solution requires flexibility, not necessarily innovation. The United States has, wrongly, decided to simply equate state ownership with un-market-like behavior without determining whether a particular state-owned company behaved like a private company or not. The WTO Appellate Body was, originally at least, equally wrong to ignore state ownership. Consequently, the Appellate Body would not see anything wrong with state ownership and would routinely find against the United States every time it equated state-owned companies with subsidizing agents.

A crisis erupted as a result, and it was not China-specific. It helped ignite the fire in Washington, D.C., that threatened the very existence of the Appellate Body and compulsory third-party adjudication at the WTO level, and the Trump administration was carrying the torch. At the very least, the Appellate Body should have asked why a state would intervene if the market would have done so anyway, since the purpose of the agreement was to compare an actual behavior with a counterfactual where the state has not intervened.

What can be done, considering the current mess we are in? Case law reversal would be helpful. The Appellate Body, for example, could introduce a presumption in situations of majoritarian state ownership. It could reverse the burden of proof and ask China to demonstrate that in such cases, SOEs/SIEs behave in accordance with commercial considerations, even though the state is the majority shareholder.

Through the Appellate Body decision of July 16, 2019, the situation has now changed. Even though the Appellate Body did not reverse prior case law as per our suggestion above, it did clear a path toward treating even private agents as SOEs, to the extent that links between the company entity and the party (government) can be established. There is, nevertheless, no guarantee that the new normal will persist.

AMENDING THE LAW IS A BETTER OPTION

Ideally, case law should be crystallized into law. We would like to see, for example, a definition of "public body" that encompasses SOEs. This could be done in various ways. As suggested above, government ownership amounts to a presumption that the entity at hand is a public body. One could add SIEs, where the state is enjoying a certain percentage of total shares.

The key, nevertheless, is the next step. Actions by SOEs will be considered subsidies if they confer a benefit. Conferral of a benefit means, as per standard case law, obtaining something that would not have been obtained under market conditions. Were SOEs to act under "commercial considerations," then benefits of that sort would have been avoided. This line of thinking brings us squarely into the text of the CPTPP.

THINK CPTPP (OR USMCA)

In our view, emulating Chapter 17 of the CPTPP (and previously of the TPP) is the appropriate way for the WTO to address this issue.[9] This chapter accomplishes precisely what a series of GATT/WTO panels should have addressed earlier. Article XVII of the GATT was designed to cover activities by entities engaging in state trading. This provision requires WTO members to ensure that their STEs

- behave in accordance with commercial considerations;
- afford interested parties adequate opportunities to compete; and
- avoid discriminatory behavior.

On its face, this provision does not state that the first two disciplines are an expression, or disaggregation, of the third discipline. A textual reading of the provision would thus suggest that these are independent obligations.

This makes sense, especially from the perspective of economics. Acting in accordance with commercial considerations often entails selling at different prices to different buyers in order to maximize profits. What Article XVII of the GATT wanted to avoid is not price discrimination but discrimination stemming from the origin of the buyer/seller with whom an STE would be transacting.

A series of GATT/WTO panels turned this test on its head when understanding the first two obligations (act in accordance with commercial considerations; afford adequate opportunities to compete) as a subset of the obligation to not discriminate.[10] By equating price differences to discrimina-

9. Hufbauer and Cimino-Isaacs (2015) discuss this point in detail.
10. The case law is discussed in detail in Mavroidis 2016, 1:397ff.

tory behavior, they have adopted a test that is not faithful to the legislative intent.

Price discrimination should be the beginning, not the end, of the analysis. When faced with price discrimination, and an allegation that Article XVII of the GATT has been violated as a result, panels should ask whether the observed discrepancy is due to discriminatory behavior. In the presence of a quota, for example, that an STE is called to administer, selling at price x to Home and 2x to Foreign should not automatically lead to a violation of Article XVII of the GATT. A further inquiry should be required in order to decide whether the differential pricing practices are (or are not) in accordance with commercial considerations.

We can return to orthodoxy, to the intended meaning of this provision, by simply reversing the current case law (which is, in fact, what the text of Chapter 17 of the CPTPP does). Nevertheless, we can ensure that the return to orthodoxy will be permanent only by preempting judicial discretion through, say, the adoption of an understanding of Article XVII of the GATT that will dissociate the two obligations (act in accordance with commercial considerations; afford adequate opportunities to compete) from the obligation to not discriminate. And, of course, the obligation to act in accordance with commercial considerations should not be confined to STEs only. It should be required from SIEs, SOEs, SOCBs, and so forth.

Chapter 22 of the United States-Mexico-Canada Agreement (USMCA), the successor to the North Atlantic Free Trade Agreement (NAFTA), goes even further than Chapter 17 of the CPTPP.[11] Its main features are the following:

- Article 22.1 includes a definition of SOEs, which covers not just cases of ownership but also cases of control of voting rights, or of the enterprise itself by the state. It makes it clear, though, that regulatory or supervisory activities of, say, a financial regulatory body are not covered.
- As in the CPTPP context, the agreement makes it clear (Article 22.4) that SOEs, when engaging in commercial activities, must act in accordance with commercial considerations.
- Article 22.1 defines "commercial considerations" to cover price, quality, marketability, and so forth of purchase or same that "would normally be taken into account in the commercial decisions of a privately-owned enterprise in the relevant business or industry."

11. The NAFTA agreement contained a few words on SOEs in Articles 1502 and 1503.

- The same provision also defines "non-commercial assistance," a term aiming to capture equity infusions, loans, guarantees, and so forth, "on terms more favourable than those commercially available."

The WTO could use these agreements as inspiration. Introducing an agreement inspired by Chapter 22 of the USMCA and/or Chapter 17 of the CPTPP would cover a great deal of ground in addressing the concerns expressed by China's trading partners.[12] At the end of the day it will, of course, be a matter for courts to decide, since they will be called upon to enforce this provision. This is quite a realistic prospect, in fact.[13] We are encouraged to think this way by the language in Chapter 11 of the EU-Vietnam FTA. Vietnam is a self-described socialist market economy, just like China. The language in this chapter recognizes the right of both parties to decide upon their own system of ownership but requires that SOEs act in accordance with commercial considerations with respect to their commercial activities.[14]

---

12. Scissors (2015) thinks otherwise, at least as far as Chapter 17 of the TPP is concerned. In his view, asking SOEs to behave like private companies is just a "pretense." He argues that if states really wanted SOEs to behave like private companies, SOEs would not exist in the first place. It is quite likely that he is dismayed by the manner in which the obligation to act on "commercial considerations" has been understood in case law concerning STEs under Article XVII of the GATT, as we discussed earlier. If this obligation was given its proper meaning (as we explained), then a number of his concerns would be addressed. The problem, however, is that the term "commercial considerations" has not received proper meaning in GATT/WTO case law and, instead, has been subsumed under a generic obligation to not discriminate. Our understanding of Chapter 17 (and even more so of the relevant part of the USMCA) is that the two obligations (commercial considerations and nondiscrimination) should be separated and treated as distinct. Future practice will be decisive in this respect. We would favor a legislative solution where acting in accordance with commercial considerations becomes the overarching obligation, and nondiscrimination should be appreciated in this context.

13. We are mindful of the fact that a reduction of the role of SOEs equals ipso facto reduction of the role of the state in the national economy. China will be reluctant to do so as long as the current regime holds the views it does on the role of the state in the national economy. If the performance gap between private Chinese companies and SOEs continues to grow, then China will be more eager to negotiate.

14. China has unilaterally taken some steps to address productivity-related concerns. Bell explains measures adopted to improve corporate governance of SOEs by opening up their recruitment in an effort to ensure that key personnel correspond to commercial, as opposed to political, considerations (2015, 71ff.). Nevertheless, such reforms aim at improving performance by SOEs, not cutting their connection to the Chinese state. They are, in Bell's expression, consistent with the "vertical democratic meritocracy" model of China, that is, "democracy at lower levels of government, with the political system becoming progressively more meritocratic at higher levels of government" (xiii).

Connecting SOEs to Transfer of Technology

Transfer of technology is sometimes but not always requested by Chinese SOEs, but if SOEs were to be viewed as "public bodies,"[15] then all requests to transfer technology would be attributable to China. In this scenario, there is no need to amend anything, as China would be violating commitments it has already accepted in its process of accession, as we explained. Conversely, if SOEs are not considered "public bodies," then the question will be to what extent the challenged measure (forced transfer of technology) should be attributed to China or not. In this case, the evidentiary requirements would be quite substantial. Without questioning Wu (2016), who points to the inexhaustible potential for China to evade its obligations, we believe that an informed judge could still appropriately attribute behavior to China by establishing the link between actions by SOEs and Chinese public policy, whenever this is the case.

Judicial discretion can, of course, be exercised in different ways when the provisions that judges are called to interpret are "incomplete." Legislators can preempt the exercise of judicial discretion by "completing" the (existing) contractual language. It is, for example, one thing to state in a legal provision that "public bodies" are required to do something without defining them. It is a different thing to provide an indicative list of "public bodies." An indicative list will help judges avoid false negatives: when in the presence of one of the examples mentioned in statutory language, judges will know they are in the presence of a "public body."

In this vein, a CPTPP-inspired solution concerning the understanding of the function of SOEs should, in our view, find its way into the WTO as well.

Last, but definitely not least, there is an issue with identifying SOEs. Even if an agreement defining them has been agreed upon along the lines described above, there is an issue with the transparency of SOEs. As Wolfe (2017) correctly underscores in his excellent account, neither the WTO nor FTAs have managed to address this issue effectively. He proposed the introduction of a reference paper (à la Telecoms Reference Paper) as a possible path toward a reduction of the problem. This proposal has much merit and should be explored further.

---

15. Ahn and Spearot (2016) offer a very comprehensive account of the way the interpretation of this term has evolved over the years in WTO practice. Branstetter (2018) discusses how General Electric was obliged to transfer technology by a Chinese SOE as a precondition for entering the Chinese market.

Enforcement

Enforcement is key to our solution, especially since claims about underenforcement of the WTO contract against China seem to have some legitimacy. Recall, for example, our discussion about the relatively low number of cases in which China has acted as a respondent in WTO litigation. If it is the share of export trade that explains the number of disputes, then the number is definitely low. But even if not, what is the point in negotiating new agreements that will remain underenforced?

The WTO is a government-to-government contract. The typical scenario is for one WTO member to challenge the consistency of measures adopted by another member before an independent (WTO) judge. However, an often overlooked provision, Article X of the GATT, provided private traders with a forum to advance their claims concerning administrative action relating to customs matters.[16] By providing private traders with a forum, Article X bypasses the need to persuade national governments to act on their behalf.

This provision has been extensively practiced and has been emulated in the realm of government procurement following the GATT dispute concerning Norway's procurement of toll-collection equipment for the city of Trondheim. Suspecting foul play in the bidding process in favor of Norwegian firms, the United States introduced a challenge against Norway. It prevailed, but by the time it did so, the toll ring system was already in place. The panel faced a dilemma as to what to recommend and opted for a soft remedy: it asked Norway to never repeat this behavior.[17]

Inspired by this incident, the WTO Agreement on Government Procurement (GPA) introduced "challenge procedures," an institution reminiscent of Article X of the GATT. The question was how to avoid inefficient remedies à la Trondheim. Fast relief would be guaranteed if private traders could appear before domestic tribunals, even in cases where transparency had not been served, since a lot of time is saved when private agents do not have to go through the government filter.

The other upshot is that private traders do not depend on their national government exercising discretion. In equilibrium, governments might privilege inaction in the name of serving other interests that are dearer to them. This is not the case in the realm of the GPA, where action depends on the

16. Hoekman and Mavroidis (2009) provide a comprehensive overview of this provision.
17. We detail this dispute in Mavroidis 1993.

sole will of the affected private agent.[18] Private agents, of course, litigate differently than governments, since action will depend on how measures affect their own, and not the country-wide, welfare.

Would the introduction of challenge procedures in the new agreements we would like to see introduced address the problem of underenforcement? On its face, one could easily say no. After all, why would incentives change by the mere introduction of new world trade laws? And yet recall our discussion of the provisions in the Chinese Protocol of Accession regarding export taxes. Clarification of rules and the assumption of unambiguous, clear-cut obligations, to the extent feasible of course, coupled with challenge procedures could provide a welcome change. Inspired by the provision of the CPTPP on SOEs, and the many examples of regulation of investment, the WTO members could go a long way in addressing similar concerns.

Nevertheless, one can never be too cautious. Therefore, we propose the establishment of "challenge procedures." The additional element compared to the existing procedures would consist in reviewing practice, and acting upon it, in cases where it is warranted. For example, the membership could establish a mechanism to review the numbers of challenge procedures raised across national jurisdictions, the quality of outcome, and so forth. Action could be recommended to address discrepancies, on conditions to be elaborated by the membership. The idea would be to increase the level of transparency with respect to practice in the realm of challenge procedures. This task could/should be entrusted to the common agent, the WTO Secretariat, ideally as a self-contained, focused exercise and not as part of the Trade Policy Review Mechanism.

Challenge procedures of the GPA could, for example, provide an inspiration for disputes concerning IP rights.[19] To some extent this provision is

---

18. A series of country-specific evaluations in Georgopoulos, Hoekman, and Mavroidis 2017 support the positive picture that the literature—and we—paint on this issue.

19. Our suggestion here is guided by concerns to avoid unrealistic first-best solutions and concentrate what can realistically be achieved and improve the current situation. As with our other suggestions, we need to be pragmatic. For starters, challenge procedures already exist in the GPA, which China, in its Protocol of Accession, has promised to join but has not yet done so. Furthermore, the introduction of challenge procedures would fill in the gap left by the TRM, which we discussed earlier. Indeed, one of the weak points of the WTO legal system is the absence (or almost) of monitoring of compliance. The WTO, unlike the EU, has no institutional watchdog to oversee implementation of assumed obligations. The TPRM is an exercise in transparency, but a very imperfect one, as suggested by the fact that TPRM reports are almost never used in dispute adjudication. In fact, the recent panel report on *Russia–Traffic in Transit* (see §§7.116ff.) is a unique exception so far. Enforcement of WTO commitments is, for all practical purposes, decentralized and largely relies on incentives of those possessing private information. Incentives, however, may

echoed in Article 41.5 of the TRIPS Agreement. Timing is crucial in protecting IP rights. Challenge procedures are geared toward providing fast relief. The WTO membership should consider the possibility of introducing multilateral reviews of decisions rendered by similar instances. This way the WTO contract will be interpreted harmoniously across the membership.

Obviously, challenge procedures will not solve the deeper issue of the liberal understanding and the rule of law in China. In this respect, one must acknowledge that the country has come a long way since the days of Chairman Mao and that it has been moving in the right direction toward establishing a system where political decisions are accountable to courts rather than the other way around, even though recent events and decisions have cast some (at times considerable) doubt on this proposition.[20] The inflection point would be the establishment of a *Rechtsstaat*, a constitutional order where the power of the state is constrained by the law, a decision that rests with China alone.[21]

Liebman's (2017) thoughtful analysis suggests that we are not there yet, and he is not alone in defending this view.[22] Other renowned experts of the

------

be lacking, as we more often than not will be facing a Prisoner's Dilemma. The experience with cross-notifications of Chinese subsidies is ample proof in this respect, as documented in Mavroidis 2016, vol. 2, chap. 3. Keep in mind, though, that, with respect to subsidies provided by subcentral entities in, say, federal states, Article XXIV.12 imposes on members only a best-endeavors, and not an obligation to withdraw them. Simon Evenett routinely reports all similar schemes in his Global Trade Alert webpage, https://www.globaltradealert.org/.

20. Economy refers in detail to the decision by President Xi, in January 2014, to the effect that "all judicial, procuratorial, and public security departments needed to uphold definitively the leadership of the party" (2018, 46). She refers to the unprecedented crackdown on lawyers during Xi's presidency, which made worldwide headlines as the "709 crackdown" because it occurred on July 9, 2015, and led to the detention of over three hundred human rights lawyers (46ff.). In her view, the rule of law in contemporary China is drastically different from the way the same term is understood in the Western world. In China, she notes, "the law is an instrument with which the Communist Party can ensure the continued dominance of the party itself" (46).

21. Alford (2018) provides some skeptical thoughts in this respect. He cites a party document (216–17) that makes it clear that law is an instrument for the Communist Party as it exercises its leadership in the name of the people. He further cites (218) pronouncements by party authorities that courts should issue "guiding" and not "binding" precedents, thus keeping discretion to adjust laws when warranted (or requested to do so by the party). McGregor (2010) provides a lot of support for this view. He cites various documents and decisions showing that the party is essentially unaccountable before domestic courts. Since the party still dominates parts of the national economy, some of its decisions remain unchallenged before domestic courts.

22. Similar thoughts have been expressed in the World Bank report (2018a, 47ff., especially 56–58). Liu, Chen, and Lin (2018) examine how the introduction of the social credit system is likely to have a profound impact on how business is conducted in China. Mattingly (2020) explains how the party had already infiltrated rural social networks even before the introduction of the

judicial system of China have for years cast doubt on its independence from the party. Peerenboom (2014) provides an excellent survey on this score.

More and more academics have joined the chorus of independent analysts casting doubt on the separation of powers in China.[23] Recently, the appointment of Zhou Qiang, a qualified lawyer, to the helm of the Chinese Supreme Court by President Xi caused observers to wonder whether China had turned a corner. Zhou Qiang, once considered a reformer, left no one in doubt as to where he actually stood on this question when he denounced judicial independence as a "false western ideal."[24]

Under the circumstances, we are under no illusion that efficient challenge procedures will be more than a nudge toward the rule of law. But sometimes a nudge is all you need to better evaluate the shortcomings of inertia and rethink the merits of change. Instead of chasing rainbows, perhaps an incremental change of this sort might tilt the balance in the right direction. Establishing forums where private agents can invoke and enforce their rights under international agreements will provide the citizenry with food for thought about enforcing and protecting their own rights in an increasingly privatized economy.[25] But we should not be blind to the fact that the WTO suffers from a general problem of transparency as far as trade measures are concerned. As long as this problem remains, it will be difficult to

---

social credit system. Finally, Kong (2002), on the other hand, provides various arguments substantiating the claim that the Chinese legal culture per se is an impediment to strict enforcement of WTO law. McGregor (2010) states that 45,000 of the 150,000 lawyers registered in China in 2009 were party members, whereas 95 percent of all law firms registered had party committees. McGregor cites Luo Gan, a member of the Politburo Standing Committee, stating, "There is no question about where legal departments should stand. . . . The correct political stand is where the Party stands" (2010, 25). Worse, in this author's account (24), Wang Shengjun, the most senior judicial official in China, never studied law but is a party member. In McGregor's account, what is called "interference" in the Western world is defended as "leadership" in China (23ff.).

23. Farbain 2016 and Feng 2016 are typical in this regard.

24. https://www.ft.com/content/60dddd46-dc74–11e6–9d7c-be108f1c1dce. Blustein quotes the same individual stating that courts should be loyal to the party and to the state (2019, 186). In 1978, a young Chinese man, Wei Jingsheng, requested a fifth modernization (next to the four chosen areas, namely, agriculture; industry; science and technology; national defense), the establishment of true democracy in China. He was imprisoned, and remained in prison until 1997, when he was exiled in the United States. He is one of the best known Chinese human rights activists and was awarded the Sakharov Prize of Freedom of Thought in 1996. https://en.wikipedia.org/wiki/Wei_Jingsheng.

25. Lei, Liebman, and Milhaupt (2016) have persuasively argued that SOEs influence the way the legal system in China is evolving, the manner in which legislative/judicial discretion has been exercised. Viewed in this light, entrusting decisions to Chinese legal procedures could be submitting to foregone conclusions. Nevertheless, such decisions are "measures" and could be challenged before WTO panels.

enforce WTO rules, whether in SCM, TRIPS, or other domains relevant to the subject of this volume.[26]

A Plurilateral Silk Road Ahead

Negotiating new multilateral agreements is an awesome task. The fact that WTO members have not managed to add anything to the multilateral arsenal other than the Agreement on Trade Facilitation since 1995 is proof enough of the difficulties associated with such endeavors.

Yet it is absolutely essential to add new rules to the WTO in order to make it fit with today's reality. In particular there is a need to translate some of the liberal understanding of the law, which was implicit in the GATT era and remains implicit today in the WTO, into operational rules so as to ensure that China and WTO members that belong to a different tradition of the law fit better with the WTO than they actually do.

Following Wu (2016), we endorse the view that the most realistic, and indeed appropriate, way forward is the path of incrementalism. It is a monumental task to prioritize. If we go by revealed preferences of the trading community, forced transfer of technology and SOEs are the natural starting points. Progress in this area will encourage cooperation elsewhere.

Given the heterogeneity of the WTO membership, and along with Hoekman and Mavroidis (2015), we believe that plurilateral agreements are the way forward to preserve and reinforce the WTO.

The leading nations of the WTO must get together and design new rules in the domains we have discussed here and probably in others. China, undeniably, is a leading nation. It must pull its weight. It belongs to the core of countries, along with Brazil, the EU, India, Japan, the United States, and eventually Russia, that should take the lead. In a context of variable geometry, China should be in the forefront. This is a must for the endeavor to succeed and ensure the sustainability of the rules-based multilateral trading system.

26. The problem is, of course, that no one is willing to provide self-incriminating information. Some regimes have been more successful than others, but they typically empower a common agent (e.g., the EU Commission) to do the job. See, for instance, Mavroidis and Wolfe 2015 for the need to expand the role of the WTO Secretariat in this area. This is not to say that all WTO members are equally non-transparent. Domestic law checks and balances do exist. China, for example, has been successful in concealing state involvement in investment overseas, as McGregor (2010, 21ff.) has shown.

7

The Time Is Now

President Xi Backtracks

The hope was that the Deng reforms were a one-way street. The global community might have had second thoughts in 1989 after the Tiananmen Square brutalities, but China demonstrated quickly that its economic course was, in principle at least, dissociated from the way it understood protection of human rights at home. The two go together in Western countries, but not in China. Alas, as time passed, the Communist Party of China tightened its grip on the economy as well. The major SOE reform, as we have seen, was initiated in the 1990s, when SASAC was called to consolidate, corporatize, and privatize SOEs.

The reform of the SOEs in the 1990s, which we briefly discussed in chapter 2, has been hailed as generally pointing in the right direction. There are voices that, while recognizing that these reforms are a positive sign overall, still deplore the fact that they did not go far enough. Berkowitz, Ma, and Nishioka (2017) make a very persuasive case in this vein, with evidence that the productivity of SOEs, even after the SOE reform, still lags behind the corresponding numbers for both foreign and Chinese private firms.

This may well be the case, but the 1990 reforms were primarily aimed at addressing productivity-related issues, albeit in an imperfect manner. Irrespective of Hu Jintao's intention, the introduction of SASAC did mark a return to more state control of the economy. The state would determine the number of players in the market, a decision left to private actors in Western economies, where antitrust competition authorities simply ensure that rivalry persists in well-defined relevant product markets, without deciding ex ante who will participate in a given product market. Blustein advances persuasive arguments that the introduction of SASAC was meant to avoid enriching a few oligarchs, as was the case during Russia's privatization (2019, 112ff.). The hope was that the whole enterprise would be more public-spirited. The necessary by-product was the strengthening of the statist hand.

The establishment of the National Development and Reform Commission (NDRC), the entity designing the five-year plans in China, was yet another harbinger of the return to a more statist economy. Suddenly, decisions that Western economies leave to the market would be decided behind the closed doors of the party's headquarters. And, to cap it all, the Central Hujin, the head of which would be appointed by the party, as is the case with the NDRC and SASAC, would oversee China's banking sector. In any event, as McGregor (2010) keenly underscores, throughout the period of reform, the party kept a stronghold on three key areas: namely, the control of personnel, the People's Liberation Army, and propaganda.[1]

Jiang Zemin (1993–2003) oversaw the 1990s reforms. Hu Jintao (2003–2013) picked up where his predecessor had left off. He did not leave all decisions to the market, however, as our preceding discussion has shown. This tendency has been exacerbated ever since President Xi came to power.[2]

In 2006, the Chinese leadership divided industries into key (defense, electricity, oil and gas, telecom, coal, shipping, aviation, and rail), pillar (auto, chemicals, construction, electronics, equipment manufacturing, non-ferrous metals, prospecting, steel, and technology), and normal (agriculture, general trade, and manufacturing).[3] The guiding principle of the reforms was that the degree of state influence would climb the ladder from normal to key industries, where the state would exercise absolute control. The Chinese state, within this framework, would limit its influence to the top of the hierarchy and exercise a more subtle monitoring of non-key industries.

As of 2013, however, with the departure of Hu Jintao, a series of actions have cast doubt on the initial belief that Deng's reforms were a one-way street and that there was no turning back. President Xi has rescinded some of the reforms undertaken in previous years, as Lardy (2019) illustrates in his

1. McGregor (2010) focuses on the role of the party in general. In a companion study, McGregor (2019a) details the backtracking of President Xi from market reforms. McGregor (2019b) provides the context that explains the changing attitudes of the Chinese leadership.

2. Hameiri and Jones (2016) advance a political science explanation for why reform has occurred in China.

3. Ye Zhang 2019. Lardy (2014) discusses the reforms up to 2013.

magnificent account. It is not easy to explain why this rollback has occurred. Lardy seems to echo the sentiment of key party members to the effect that the party would become irrelevant if privatization proceeded at a fast pace. A more benign (for party members) explanation is that, absent the steering provided by the party, the whole privatization endeavor risked being derailed.

PRESIDENT XI ROLLS BACK THE YEARS

In 2013, at the 18th Congress of the Chinese Communist Party, one year after Xi Jinping acceded to the post of general secretary of the Communist Party, the Third Plenum signaled its intentions that "we must ensure that the market has a decisive role in the allocation of resources, unswervingly consolidating and developing the public economy, persisting in the dominant position of public ownership, giving full play to the leading role of the state sector, continuously increasing its vitality, controlling force and influence." This passage, which we borrowed from Lardy (2019, 17–18), made many observers wonder whether China was indeed going back after all. Skepticism was soon replaced by persuasive evidence that something was indeed changing in China. In 2015, the Chinese government enacted an important policy document, titled "Guiding Opinions of the Central Committee on Deepening the Reform of State-Owned Enterprises."[4] Since SOEs had been performing below par, there was certainly a need for action on a purely economic basis. Instead of moving toward privatization, however, this document called for a combination of mixed ownership and mergers and acquisitions as an appropriate means to redress the situation.

Kroenig mentions that President Xi has reversed course in eight of the ten key areas where the party had promised reforms (2020, 183). At the same time, he has aggressively pushed for China to become a regional and global power through the Belt and Road Initiative and the Asian Infrastructure Investment Bank (AIIB). In Haass's view, the U.S. government pushed back against the AIIB precisely because it wanted to put a dent in President Xi's hope of turning China into a global player (2017, 90ff.).

The reforms initiated by President Xi in the 2015 document, and other policy instruments as well, rest on two interlinked legs. The first concerns the size of SOEs. The prevailing view in the Chinese Communist Party was

4. http://english.gov.cn/policies/latest_releases/2015/09/13/content_281475189210840 .htm.

that unless SOEs increased in size, they would find it difficult to compete on the international scene. Since China had adopted an export-led growth model, size mattered in the eyes of the leadership. The second leg consists mainly of strengthening the role of the party in controlling the management of SOEs, so the party retains a means to impose its policy priorities.[5]

It seems to us that there are still two camps in China, even though some prominent reformers have perhaps been less influential over the years. President Xi is not part of the liberal-minded reformist camp. His camp won kudos, important kudos we would add, when the financial crisis hit the West. The pushback against reforms should not, then, come as a surprise. In fact, President Xi has, for now at least, consolidated the position of his camp, since his attitude and policy choices have paid dividends. China did not leave the financial crisis behind completely unscathed. But it certainly did not pay the same heavy economic price as the European Union and the United States did.

President Xi knew that his pushback against reforms was music to the ears of influential party members. Madden (1998), for example, has argued that many in the party who were considered reformers were still also fans of Han Fei Tzu, an ancient Chinese philosopher who believed that states can prosper only when an authoritarian regime is in place.

BUILDING BEHEMOTHS

If the Chinese hierarchy was indeed displeased with the development of SOEs and believed they were underperforming, it could, in principle at least, have addressed the issue in various ways. It could have, for example, broken up a few of the already gigantic SOEs and thereby incite more competition between them. And yet, as Yu (2019) has argued, the opposite has happened. Yu explains how the party's strategy in recent years has been to scale up the SOEs through mergers. He cites, as an illustration, the very telling merger of two rolling-stock manufacturers, China NCR and China Southern Locomotive (CSR). The merger of these two giants involved a market capitalization of $26 billion. And there are many more cases like this. Sokol (2013) reviews merger control in China and provides conclusive

---

5. By this we do not mean to suggest that President Xi's reforms are a one-way street. As of 2015 China launched its "Mass Entrepreneurship Initiative" aiming to reduce market restrictions, even though tangible results thus far are meager, at least as per the evaluation of the World Bank (2019b).

evidence supporting the thesis that the role of the Ministry of Commerce is quite decisive throughout the process.

Consolidation to fewer and fewer players facilitates control by the party. In a similar vein, Li (2016) concludes that we are observing the rise of *Yangqi*—that is, the centrally controlled business. Various contributions in the work by Brandt and Rawski (2019) underscore this point. They provide much empirical evidence of increased subsidies in two key sectors, telecoms and electricity, which, of course, exhibit network effects for the rest of the economy.[6] The Chinese response has been to transform SOEs into corporate behemoths, instead of overhauling them completely, and thereby increase their potential to influence international trade.

THE PARTY MAKES A COMEBACK

The reforms of President Xi are multifaceted and focus on a more effective surveillance of SOEs by the party. The statutory underpinnings for reforms are to some extent transparent (like the 2015 "Guiding Opinions" we cited earlier) and to some extent a development occurring in practice (that is, some reforms happened even without explicit mandate to this effect).

Brødsgaard (2018) has provided a succinct and accurate description of the thrust of reforms:

> The Party controls SOEs in various ways. All enterprises must have a Party organization headed by a Party secretary. Recent Party documents stipulate that all important decisions must first be studied and discussed by the Party committee of the enterprise. Only after that committee has forwarded a recommendation can the matter be decided by the board and an action implemented. This ensures that the CCP has a decisive say on enterprise operation and management.
>
> In enterprises where a board has been established, the Party secretary and chairman of the board must be the same person. Members of the company's Party committee should also serve on the board of directors, management team, and supervisory board.

6. It is particularly interesting to compare subsidization in the Xi years with the earlier situation. In a previous study, Brandt and Rawski (2008) included various contributions demonstrating less presence of the state in key industries than what they find in their 2019 volume. Liu (2019) discusses the decision of the Chinese state to subsidize upstream industries, based on the belief that such intervention will benefit vast areas of the national economy.

This principle of overlapping positions and cross appointments has been at the centre of recent discussions on enterprise management in Chinese media. The former chairman of the State Council's State-Owned Assets Supervision and Administration Commission (SASAC), Li Rongrong, praised the cross-appointment system as an "effective measure to combine corporate governance with the Party, which is the political core of the company."

Since 2015, cross-appointment has become a key concept in the Party's management of state-owned businesses and government institutions. Former Chinese leader Deng Xiaoping's policy of separating Party and government has been officially abandoned and the notion of separating government and business has also largely disappeared from public discourse.

Cross-appointments are but one of the instruments that President Xi used to reclaim the dominance of politics over the Chinese economy. Leutert (2018) mentions two more policy instruments designed to achieve this objective.

First, China has established a series of "leading small groups." These consist of supraministerial and extraconstitutional organizations that bring together high-ranking government officials, party organs (committees), SOE personnel, and sometimes even the military. The Chinese Communist Party charges them with specific mandates that they must implement. Leutert cites a government document (2018, 231) as evidence of the increased participation of the party in the corporate governance of SOEs, where the SASAC's party committee clarifies that all major decisions will first be discussed at the level of the party committee of the SOE.

Second, political dominance has increased through the introduction of the new "three committees" at the holding company level: the board of directors, the supervisory committee, and the shareholders' meeting. Through this mechanism as well, the party's committees exert increased influence in the day-to-day workings of SOEs.[7]

Thus the SOE reform that was initiated in 2013 and continues today could be succinctly described as consisting of a two-tiered system:

- On the one hand, a mixed ownership strategy of increasing capital investment in SOEs aiming to improve corporate governance and, ultimately, profitability.

---

7. Naughton (2018) provides a detailed account of the extent of oversight that the party exercises today as a result of SOE reform under President Xi.

- On the other hand, a "party building" movement, as Lin and Milhaupt (2019) call it (*dangjian*), which leads SOEs to expressly give party leadership and committees a legal status inside the company.[8]

Perhaps the most obvious demonstration of *dangjian* was the issuance of the "Guiding Opinions of the Central Committee on Deepening the Reform of State-Owned Enterprises," the 2015 document that we discussed earlier. The main objective of this document was to strengthen the role and influence of the party in SOEs. It effectively formalized the legal position of party cells in SOEs, as well as the role they would be called to play in corporate governance. Lin and Milhaupt (2019) correctly underscore the fact that this document explicitly endorses the "party cadre management principle," that is, the identity of key executives of SOEs.[9] In their empirical survey, which postdates the issuance of the 2015 document, Lin and Milhaupt (2019) have estimated that 90 percent of listed SOEs and 7 percent of large privately owned enterprises (predominantly big players, which have not benefited from government subsidies) have amended their statutes to include some form of "party building" provisions.

Wu (2016) makes a persuasive case that six distinct elements that President Xi either implemented or strengthened have turned China into even more of an idiosyncratic case than before and have increased its threat to the WTO regime. These six elements are: a state holding company for key industries; state dominance of the banking sector; the planning agency (NDRC) with its broad powers; nimble linkages across firms coordinated by SASAC; state control over appointments of key companies (SOEs); and embedding the party (state) within private enterprises, for which he cites Jack Ma, the founder of Alibaba who confessed his allegiance to the party, as an appropriate illustration.

There are undoubtedly various countries that have instituted one or more of these elements, but none have implemented all of them simultaneously, and none, of course, have the size or economic potential of China. The overall result has been to ensure that the Chinese economy can easily be steered in whatever direction the state (or the party) wishes.

To be sure, change in some direction was required. As the Chinese economy was lagging compared to its earlier rate of growth, critics were

---

8. Although recent WTO case law distances itself from earlier case law when it comes to understanding SOEs as "public bodies," it has not paid any attention to these initiatives.

9. See Economy 2018, 13ff.

quick to blame SOEs, the motor of the economy, for its sluggishness. The gap between people's expectations and actual deliveries was widening. The question was what do about it, and President Xi obviously took the view that more effective state control could be the correct antidote and reignite the economy. As Kroeber correctly underlines, even the most reform-oriented Chinese officials espoused the view that a strong role for the state in the national economy was warranted (2016, 91ff.). They saw this role more in direct ownership of assets than in regulatory function or control of distribution of resources, as in Japan. It remains to be seen whether this plan will work.[10]

One additional element has tightened state control over the Chinese economy even further: the Communist Party Central Organization Department. This is a trusted agency of extreme secrecy that has been determining the nomenklatura jobs in SOEs and the private sector for a few years now. In fact, McGregor (2010) provides much evidence to this effect, citing studies that have seen the light of day during the 1990s and the first decade of the twenty-first century. The agency has proceeded to reshuffle top jobs in big state-owned telecom companies, like China Mobile, China Unicom, and China Telecom, all without prior warning (McGregor 2010, 80ff.). Yu (2019) submits reliable evidence underscoring the (new) authority of the Chinese Communist Party Central Organization Department, as well as of the SASAC, to appoint, transfer, and/or sack the core managers in key SOEs.

Taken as a whole, there is undeniably a change under way in the structure and control of China's economy. The separation of government from the economy, even if not perfect during Deng's years, is a thing of the past in the current regime.[11] We started this discussion stating that the objective sought through President Xi's reforms was to reinvigorate SOEs and make them genuine global players while, at the same time, tightening the grip of the state around them. The evidence that we have submitted supports this

10. Compare the thoughts of Economy (2018, 105ff.), who details the "Made in China 2025" initiative, the very ambitious strategy to establish ten priority sectors for the Chinese economy (including aviation, information technology, etc.), where domestic content should rise from the current 40 to 70 percent by 2025. Kroeber has taken the view that this initiative has been inspired at least in part by Germany's "Industry 4.0," which aims to upgrade industry through a systematic use of information technology (2016, 52ff.). More generally, on the resurgence of statism in China, see Kurlantzick 2016.

11. McGregor cites an unnamed high-ranking Chinese official who stated that the party is like the "panopticon"; it is everywhere watching everything but cannot be seen (2010, 17). In his 2019 study McGregor reinforces this point.

view and raises a further question: Is there a hierarchy between the two objectives? Which is more important to the Chinese state?

ECONOMY OR STATE?

Ye Zhang examined the effect of President Xi's reforms thus far and concluded that "the leadership in Beijing was reluctant to withdraw the 'visible' hand of the state" (2019, 4). This opinion is probably not far from the truth. A recent report by the Rhodium group (2018) has found that as of June 2018, whereas return for private investment in China was hovering around 9.9 percent, return on assets for SOEs had been limited to 3.9 percent.[12] While a strong case can be made that the reforms have shortened the distance between the Chinese bureaucracy and the marketplace, the economic efficiency of the reforms is doubtful.

In a way, the Chinese hierarchy should have anticipated that this would eventually be the case. Naughton (2017), in his astute account of the SOE reform under President Xi, has explained that the chances of success were always limited, since China was pursuing an impossible hierarchy:

- Increase firm (SOE) autonomy
- Improve oversight of firms
- Assign new developmental mission to firms

Something had to give, and this something, so far, has been the autonomy of SOEs. Take the example of FDI in goods, an area where China is unconstrained by WTO rules. The Ministry of Commerce and NDRC jointly manage this area. FDI is divided into "encouraged," "permitted," "restricted," and "prohibited." This list corresponds to the need to import technology, for example, in the realm of train or automobile construction. Now that China has managed to reach the technological frontier, FDI in these areas has been downgraded from "encouraged" to "permitted."[13]

This is part of a wider reinvigoration of industrial policy in China. "Industrial policy" is, of course, hard to define as it encompasses both measures of a horizontal nature (such as R&D subsidies) and measures of specific support. The FDI example cited above is part of this wider reinvigorated

12. This report is available at https://aspi.gistapp.com/spring-2018/page/state-owned -enterprise.

13. According to the OECD FDI Restrictiveness Index, China is one of the countries most hostile toward FDI. Only the Philippines, Indonesia, Russia, South Africa, and Malaysia are more restrictive; see https://data.oecd.org/fdi/fdi-restrictiveness.htm.

industrial policy. There are more. There is evidence of selective enforcement of merger control, aiming to support the Chinese quest for homegrown behemoths.

In part, the changes are motivated by an apprehension that something needs to be done since growth rates have been slowing. In part, this is also because of the need to ensure some level of social justice. If so, is this the way forward? Schleifer (1998) had provided the perfect response to the Chinese quest for achieving both economic development and social justice: social goods are more easily attained through regulation than through ownership. China chose the latter.

Each and every major initiative undertaken by the Chinese hierarchy points in the same direction: the increase of state participation in the national economy. China targets self-sufficiency first and global dominance later. Nothing captures this attitude better than the "Made in China 2025" initiative: China aims for 70 percent self-sufficiency in high-tech industries by 2025 and global dominance by 2049.[14]

At this stage, not even China insiders can predict what the next steps will be. Undeniably, there is a "party vs. economy" struggle going on in Beijing. President Xi seems to be walking a tightrope. The gains from liberalization are there for everyone to see, but continuing down this road might entail the reduction of influence of the Communist Party. President Xi does not seem to be ready to head in this direction and eviscerate the grip of the party on the economy. Then again, we have been surprised quite often by China.

China has undeniably come a long way since Deng Xiaoping became the country's leader. The WTO accession was hailed as the apex of a long transformation process. Its transformation, though, has stopped short of espousing market economics the way they are typically understood in the Western world. Now that China seems to be making *marche arrière* under the leadership of President Xi, strengthening the control of the state on the domestic economy, doubts over the commitment of the present leadership to the Deng reforms have been multiplying. Its self-proclaimed "socialist market economy" system has alienated its trading partners and ultimately

---

14. The idea is that China progresses in ten sectors ranging from aerospace and aeronautics to advanced medical devices and agricultural machinery, and self-sufficiency in these areas permeates the whole plan; see https://www.cfr.org/backgrounder/made-china/2025-threat-global-trade.

represents a threat, even though this word might sound like an exaggeration to the multilateral trading regime.[15]

Whether China will continue down the road toward liberalization that the Deng reforms opened up or retreat to a more state-managed economic model remains an open question.[16] The WTO incumbents had likely taken it for granted that there was no going back from reforms. Recent experience put the lie to this assumption; nothing should be taken for granted when it comes to Chinese politics. There is a need to better understand what is going on. In the words of Szonyi, "Because China matters, understanding China matters" (2018, 2).

China Corporatization and Privatization

In his excellent survey of technological evolution, Mokyr explains why there is nothing paradoxical about the important role that the Chinese Communist Party plays in everyday life. In his words, "China has . . . always been a 'one-party state' and for 2,000 years it was ruled by the 'Confucian party'" (1990, 236). The Communist Party is a natural continuation of this tradition. Privatization of the economy inevitably calls into question this model, and it did not take long for the party to react. McGregor explains why President Xi was the appropriate man to do just that:

> Xi has always been a true believer in the party's right to rule China. . . . In Xi's eyes, a Chinese leader must be above all Red, meaning loyal to the Communist Party, its leader, and its ideological roots, in good times and bad. By the time he took office, Xi seemed possessed by a deep fear that the pillars of party rule—the military, the state-owned enterprises, the security apparatus, and the propaganda machine—were corrupt and crumbling. So, he set out on a rescue mission. He would be the Reddest leader of his generation. And he expected all Party members to follow in his footsteps, or else. (2019b, 20)

In this analysis, there seems to be no doubt that China has, and will continue to, put party above economy when necessary.

---

15. Blustein provides some evidence that President Xi holds both Chairmen Mao and Deng in high esteem, so he feels that he can achieve market reforms without jeopardizing the predominance of the party (2019, 172ff.).

16. Shambaugh (2016) offers an excellent, succinct analysis on this score.

McGregor explains (2019b, 22ff.) that President Xi viewed the fall and disappearance of the Soviet Communist Party as a warning. He was flabbergasted by the inertia at all levels and by the inability to resist forces for change, forces that ultimately led to the demise of a behemoth, the Soviet Communist Party and the Soviet Union. In Xi's words, quoted by McGregor, "To dismiss the history of the Soviet Union and the Soviet Communist Party, to dismiss Lenin and Stalin, and to dismiss everything else, is to engage in historic nihilism. It confuses our thoughts and undermines the party's organizations at all levels" (2019b, 23). In that, President Xi sees eye to eye with Deng, who had expressed similar views, as we saw in chapter 1. So President Xi accordingly rebranded his "Chinese dream" and committed to a reinvigoration of the role of the state in the workings of the Chinese economy. By adding grandiose projects, like the Belt and Road Initiative, which harkens back to the original Silk Road connecting Europe to Asia centuries ago, he managed to capture the imagination of the masses.[17] He also reaffirmed national pride by establishing the Asian Infrastructure Investment Bank, against the wishes of the United States.[18] President Xi, through these actions, seemed to undo Deng's famous saying "hide your strength, bide your time."

Westad (2019) argues in support of the view that the persisting underlying principle in the way the Chinese Communist Party has been reigning over the economy is that there is no need to become democratic in order to prosper. Democracy is no *passage obligé* on the road to prosperity in the eyes and mind of the Chinese leadership. In fact, the Chinese hierarchy looks at democracy with disdain. Westad mentions that, in the logic of the current leadership of the Chinese Communist Party, "democracy is simply a pretext for robbing poorer countries of their sovereignty and economic potential" (2019, 87). The same author quotes from a speech of President Xi indicating that Beijing is "blazing a new trail for other developing countries to achieve modernization . . . and offers a new option for other countries and nations who want to speed up their development while preserving their

17. Seventy-one countries participate in the Belt and Road Initiative, representing 40 percent of world trade and 35 percent of investment inflows. They are corridor economies linking China to the world. On the trade impact of the Belt and Road Initiative, see World Bank 2019a, which estimates that trade increase will be 9 percent for participating countries and 6 percent for the rest of the world. The same study estimates that 60 percent of all projects under the aegis of this initiative have been entrusted to Chinese companies. If the corridor economies had all joined the WTO Agreement on Government Procurement, the outcome could have been different.

18. The United States has put pressure on others not to join this bank. Vogel mentions that Japan, for example, has followed the U.S. wishes on this score, even though it has kept some informal ties with the bank (2019, 402–3).

independence" (87). It is not the purpose of this volume to engage in detail the background driving current Chinese trade policies. It is good to keep this background in mind, however. President Xi has, of course, operated at a much more granular level as well, and it is this level that is of interest to us.

Lin and Milhaupt (2013) and Howson (2017) draw a distinction between corporatization and privatization, explaining that reducing the importance of state ownership in China did not always lead economic agents to behave like Western private companies.

According to Milhaupt and Zheng, the role of ownership was relegated to a second-order concern. The authors note (and we quote, approvingly) that "large firms in China exhibit substantial similarities in their relationship with the state that distinctions based on corporate ownership simply do not pick up" (2015, 669). To some extent, this view has been endorsed recently by the WTO adjudicating bodies, as we have seen. The distinction between corporatization and privatization is largely attributable to President Xi, who wants to reassert the role of the party in the Chinese national economy, as Lin and Milhaupt (2019) aptly detail.[19] In the words of Liu Yongxing, cited by McGregor (2010, 194): "Government support for private enterprises is less than that given to the state sector. We take this as rule of nature." The Chinese state will not, in other words, relinquish its control of the economy anytime soon, and the world trading community will continue to need to take that fact—that "rule of nature"—into account. Nevertheless, we remain convinced there is a way forward, despite the critical current situation and the strident—and counterproductive—complaints raised against China.

Negotiating Anew

Our discussion in the previous chapters has, we hope, demonstrated the inefficacy of currently adopted approaches to address the China issues. Here we add one more dimension. Instead of inciting China to continue down the road of reforms, the policies adopted vis-à-vis China have produced the opposite effect. China has retrenched, recoiling from the vision of the liberal understanding. Staying idle, therefore, is not an option, as the problems will continue to haunt the world trading system and might even be exacerbated.

---

19. Upon becoming president of China, Xi made all the right noises. He even traveled to the South, to Shenzhen and Guangzhou, in a move reminiscent of Deng's "southern tour," where Deng had announced the definitive turn toward pro-market reforms. He subsequently, for reasons discussed in various publications (including Economy 2018, 97ff.), backtracked. See also Shambaugh 2013 and Kroeber 2016 on this score.

Forced unilateral or bilateral solutions, on the other hand, as was the case with Japan, have not produced the expected results in the case of China.

Undeniably, the current crisis can partly be addressed through better enforcement of existing rules, including commitments taken by China in its Protocol of Accession. But there is only so much that can be done through the current rules, as we have shown, and, in light of the current contract incompletion with respect to the two key issues discussed in this volume, there is uncertainty as to whether litigation will be successful.

In our view, changing some of the WTO rules in order to translate at least some of the implicit GATT/WTO liberal understanding into explicit treaty language is inevitable, if the trading community is serious, as it seems to be, on the issue of SOEs and forced TT. In this volume, we have proposed functionalist solutions in line with the objectives and targets of the WTO.[20] Realistically, a reworking of the WTO, inspired by solutions that already exist in preferential and plurilateral agreements, can help the regime move out of the current crisis.

The most promising avenue is the one that the world community has not tried so far: negotiation (ideally multilaterally, or plurilaterally, if need be, but with the participation of the key players secured) of new agreements under the auspices of the WTO. The role of the state in trade relations needs to be curtailed, not by imposing a regime change on socialist countries like China but by enacting new WTO rules that will change their trade behavior. SOEs and transfer of technology are the prime candidates for reform in this context.

For this to happen, a few prerequisites need to be met. What is clear to us is that the participation of China and the United States is the sine qua non of the whole enterprise. Without being contemptuous toward any other trading nation, realistically, these two, the leading world trading powers, need to take the initiative and pull other countries in their wake.

How can this happen? The United States needs to dissociate its trade policy from its national security concerns. The Trump administration increasingly conflates the two issues, and undoing the current trend is one of the key conditions for succeeding in what we propose. The United States obviously wishes to keep China far enough from reaching the technological frontier in a long line of industries. Economic history teaches otherwise, so this

---

20. In similar vein, Diamond and Schell (2018) have argued for "constructive vigilance," a cooperative approach vis-à-vis China aiming to increase transparency and awareness.

strategy must be rethought in terms of interdependence and coexistence, rather than dominance and exclusion.

China must pull its weight too. We do not know whether China would accept participation in a multilateral or even plurilateral negotiation that would modify WTO rules on SOEs and technology transfer. We are fully aware that this is a crucial and difficult question and that progress depends on an affirmative answer. At the same time, we strongly believe that China is committed to a rules-based multilateral trading system.

The partial, or even total, breakdown of the multilateral trading system cannot be ruled out at this stage. China has profited a great deal from its participation in the WTO, and, as a responsible world leader, it is now time that it acts to prevent the WTO's demise. It must sit at the negotiating table in Geneva and play a central role in drafting new WTO rules. China should propose a package of measures that, together with SOEs and technology transfer, could form the basis of new multilateral or plurilateral negotiations.

Of course, we do not believe that the survival of the current regime depends solely on feelings of altruism. China's participation in new talks could be greatly aided by a few carrots and some sticks. Reopening the Trade in Services Agreement (TiSA), with China occupying a seat at the table, could provide a boost in this direction. Inviting China to the CPTPP could further act as a quid pro quo for negotiating forced transfer of technology (an investment agreement that is in the WTO context) and disciplining of SOEs. And China might, anticipating a thawing of the Transatlantic Trade and Investment Partnership (TTIP) talks between the EU and the United States, be willing to lock in reforms at the WTO level that would reduce the urge to "go the TTIP way." But we should not set such hopes too high.

Wu (2019), for one, doubts that China would be willing to join the CPTPP or that TTIP and similar free-trade agreements (FTAs) from which it is excluded would induce China to accept making changes to global trading rules. One of his arguments in support of this thesis is that the loss of competitiveness from being excluded from those FTAs is likely to be small and that China would be able to compensate for this loss through FTAs of its own.

At the end of the day, as we have repeatedly emphasized in this volume, we have to face the reality that China is different from other countries. China is a socialist country, a massive country with a correspondingly gargantuan population, and is soon to be number one in the world in terms of economic activity. There is little chance, therefore, that it will be amenable to pressure, including from the current world economic leader, the United States, the way Japan was when it threatened that leadership. At the same time, China is unlikely to want to see the collapse of the multilateral system because it would mean the end of the rules-based trading system and the return to an earlier power-based system that would set it on a collision course with the other big power, the United States. In our view, therefore, the best hope for making progress and bringing both China and the United States to the multilateral table in Geneva rests with the "friends of the WTO," liberal trading nations that seek peace and prosperity through multilateral cooperation and liberal voices in the United States and China.[21]

21. See Mattoo and Staiger 2019 for a discussion of why the United States has initiated a shift from rules-based to power-based trade relations, and why its enlightened self-interest could make it revert to its earlier preference for a rules-based system.

Concluding Remarks

THIS TIME IT IS DIFFERENT INDEED

In 1992, Deng took his second Southern Tour. He visited Shenzhen and Zuhai, where the transformation of the Chinese economy had all started, but also Shanghai and Wuhan, where the market transformation had been transplanted. The changes on the face of China were dramatic and there for anyone to see.

Deng delivered a series of speeches during this tour, calling for accelerated growth. He had solid arguments to this effect, as he could point to the improbable success of the first four SEZs, as well as those that followed. Shanghai was very much his focus, as he believed, like others did, that the transformation of Shanghai would contribute immensely to the growth of China.

This second Southern Tour is widely perceived as the signal for the second generation of Chinese reforms. At a moment when some party insiders were getting cold feet and wanted to limit reforms, Deng pointed to the opposite direction. We know by now, as we are living in the fifth decade of *gaige kaifang*, that the ongoing reforms yielded unprecedented benefits for the Chinese economy. As China kept growing at rates that it had never experienced before, its success was becoming controversial, at least as far as its trading partners were concerned.

Lessons for the World from the Past

The GATT/WTO regime was predicated on the liberal ideals that dominated thinking and practice in the Western world in the post–World War
II era. It is hard to imagine how the basic legal instruments committed to
the endeavor to liberalize international trade, the GATT's primary objective, could function absent market economies to support them. The GATT
did make room for state involvement in the economy, and the provision
on STEs is the culmination point. The assumption, nevertheless, was that
participants would be market economies with occasional tinkering by the
state.

For reasons having to do with a quest for independence by acceding
countries, or the corresponding belief of the incumbents that opening the
door to them would eviscerate the cohesion of the Soviet bloc, the GATT
welcomed centrally planned economies. It did not impose economy-wide
reforms on these countries—it could not do that anyway. The assumption
of the incumbents was that the acceding countries would change once they
had realized the gains associated with increased trade within the GATT.
And in any event, these countries represented an infinitesimal percentage
of world trade, so no matter how they ran their economy, they would not
affect the workings of the world trading system.

Japan was a more significant challenge for the GATT. It was of course
not a centrally planned economy and was a heavy hitter in world trade.
What made Japan a special case was that its economic model was more of
a public-private partnership than that of any Western country member of
the GATT. It was Japan Inc., in the eyes of the incumbents at least. Once
again there was no reform of the GATT because of Japan's accession. In this
case, nonetheless, reform was unnecessary for a different reason. Japan quite
quickly espoused the liberal understanding implicit in the GATT agreement
by, for instance, joining OECD, the exclusive club of Western economies.

The accession of China to the WTO combined the most problematic
features of the two categories above. China was both a leader in world trade
and it was centrally planned. This time the challenge was different, and the
response to that challenge was different as well.

An elaborate Protocol of Accession was agreed to that included a number
of obligations that China was required to undertake in order to accede to the
WTO. There was worldwide exuberance when the news broke that China
had joined this bastion of liberalism. For some, the Protocol of Accession
marked what had to be the transition toward a full-fledged market economy.

A date was even set, 2016, as of which China would, it was assumed, no longer be a non-market economy.

And yet only a few years later, doom and gloom reigned over the WTO in Geneva. Protests against China originated in Washington, D.C., but a few others joined in (albeit not as stridently). Some pointed to China not playing fairly, and some complained that there was underenforcement of the Protocol of Accession. One thing was certain: China had not changed, and as it turned out, that retrenchment would continue.

Drawing the line between the private and public spheres in China is never easy. The most successful private entrepreneurs, from Zhang Ruimin, who heads Haier, to Jack Ma, who established Alibaba, are also party members. UBS, the Swiss banking giant, in its report on the Chinese economy in 2005 concluded that critical sectors (oil, petrochemicals, mining, banks, insurance, telecoms, steel, aluminum, electricity, aviation, airports, railways, ports, highways, autos, health care, education, and civil service) were either 100 percent or majority controlled by the Chinese state. And then, for the remainder of the economy, the distinction between *siying* (privately run) and *miying* (run by the people) is often blurred.[1]

Lessons for China from Russia

Deng did not think highly of Gorbachev. In his view, it was a huge error, a mistake of gigantic proportions, to give up the party while restructuring the economy. President Xi follows Deng on this score.

When the liberalization of the economy threatened the dominance of the party, there was a pushback. The complaints about SOEs and forced TT are, for all practical purposes, complaints about the renewed heavy involvement of the Chinese state in the economy. And the distance is not far between those complaints and deleterious economic effects across China's trading partners. A solution to this conundrum is crucial for today's global economy, just as it was twenty years ago before China's accession to the WTO.

Dealing with China

Every now and then, voices are raised about the eventual moral victory of liberal ideas. China is no attractive model, these voices argue, hence it can never provide an example for the rest of the world. Eventually, it will have to change.

1. McGregor 2010, 199ff.

But "eventually" is a long way from today. It might be sooner or later depending on how the party versus economy struggle will evolve in China, but it certainly does not appear to be imminent. Furthermore, much damage can be done between now and then by simply delaying a resolution of the issues involved.

There are voices that argue for a "do nothing" approach. These voices are incorrect, as we hope we have demonstrated, when evaluated in light of the GATT liberal understanding. Furthermore, doing nothing has its own problems—it amounts, in effect, to a negative action. The moralizing justification of President Trump to "take on" China is, in fact, multilateral passivity. It is an argument that since the WTO will not solve the problem (whatever the problem is), the United States should take justice into its own hands. What has been the outcome? Besides increasing geopolitical tensions, tariff impositions on an ever-widening series of products have harmed U.S. consumers, some U.S. producers, some Chinese producers, and many producers, investors, and traders outside China and the United States. What is worse is that the issue is still ahead of us, since these tariff impositions have not curbed China's behavior.

But even if tariffs worked, what is the likelihood that they would have solved the China problem? If the problem is SOEs and forced TT, then we should have seen somewhere in the pronouncements of the U.S. administration something to this effect. All we have seen is an effort to reduce the U.S. trade deficit. President Trump is no messenger for the world trading community. In fact, he has neither the incentive nor the mandate to act as such.

Be Inclusive and Prudent

Article 32.10.5 of the USMCA reads:

> Entry by a Party into a free trade agreement with a non-market country will allow the other Parties to terminate this Agreement on six months' notice and replace this Agreement with an agreement as between them (bilateral agreement).

The same provision (Article 32.10) defines an NME as:

a country:

(a) that on the date of signature of this Agreement, a Party has determined to be a non-market economy for purposes of its trade remedy laws; and

(b) with which no Party has signed a free trade agreement.

China is undoubtedly the target here. This is exactly what we believe should not happen. Excluding China from various initiatives (TiSA being the most prominent example, but from potential FTAs as well, as this example amply demonstrates) is a strategy that has not paid off. Instead, including China, probably with a reconsideration of the security interests involved, in the solution is the way forward.

Acheson includes the following passage from a speech by Townsend Hoopes, undersecretary of the U.S. Air Force, which perfectly encapsulates the spirit of our argument here:

> Our difficulty is that as a nation of short-term pragmatists accustomed to dealing with the future only when it has become the present, we find it hard to regard future trends as serious realities. We have not achieved the capacity to treat as real and urgent—as demanding action today—problems which appear in critical dimension only at some future date. Yet failure to achieve this new habit of mind is likely to prove fatal. (1969, 16)

What Hoopes claimed about U.S. society perfectly captures the current zeitgeist as far as the WTO membership is concerned.

Be Bold and Realistic

Doing nothing is untenable and creates all sorts of problems, including "go it alone" strategies that we have discussed in this volume. We need a new strategy instead. The world trade community must turn the page on the unilateral and bilateral actions it has been practicing in recent years. This is where our proposals for multilateral agreements come in. This is no time for Trumpian bullying or marking of territory, nor is it a *weiqi* (go) game. It is even more unrealistic to attempt to change China. Instead, we believe it is high time that the world trade community sat around the table to address these issues, which might be predominantly—but are certainly not exclusively—China issues. There is a genuine need to negotiate a new WTO deal, starting with the currently pressing issues of SOEs and forced TT.

Recently there have been multiple cases dealing more or less with the same question: the (impermissible, in the eyes of complainants) degree of state intervention in the workings of the Chinese economy. Following a few defeats, the United States managed to score a clear victory in *U.S.–Countervailing Measures (China)* (DS437) regarding the understanding of the term "public body," where even private firms, assuming they are inter-mingled with the state, could be characterized as such. This could be the case, for example, of an agent with no state ownership whose board members are selected by the Chinese Communist Party.

Why, then, do we not recommend leaving it to adjudication? There are various reasons. For one thing, there is no guarantee that this case law will be reproduced in the future as well. Indeed, because of the lack of clarity in the way the Appellate Body report on *U.S.–Countervailing Measures (China)* addresses the issue, it could very well be that future case law will divert. To provide but one illustration, in the "entity vs. conduct" debate that we cited earlier, case law has failed to draw a boundary between inter-mingling with the state and accepting directives by the state to behave in a particular way.

Furthermore, there is no guarantee that case law will be internally coher-ent. Understanding private entities as SOEs could and indeed should have implications not only for our discussion regarding treatment of SOEs but also for our discussion concerning forced TT. There is no certainty, though, that case law will evolve in this way. There is no guarantee, in other words, that the understanding of "public bodies" will be the same, irrespective of whether we discuss an SOE- or a forced TT-related case.

Dispute adjudication is, finally, not immune to glitches. In *EU–Provisional Methodologies*, China was attacking the way the EU authori-ties had treated it as an NME. Following the issuance of the interim report, China requested that the panel suspend its proceedings, as it could do under Article 12.12 of DSU.[2] Because of China's actions, though, an oppor-tunity to bring some coherence into the conditions under which China can lawfully be treated as an NME was lost. This could happen in other areas as well.

Our point, in a nutshell, is this: even if those attacking China before WTO courts are quite strategic about it, the risk of inconsistent/incoherent case law argues against privileging this method for addressing the China issues. A legislative amendment explaining under what conditions SOEs are private bodies, and how they should act if so, is warranted. The "public bodies" characterization should hold for forced TT purposes as well.

And, of course, the next logical question, the next frontier so to speak, would be whether all of the above can meaningfully be implemented by China (as opposed to being adjudicated before the WTO) if it has not first

2. https://www.wto.org/english/tratop_e/dispu_e/cases_e/ds516_e.htm.

adopted a well-functioning competition law. Attempts to internationalize competition law have been recorded since the ITO negotiation, and more recently with the establishment of the WTO Group on the Interaction between Trade and Competition Policies.[3] Unfortunately, this discussion ended up leading nowhere.

It is unclear to us whether multilateral (or plurilateral) disciplinary rules are necessary. What is clear is that any disciplinary regime on SOEs and forced TT will be undermined if it is not supported by competition law. This could very well be Chinese competition law, but it needs to be inspired by practice in the most advanced quarters. Whether some international disciplines are necessary to ensure that this has indeed been the case could very well be a matter for debate and, eventually, negotiation.

And we should not underestimate China's potential to extract rents through other instruments. There is recent evidence, indeed, that despite having on paper a competition regime similar to that of the EU, China nonetheless manages to treat Chinese companies differently from foreign companies operating in its market through other instruments.[4]

Finally, we are not oblivious to the fact that China is a behemoth, and one with a different profile than that of the Western world. Security concerns will and do naturally arise. But they should not be exaggerated either. Under the guise of national security, we would not like to see an expansion of the term "strategic industries" in order to cover each and every domestic industry.

National investment regimes, like CFIUS, which we discussed earlier, provide a framework for scrutinizing foreign investment in light of security concerns that might arise. A CFIUS-type approach could provide useful inspiration for the WTO context as well.

The main winner from this endeavor will be the multilateral regime itself. Unilateral actions, retaliation to unilateral actions, and inaction by the WTO have all contributed to reducing the relevance of the multilateral regime. Now is the time to turn the tide. The world leadership needs to bring interested parties to the table and, by doing that, to renew their belief in the multilateral procedures. Blustein, in a similar vein, suggests in more graphic terms that the correct response to the China challenge is to double down on multilateralism (2019, 7).

3. https://www.wto.org/english/tratop_e/comp_e/comp_e.htm.
4. See Zhang and Wu 2019 and Lyu, Buts, and Jegers 2019.

Will China Oblige?

We should not underestimate China's potential to extract rents through other instruments. What we have discussed here is what to do with respect to priority issues and is by no means a blueprint for addressing all grievances about China. One example concerns China's competition regime, which prima facie closely resembles the EU's regime. Zhang and Wu (2019) and Lyu, Buts, and Jegers (2019) both explain how China, despite this resemblance, manages to extract profits from foreign companies operating in its market.

We understand, of course, that there is no guarantee that China will take a seat at the table of negotiations, when it is feeling increasingly strong. Indeed, seasoned experts have become much more cautious and even skeptical about the role of China in international relations. Kissinger (2011) seemed quite optimistic, and only one year later, following the ascent to power of President Xi, he adopted a more cautious attitude (Kissinger 2012). And of course, at the furthest end of the spectrum, more skeptical, equally respectable voices believe that conflict is almost unavoidable. Mearsheimer (2001) is probably the most eloquent voice in this line of thinking.

We also understand that trade is part of a wider game in the realm of international relations. Even though our focus in this volume has been on trade issues, we are mindful of what is more generally at stake. Indeed, we focused on trade because we believe that it provides a very appropriate mechanism to avoid conflict by increasing the existing level of cooperation. The WTO is undeniably the most far-reaching institutional arrangement promoting cooperative attitudes. And we believe China, which has gained a lot from its participation in the WTO, has (or at least should have) an interest in promoting the reinforcement of WTO disciplines along the lines we propose in this book. This is how we see China behaving as a "responsible stakeholder": by taking a seat at the negotiating table and attempting to smooth over the thorny subjects put on the table. Paraphrasing Zoellick (2005), who linked China's "responsible stakeholder" status to its attitude essentially vis-à-vis the United States, we would like to see China take more initiative within the multilateral system. This would mean obviously not only responding to demands from its partners but also making its own demands of them.

In the same line of thinking, White had already observed (2012, 48ff.) that China faces a dilemma: it needs stable international relations in order to continue to grow and catch up to rich countries, but it also needs an international framework that accommodates its idiosyncratic system. He quotes in this respect Admiral Jacky Fisher, who built the Royal Navy and famously quipped: "All nations want peace, but they want the peace that suits them" (125). The argument in this book is the peace that suits not only China but also the world passes through multilateral institutions and organizations. Martin Wolf (2017) has perceptively argued that

> we are, in short, at the end of both an economic period—that of Western-led globalization—and a geopolitical one, the post–Cold War "unipolar moment" of a U.S.-led global order. The question is whether what follows will be an unravelling of the post–Second World War era into a period of deglobalization and conflict, as happened in the first half of the 20th century, or a new period in which non-Western powers, especially China and India, play a bigger role in sustaining a cooperative global order.

Thucydides's Trap Redux

In Allison's (2017) account, only a handful of transitions from the old to the new hegemon have taken place in a peaceful manner. What is different now is the existence of a multilateral rules-based system. International cooperation in the post–World War II era is an unprecedented phenomenon in world history. A web of agreements has cemented international relations into concrete legal obligations and, by increasing interdependence, has also increased the cost of unilateral warlike behavior. Past transitions could not have benefited from a similar context.

When endorsing Allison's book (2017), Henry Kissinger expressed the hope that readers, influenced by the message and the lessons history can teach us, will be inspired to ensure that the U.S.-China relationship will add up to the four cases where the rising power and the incumbent avoided Thucydides's trap, rather than to the twelve where, alas, the opposite happened. Reinvigorating the multilateral system, through negotiations of the kind that we propose, is certainly in line with this view.

Brunnermeier, Doshi, and James conclude their essay comparing today's China with Bismarckian Germany at the end of the nineteenth century with the following words:

> That American response should neither be blindly confrontational nor naively cooperative; instead it should be competitive. The right approach, in contrast to tariffs, would be to work with allies to strengthen rules, set

standards, punish Chinese industrial policy and technology theft, invest in research, welcome the world's best and brightest, and create alternatives to its geo-economic statecraft. China is playing a good hand well, but the United States and its allies have an even better one—but only if they work together. (2020, 176)

This is in essence what we have argued in this volume, except for a key feature: in our scheme of things, the game should not be played between Beijing and Washington, D.C., with some stopovers in Brussels, the EU capital. For all the reasons mentioned in this volume, the game should be played in Geneva, at the WTO headquarters. The WTO is at the forefront of genuinely multilateral cooperation. Transition, if it has to occur, should be managed within its confines. Ideally, we should even drop the term "transition" and return to the mundane, but quite necessary, idea of enduring cooperation.

REFERENCES

Acheson, Dean. 1969. *Present at the Creation: My Years in the State Department.* New York: W. W. Norton.

Ahn, Dukgeun, and Alan Spearot. 2016. "US-Carbon Steel (India), Multi-product Firms and the Cumulation of Products." *World Trade Review* 15:351–73.

Alford, William P. 2018. "Does Law Matter in China?" In *The China Questions: Critical Insights into a Rising Power*, ed. Jennifer Rudolph and Michael Szonyi, 212–18. Cambridge, MA: Harvard University Press.

Aliber, Robert Z., and Charles P. Kindleberger. 2015. *Manias, Panics, and Crashes: A History of Financial Crises.* New York: Palgrave Macmillan.

Allison, Graham. 2017. *Destined for War: Can America and China Escape Thucydides's Trap?* New York: Houghton Mifflin Harcourt.

Amiti, Mary, Stephen J. Redding, and David Weinstein. 2019. "The Impact of the 2018 Trade War on US Prices and Welfare." NBER Working Paper No. 25672. Cambridge, MA: NBER.

Anderson, Robert D., Philippe Pelletier, Kodjo Osei-Lah, and Anna Caroline Müller. 2011. "Assessing the Value of Future Accessions to the WTO Agreement on Government Procurement (GPA): Some New Data Sources, Provisional Estimates, and an Evaluative Framework for Individual WTO Members Considering Accession." WTO Staff Working Paper, ERSD-2011–15, Geneva.

Appelbaum, Binyamin. 2019. *The Economists' Hour: False Prophets, Free Markets, and the Fracture of Society.* New York: Little, Brown.

Autor, David H., David Dorn, and Gordon H. Hanson. 2013. "The China Syndrome: Local Labor Market Effects of Import Competition in the United States." *American Economic Review* 103:2121–68.

Bacchus, James, Simon Lester, and Han Zhu. 2018. "Disciplining China's Trade Practices at the WTO." Cato Institute Policy Analysis No. 856, Washington, DC.

Bader, Jeffrey A. 2012. *Obama and China's Rise: An Insider's Account of America's Asia Strategy.* Washington, DC: Brookings Institution.

Bagwell, Kyle, and Robert W. Staiger. 2001. "Domestic Policies, National Sovereignty, and International Economic Institutions." *Quarterly Journal of Economics* 116:519–62.

Baker, James A. III, with Thomas M. DeFrank. 1995. *The Politics of Diplomacy: Revolution, War, and Peace, 1989–1992.* New York: G. P. Putnam's Sons.

Baldwin, Robert E. 1970. *Non-Tariff Distortions of International Trade.* Washington, DC: Brookings Institution.

Barfield, Claude E. 2003. *High-Tech Protectionism: The Irrationality of Antidumping Laws.* Washington, DC: American Enterprise Institute.

Bayard, Thomas O., and Kimberly Ann Elliott. 1994. *Reciprocity and Retaliation in US Trade Policy.* Washington, DC: Peterson Institute for International Economics.

Bell, Daniel A. 2015. *The China Model: Political Meritocracy and the Limits of Democracy*. Princeton: Princeton University Press.

Berkowitz, Daniel, Hong Ma, and Shuishiro Nishioka. 2017. "Recasting the Iron Rice Bowl: The Return of China's State-Owned Enterprises." *Review of Economics and* Statistics 99:735–47.

Bhagwati, Jagdish. 1965. "On the Equivalence of Tariffs and Quotas." In *Trade, Growth, and the Balance of Payments: Essays in Honor of Gottfried Haberler*, ed. Robert E. Baldwin et al., 53–67. Chicago: Rand McNally.

Bhagwati, Jagdish, and Hugh T. Patrick, eds. 1990. *Aggressive Unilateralism: America's 301 Trade Policy and the World Trading System*. Ann Arbor: University of Michigan Press.

Bhala, Raj. 2000. "Enter the Dragon: An Essay into China's WTO Accession Saga." *American University International Law Review* 15:1469–1538.

Blanchard, Emily J., Chad P. Bown, and Robert C. Johnson. 2017. "Global Value Chains and Trade Policy." http://faculty.tuck.dartmouth.edu/images/uploads/faculty/emily-blanchard/BBJ -August2017.pdf.

Blustein, Paul. 2019. *Schism: China, America, and the Fracturing of the Global Trading System*. Waterloo, Ontario: Centre for International Governance Innovation.

Bown, Chad P. 2011. "Import Protection and the Great Recession." VOX, CEPR Policy Portal. https://voxeu.org/article/import-protection-and-great-recession.

———. 2017. "Rogue 301: Trump to Dust Off Another Outdated US Trade Law?" https://piie .com/blogs/trade-investment-policy-watch/rogue-301-trump-dust-another-outdated-us -trade-law.

———. 2018. "Trade Policy toward Supply Chains after the Great Recession." *IMF Economic Review* 66:602–16.

———. 2019. "US-China Trade War: The Guns of August." https://www.piie.com/blogs/trade -and-investment-policy-watch/us-china-trade-war-guns-august.

Bown, Chad P., and Doug Irwin. 2019. "Trump's Assault on the Global Trading System." *Foreign Affairs* 98 (September–October): 125–36.

Brandt, Loren, and Thomas J. Rawski. 2008. *China's Great Economic Transformation*. New York: Cambridge University Press.

———. 2019. *Policy, Regulation, and Innovation in China's Electricity and Telecom Industries*. New York: Cambridge University Press.

Brandt, Loren, Johannes Van Biesebroeck, Luhang Wang, and Yifan Zhang. 2017. "WTO Accession and Performance of Chinese Manufacturing Firms." *American Economic Review* 107:2784–2820.

Branstetter, Lee. 2018. "China's Forced Technology Problem—And What to Do About It." Washington, DC: Peterson Institute for International Economics. https://www.piie.com/system /files/documents/pb18-13.pdf.

Branstetter, Lee, Ray Fisman, Fritz Foley, and Kamal Saggi. 2011. "Does Intellectual Property Rights Reform Spur Industrial Development?" *Journal of International Economics* 83:27–36.

Branstetter, Lee, and Kamal Saggi. 2011. "Intellectual Property Rights, Foreign Direct Investment, and Industrial Development." *Economic Journal* 121:1161–91.

Brødsgaard, Kjeld Erik. 2018. "Can China Keep Controlling Its SOEs?" *The Diplomat*, March 5. https://thediplomat.com/2018/03/can-china-keep-controlling-its-soes/.

Brown, Chris. 1994. "China's GATT Bid: Why All the Fuss about Currency Controls?" *Pacific Rim Law & Policy Journal* 3:57–103.

Brown, William Adams, Jr. 1950. *The United States and the Restoration of World Trade*. Washington, DC: Brookings Institution.

Brunnermeier, Marcus, Rush Doshi, and Harold James. 2020. "Beijing's Bismarckian Ghosts: How Great Powers Compete Economically." *Washington Quarterly* 41:161–76.

Campbell, Kurt M., and Jake Sullivan. 2019. "Competition without Catastrophe: How America Can Both Challenge and Coexist with China." *Foreign Affairs* 98 (September–October): 96–111.

Cartland, Michael, Gérard Depayre, and Jan Woznowski. 2012. "Is Something Going Wrong in the WTO Dispute Settlement?" *Journal of World Trade* 46:979–1015.

Cass, Deborah, Brett Williams, and George Barker, eds. 2003. *China and the World Trading System: Entering a New Millennium.* Cambridge: Cambridge University Press.

Cerutti, Eugenio, Shan Chen, Pragyan Deb, Albe Gjonbalaj, Swarnali A. Hannan, and Adil Mohommad. 2019. "Managed Trade: What Could Be Possible Spillover Effects of a Potential Trade Agreement between the U.S. and China?" IMF Working Paper WP/19/251. Washington, DC: International Monetary Fund.

Charnovitz, Steve. 2008. "Mapping the Law of WTO Accession." In *The WTO: Governance, Dispute Settlement and Developing Countries,* ed. Merit E. Janow, Victoria Donaldson, and Alan Yanovich, 855–920. Huntington, NY: Juris Publishing.

Chen, Hejing, and John Whalley. 2011. "The WTO Government Procurement Agreement and Its Impacts on Trade." NBER Working Paper 17365. Cambridge, MA: NBER.

Cheng, Yao Lei. 2014. "The Reform of SOCBs in China: A Political Economy Perspective." *Economics & Political Studies* 2:67–88.

Chow, Gregory. 2018. "China's Economic Transformation." In *China's 40 Years of Reform and Development, 1978–2018,* ed. Ross Garnaut, Ligang Song, and Cai Fang, 93–116. Acton: Australia National University Press.

Chowdhry, Sonali, and Gabriel Felbermayr. 2020. "The US-China Trade Deal and Its Impact on China's Key Trading Partners." Kiel Policy Brief No. 134, Kiel Institute for the World Economy. Kiel, Germany.

Christiansen, Hans, and Yunhee Kim. 2014. "State-Invested Enterprises in the Global Marketplace: Implications for a Level Playing Field." OECD Corporate Governance Working Papers, No. 14. Paris: OECD Publishing. http://dx.doi.org/10.1787/5jz0xvfvl6nw-en.

Clintworth, Gary. 1995. "China's Evolving Relationship with APEC." *International Journal* 50:488–515.

Cooper, Richard N. 2018. "Can China's High Growth Continue?" In *The China Questions: Critical Insights into a Rising Power,* ed. Jennifer Rudolph and Michael Szonyi, 119–25. Cambridge, MA: Harvard University Press.

Copelovitch, Mark, and David Ohls. 2012. "Trade, Institutions, and the Timing of GATT/WTO Accessions in Post-Colonial States." *Review of International Organizations* 7:81–107.

Cousin, Violaine. 2007. *Banking in China.* New York: Palgrave Macmillan.

Dallmeyer, Dorinda G. 1989. "The United States–Japan Semiconductor Accord of 1986: The Shortcomings of High-Tech Protectionism." *Maryland Journal of International Law* 13:179–222.

Davis, Christina L., and Meredith Wilf. 2017. "Joining the Club: Accession to the GATT/WTO." *Journal of Politics* 79:964–78.

Diamond, Larry, and Orville Schell. 2018. *Chinese Influence & American Interests: Promoting Constructive Vigilance.* Stanford: Hoover Institution Press.

Drezner, Daniel W. 2000. "Ideas, Bureaucratic Politics, and the Crafting of Foreign Policy." *American Journal of Political Science* 44:733–49.

Drysdale, Peter, and Samuel Hardwick. 2018. "China and the Global Trading System, Then and Now." In *China's 40 Years of Reform and Development, 1978–2018,* ed. Ross Garnaut, Ligang Song, and Cai Fang, 545–74. Acton: Australia National University Press.

Eckes, Alfred E. 1995. *Opening America's Market: US Foreign Trade Policy since 1776.* Chapel Hill: University of North Carolina Press.

Economy, Elizabeth C. 2018. *The Third Revolution: Xi Jinping and the New Chinese State.* New York: Oxford University Press.

European Commission. 2001. Explanatory Memorandum of the Proposal for a Council Decision Establishing the Community Position within the Ministerial Conference Set Up by the Agreement Establishing the World Trade Organization on the Accession of the People's Republic of China to the World Trade Organization. COM (2001) 517 final—2001/0218(CNS). Official Journal of the European Communities, 51 E, 26.2.2002, pp. 314–15.

———. 2020. *White Paper on Levelling the Playing Field as Regards Foreign Subsidies.* COM (2020) 253 final. Brussels: European Commission.

Evenett, Simon J., and Carlos A. Primo Braga. 2006. "WTO Accession: Moving the Goalposts?" In *Trade, Doha, and Development: A Window into the Issues*, ed. Richard Newfarmer, 231–43. Washington, DC: World Bank Group.

Farah, Paolo Davide, and Elena Cima. 2012. "The Implementation of the WTO Agreement on TRIPS in China." *Tsinghua Law Review* 2:317–51.

Farbain, William. 2016. "An Examination of Judicial Independence in China." *Journal of Financial Crime* 23:819–32.

Feenstra, Robert, and Akira Sasahara. 2018. "The 'China Shock,' Exports, and US Employment: A Global Input-Output Analysis." *Review of International Economics* 26:1053–83.

Feng, Lin. 2016. "The Future of Judicial Independence in China." Working Paper Series No. 2, Centre for Judicial Education and Research, City University of Hong Kong.

Feng, Ling, Zhiyuan Li, and Deborah L. Swenson. 2017. "Trade Policy Uncertainty and Exports: Evidence from China's WTO Accession." *Journal of International Economics* 106:20–36.

Forsberg, Aaron. 1996. "Eisenhower and Japanese Economic Recovery: The Politics of Integration with the Western Trading Bloc." *Journal of American–East Asian Relations* 5:57–75.

———. 1998. "The Politics of GATT Expansion: Japanese Accession and the Domestic in Japan and the United States, 1948–1955." *Business and Economic History* 27:185–95.

Gaddis, John Lewis. 2000. *The United States and the Origins of the Cold War, 1941–1947.* New York: Columbia University Press.

Gao, Henry, and Donald Lewis. 2005. *China's Participation in the WTO.* London: Cameron May.

Garcia-Herrero, Alicia, and Jianwei Xu. 2017. "How to Handle State-Owned Enterprises in EU-China Investment Talks?" Bruegel Policy Contribution No. 18. Bruegel: Brussels.

Georgopoulos, Aris, Bernard M. Hoekman, and Petros C. Mavroidis. 2017. *The Internationalization of Government Procurement Regulation.* Oxford: Oxford University Press.

Gertler, Jeffrey L. 2003. "China's WTO Accession: The Final Countdown." In *China and the World Trading System: Entering a New Millennium*, ed. Deborah Cass, Brett Williams, and George Barker, 55–67. Cambridge: Cambridge University Press.

Gewirtz, Julian. 2017. *Unlikely Partners: Chinese Reformers, Western Economists, and the Making of Global China.* Cambridge, MA: Harvard University Press.

Gewirtz, Paul. 2003. "The US-China Rule of Law Initiative." *William & Mary Bill of Rights Journal* 11:603–21.

Gilbert, Richard. 2006. "Looking for Mr. Schumpeter: Where Are We in the Competition-Innovation Debate?" *Innovation Policy and the Economy* 6:159–215.

Goldman, Marshall I. 2003. *The Privatization of Russia: Russian Reforms Going Awry.* London: Routledge.

Goldstein, Judith L., Douglas Rivers, and Michael Tomz. 2007. "Institutions in International Relations: Understanding the Effects of the GATT and the WTO on World Trade." *International Organization* 6:37–67.

Goldstein, Morris, and Nicholas R. Lardy. 2009. "The Future of China's Foreign Exchange Rate Policy." Policy Analysis in International Economics 87. Washington, DC: Peterson Institute for International Economics.

Grier, Jean H. 1992. "The Use of Section 301 to Open Japanese Markets to Foreign Firms." *North Carolina Journal of International Law and Commercial Regulation* 17:1–44.

Grzybowski, Kazimierz. 1977. "East-West Trade Regulations in the United States: The 1974 Trade Act, Title IV." *Journal of World Trade Law* 11:506–25.

Haass, Richard N. 2017. *A World in Disarray: American Foreign Policy and the Crisis of the Old Order*. New York: Penguin Books.

Haddad, Mona, and Ben Shepherd. 2011. "Export-Led Growth: Still a Viable Strategy after the Crisis?" https://voxeu.org/article/export-led-growth-still-viable-strategy-after-crisis.

Halverson, Karen. 2004. "China's WTO Accession: Economic, Legal, and Political Implications." *Boston College International and Comparative Law Review* 27:319–71.

Hamada, Koichi, Anil K. Kashyap, and David E. Weinstein, eds. 2010. *Japan's Bubble, Deflation, and Long-Term Stagnation*. Cambridge, MA: MIT Press.

Hameiri, Shahar, and Lee Jones. 2016. "Rising Powers and State Transformation: The Case of China." *European Journal of International Relations* 22:72–98.

Hearden, Patrick J. 2002. *Architects of Globalism: Building a New World Order during World War II*. Fayetteville: University of Arkansas Press.

Herzstein, Robert. 1999. "Is China Ready for the WTO's Rigors?" *Wall Street Journal*, November 16.

Hillmann, Jennifer. 2018. Testimony before the U.S.-China Economic and Review Security Commission. U.S. Senate. Washington, DC. https://www.uscc.gov/sites/default/files/Hillman%20Testimony%20US%20China%20Comm%20w%20Appendix%20A.pdf.

Hoekman, Bernard M., and Petros C. Mavroidis. 1994. "Competition, Competition Policy, and the GATT." *World Economy* 17:121–50.

———. 2009. "Nothing Dramatic (Regarding Administration of Customs Laws): A Comment on the WTO Appellate Body Report EC-Selected Customs Matters." *World Trade Review* 9:31–44.

———. 2015. "WTO 'à la carte' or WTO 'menu du jour'? Assessing the Case for Plurilateral Agreements." *European Journal of International Law* 26:319–43.

Hoekman, Bernard M., and Niall Meagher. 2014. "China-Electronic Payments Services, Discrimination, Economic Development and the GATS." *World Trade Review* 13:409–42.

Hoekman, Bernard M., and Douglas Nelson. 2020. "Subsidies, Spillovers and Multilateral Cooperation." EUI Working Papers, RSCAS 2020/12. Florence: European University Institute.

Holslag, Jonathan. 2019. *The Silk Road Trap: How China's Trade Ambitions Challenge Europe*. Cambridge: Polity Press.

Hook, David H., and John Spanier. 2013. *American Foreign Policy since World War II*. Thousand Oaks, CA: CQ Press.

Horn, Henrik, Giovanni Maggi, and Robert W. Staiger. 2010. "Trade Agreements as Endogenously Incomplete Contracts." *American Economic Review* 100:394–419.

Horn, Henrik, Petros C. Mavroidis, and Håkan Nordstrøm. 2005. "Is the Use of the WTO Dispute Settlement System Biased?" In *The WTO and International Trade Law Dispute Settlement*, ed. Petros C. Mavroidis and Alan O. Sykes, 454–86. Aldershot: Elgar Publishing.

Horn, Henrik, Petros C. Mavroidis, and André Sapir. 2010. "Beyond the WTO? An Anatomy of the US and EU Preferential Trade Agreements." *World Economy* 33:1565–88.

Howson, Nicholas Calcina. 2017. "China's Corporatization without Privatization and the Late Nineteenth Century Roots of a Stubborn Path Dependency Symposium: Sovereign Conduct on the Margins of Law." *Vanderbilt Journal of Transnational Law* 50:961–1006.

Hudec, Robert E. 1975. *The GATT Legal System and the World Trade Diplomacy*. New York: Praeger.

Hufbauer, Gary C. 1998. "China as an Economic Actor on the World Stage: An Overview." In *China in the World Trading System: Defining the Principles of Engagement*, ed. Frederick M. Abbott, 47–51. Boston: Kluwer International.

Hufbauer, Gary C., and Cathleen Cimino-Isaacs. 2015. "How Will TPP and TTIP Change the WTO System?" *Journal of International Economic Law* 18:679–96.

Hufbauer, Gary C., and Zhiyao (Lucy) Lu. 2017. "The Payoff to America from Globalization: A Fresh Look with a Focus on Costs to Workers." Policy Brief 17–16. Washington, DC: Peterson Institute for International Economics:

Hvistendahl, Mara. 2020. *The Scientist and the Spy*. New York: Riverhead Books.

Irwin, Douglas A. 2013. "The Nixon Shock after Forty Years: The Import Surcharge Revisited." *World Trade Review* 12:29–56.

———. 2017. *Clashing Over Commerce: A History of U.S. Trade Policy*. Princeton: Princeton University Press.

Irwin, Douglas A., Petros C. Mavroidis, and Alan O. Sykes. 2008. *The Genesis of the GATT*. Cambridge: Cambridge University Press.

Jackson, John H. 1969. *World Trade and the Law of the GATT*. Indianapolis: Bobbs-Merrill.

———. 2003. "The Impact of China's Accession on the WTO." In *China and the World Trading System*, ed. Deborah Z. Cass, Brett G. Williams, and George Barker, 19–30. Cambridge: Cambridge University Press.

Jakobson, Harold K., and Michael Oksenberg. 1990. *China's Participation in the IMF, the World Bank, and the GATT*. Ann Arbor: University of Michigan Press.

Jaravel, Xavier, and Eric Sager. 2019. "What Are the Price Effects of Trade? Evidence from the US and Implications for Quantitative Trade Models." CEPR Discussion Paper, DP No. 13902. htpps://ssrn.com/abstract=3439455.

Johnson, Chalmers. 1982. *MITI and the Japanese Miracle: The Growth of Industrial Policy, 1925–1975*. Stanford: Stanford University Press.

Kaufman, Burton I. 1982. *Trade and Aid: Eisenhower's Foreign Economic Policy, 1953–1961*. Baltimore: Johns Hopkins University Press.

Kissinger, Henry. 2011. *On China*. New York: Penguin Books.

———. 2012. "The Future of U.S.-Chinese Relations: Conflict Is a Choice, Not a Necessity." *Foreign Affairs* 91:44–55.

Kneissel, Juta. 1974. "The Convergence Theory: The Debate in the Federal Republic of Germany." *New German Critique* 2:16–27.

Kong, Qingjiang. 2002. *China and the World Trade Organization: A Legal Perspective*. Singapore City: World Scientific Publishing.

Kostecki, Michel M. 1978. "State Trading in Industrialized and Developing Countries." *Journal of World Trade Law* 12:187–207.

———. 1979. *East-West Trade and the GATT System*. London: Palgrave Macmillan.

Kroeber, Arthur R. 2016. *China's Economy: What Everyone Needs to Know*. New York: Oxford University Press.

Kroenig, Matthew. 2020. *The Return of Great Power Rivalry*. New York: Oxford University Press.

Krueger, Anne O. 1964. "The Political Economy of the Rent Seeking Society." *American Economic Review* 64:291–303.

Kurlantzick, Joshua. 2016. *State Capitalism: How the Return of Statism Is Transforming the World*. Oxford: Oxford University Press.

Kurtz-Phelan, Daniel. 2018. *The China Mission: George Marshall's Unfinished War, 1945–1947*. New York: W. W. Norton.

Lardy, Nicholas R. 2002. *Integrating China into the Global Economy*. Washington, DC: Brookings Institution.

———. 2014. *Markets over Mao: The Rise of Private Business in China*. Washington, DC: Peterson Institute for International Economics.

———. 2019. *The State Strikes Back: The End of Economic Reform in China?* Washington, DC: Peterson Institute for International Economics.

Leddy, John. 1958. "GATT—A Cohesive Influence in the Free World." *American Journal of Agricultural Economics* 40:228–37.

Lefebvre, Kevin, Nadia Rocha, and Michele Ruta. 2019. "Containing Chinese SOEs? The Impact of Deep Trade Agreements on Firms' Exports." Mimeo.

Lei, Zheng, Benjamin Liebman, and Curtis J. Milhaupt. 2016. "SOEs and State Governance: How China's State Enterprises Influence China's Legal System." In *Regulating the Visible Hand? The Institutional Implications of China's State Capitalism*, ed. Benjamin Liebman and Curtis J. Milhaupt, 203–23. Oxford: Oxford University Press.

Leutert, Wendy. 2018. "Firm Control: Governing the State-Owned Economy under Xi Jinping." *China Perspectives* 1:227–36.

Levy, Phil. 2019. "The Endless China Trade War." *Forbes*, March 20.

Li, Chen. 2016. "Holding China Inc. Together: The CCP and the Rise of China's Yangqi." *China Quarterly* 228:927–49.

Liang, Wei. 2002. "China's WTO Negotiation Process and Its Implications." *Journal of Contemporary China* 11:683–719.

Liang, Yand, Mary E. Lovely, and Hongsheng Zhang. 2019. "Techno-Industrial Policy and China's Export Surge." Mimeo.

Liebman, Benjamin. 2017. "Authoritarian Justice in China: Is There a 'Chinese Model'?" In *The Beijing Consensus? How China Has Changed Western Ideas of Law and Economic Development*, ed. Weitsang Chen, 225–48. Cambridge: Cambridge University Press.

Lighthizer, Robert E. 2010. "Evaluating China's Role in the World Trade Organization over the Past Decade." Testimony before the US-China Economic and Security Review Commission. https://www.uscc.gov/sites/default/files/Robert%20Lighthizer.pdf.

Lin, Li-Wen, and Curtis J. Milhaupt. 2013. "We Are the (National) Champions: Understanding the Mechanisms of State Capitalism in China." *Stanford Law Review* 65:697–760.

Lin, Yu-Hsin, and Curtis J. Milhaupt. 2019. "Party Building or Noisy Signalling? The Contours of Political Conformity in Chinese Corporate Governance." Mimeo.

Liu, Ernest. 2019. "Industrial Policies in Production Networks." *Quarterly Journal of Economics* 134:1883–1948.

Liu, Han-Wei, Yu-Jie Chen, and Ching-Fu Lin. 2018. "'Rule of Trust': The Power and Perils of China's Credit System." *Columbia Journal of Asian Law* 32:1–36.

Lovely, Mary E., and Yang Liang. 2018. "Trump Tariffs Primarily Hit Multinational Supply Chains, Harm Competitiveness." Policy Brief 18–12. Washington, DC: Peterson Institute for International Economics. https://www.piie.com/publications/policy-briefs/trump-tariffs-primarily -hit-multinational-supply-chains-harm-us.

Luo, Dan. 2016. *Evolution of the Chinese Banking System*. Nottingham China Policy Institute Series. London: Palgrave Macmillan.

Lyu, Shuping, Caroline Buts, and Marc Jegers. 2019. "Comparing China's Fair Competition Review System to EU State Aid Control." *European State Aid Law Quarterly* 1:37–54.

Madden, Kirsten M. 1998. "The Political Economy of Han Fei Tzu and Adam Smith: A Comparative Analysis and Implications for Chinese Economic Transition." In *China's Transition to a Socialist Market Economy*, ed. Osman Suliman, 1697–94. Westport, CT: Quorum Books.

Martin, Will, and Christian Bach. 1998. "The Importance of State Trading in China's Trade Regime." In *China in the World Trading System: Defining the Principles of Engagement*, ed. Frederick M. Abbott, 155–71. The Hague: Kluwer Law.

Maskus, Keith. 2004. "Intellectual Property Rights in the WTO Accession Package: Assessing China's Reforms." In *China and the WTO: Accession, Policy Reform, and Poverty Reduction Strategies*, ed. Deepak Bhattasali, Shantong Li, and Will Martin, 49–61. Washington, DC: World Bank and Oxford University Press.

Mason, Mark. 1992. *American Multinationals and Japan: The Political Economy of Japanese Capital Controls, 1899–1980*. Cambridge, MA: Harvard University Press.

Matsushita, Mitsuo. 1991. "The Structural Impediments Initiative: An Example of Bilateral Trade Negotiation." *Michigan Journal of International Law* 12:436–49.

Matsushita, Mitsuo, Thomas J. Schoenbaum, Petros C. Mavroidis, and Michael J. Hahn. 2015. *The World Trade Organization: Law, Practice, and Policy.* Oxford: Oxford University Press.

Mattingly, Daniel C. 2020. *The Art of Political Control in China.* New York: Cambridge University Press.

Mattoo, Aditya, and Robert W. Staiger. 2019. "Trade Wars: What Do They Mean? Why Are They Happening Now? What Are the Costs?" Policy Research Working Paper 8829. Washington, DC: World Bank Group.

Mattoo, Aditya, and Arvind Subramanian. 2009. "Currency Undervaluations and Sovereign Wealth Funds: A New Role for the World Trade Organization." *World Economy* 32:1135–64.

Mavroidis, Petros C. 1993. "Government Procurement Agreement; the Trondheim Case: The Remedies Issue." *Aussenwirtschaft* 48:77–94.

———. 2016. *The Regulation of International Trade.* Vols. 1 and 2. Cambridge, MA: MIT Press.

Mavroidis, Petros C., and Merit E. Janow. 2017. "Free Markets, State Involvement, and the WTO: Chinese State-Owned Enterprises in the Ring." *World Trade Review* 16:571–81.

Mavroidis, Petros C., and Damien J. Neven. 2019. "Greening the WTO: Environmental Goods Agreement, Tariff Concessions and Policy Likeness." *Journal of International Economic Law* 32:373–88.

Mavroidis, Petros C., and Robert Wolfe. 2015. "From Sunshine to a Common Agent: The Evolving Understanding of Transparency in the WTO." *Brown Journal of World Affairs* 21:117–29.

McGregor, Richard. 2010. *The Party: The Secret World of China's Communist Rulers.* New York: Allen Lane, Penguin.

———. 2019a. *Xi Jinping: The Backlash Party.* The Penguin Specials. Sydney, Australia: Penguin Random House.

———. 2019b. "Xi Jinping's Quest to Dominate China." *Foreign Affairs* 98 (September–October): 18–25.

McKenzie, Francine. 2008. "GATT in the Cold War: Accession Debates, Institutional Development, and the Western Alliance, 1947–1959." *Journal of Cold War Studies* 10:78–109.

McMahon, Dinny. 2018. *China's Great Wall of Debt.* New York: Houghton Mifflin Harcourt.

Mearsheimer, John. 2001. *The Tragedy of Great Power Politics.* New York: W. W. Norton.

Melitz, Marc. 2003. "The Impact of Trade on Intra-industry Reallocations and Aggregate Industry Productivity." *Econometrica* 71:1695–1725.

Milhaupt, Curtis J., and Mariana Pargendler. 2017. "Governance Challenges of Listed State-Owned Enterprises around the World: National Experiences and a Framework for Reform." *Cornell International Law Journal* 50:473–542.

Milhaupt, Curtis J., and Wentong Zheng. 2015. "Beyond Ownership: State Capitalism and the Chinese Firm." *Georgetown Law Journal* 103:665–722.

Miller, Jennifer M. 2019. *Cold War Democracy: The United States and Japan.* Cambridge, MA: Harvard University Press.

Mokyr, Joel. 1990. *The Lever of Riches: Technological Creativity and Economic Progress.* New York: Oxford University Press.

Naughton, Barry. 2017. "The Current Wave of State Enterprise Reform in China: A Preliminary Appraisal." *Asian Economic Policy Review* 12:282–98.

———. 2018. "State Enterprise Reform Today." In *China's 40 Years of Reform and Development, 1978–2018,* ed. Ross Garnaut, Ligang Song, and Cai Fang, 375–94. Acton: Australia National University Press.

Nye, Joseph S., Jr. 2020. *Do Morals Matter?* New York: Oxford University Press.

Ostry, Sylvia. 2003. "WTO Membership for China: To Be and Not to Be—Is That the Answer?" In *China and the World Trading System: Entering a New Millennium,* ed. Deborah Cass, Brett

Williams, and George Barker, 257–65. Cambridge: Cambridge University Press. www.csls .ca/events/slt01/ostry.pdf.

Paemen, Hugo, and Alexandra Bentsch. 1995. *From the GATT to the WTO: The European Community in the Uruguay Round.* Leuven: Leuven University Press.

Parsons, Craig A. 2005. "The Effect of the Semiconductor Trade Agreement on Japanese Firms." *Singapore Economic Review* 50:117–29.

Patrick, Hugh T. 1990. "Section 301 and the United States–Japan Economic Relationship: Reflections on Kuroda." In *Aggressive Unilateralism: America's 301 Trade Policy and the World Trading System,* ed. Jagdish Bhagwati and Hugh T. Patrick. Ann Arbor: University of Michigan Press.

Patterson, Stewart. 2018. *China, Trade and Power: Why the West's Economic Engagement Has Failed.* London: London Publishing Partnership.

Paulson, Henry M., Jr. 2015. *Dealing with China: An Insider Unmasks the New Economic Superpower.* New York: Twelve.

Peerenboom, Randall. 2014. "The Battle Over Legal Form in China: Has There Been a Turn against Law?" *Chinese Journal of Comparative Law* 2:188–212.

Pelkmans, Jacques. 2018. "China and the EU: The Contradictions of Exercising Joint Leadership." Brussels: CEPS. https://www.ceps.eu/wp-content/uploads/2018/09/China%20and%20 the%20EU.pdf.

Perkins, Dwight H. 2018. "Is the Chinese Economy Headed toward a Hard Landing?" In *The China Questions: Critical Insights into a Rising Power,* ed. Jennifer Rudolph and Michael Szonyi, 126–32. Cambridge, MA: Harvard University Press.

Pollard, Robert A. 1985. *Economic Security and the Origins of the Cold War, 1945–1950.* New York: Columbia University Press.

Puchniak, Dan W., and Luh Lan. 2017. "Independent Directors in Singapore: Puzzling Compliance Requiring Explanations." *American Journal of Comparative Law* 65:265–333.

Qin, Julia Ya. 2004. "WTO Regulation of Subsidies to State-Owned Enterprises (SOEs): A Critical Appraisal of the China Accession Protocol." *Journal of International Economic Law* 7:863–919.

———. 2010. "The Challenge of Interpreting 'WTO-Plus' Provisions." *Journal of World Trade* 44:127–72.

Raballand, Gael J.R.F., Gilles Marie Veuillot, Lydia Habhab, and Philippe de Meneval. 2015. *Middle East and North Africa: Governance Reforms of State-Owned Enterprises (SOEs): Lessons from Four Case Studies.* Washington, DC: World Bank Group.

Reuland, James M. 1975. "GATT and State-Trading Countries." *Journal of World Trade Law* 9:318–33.

Rodrik, Dani. 2018. "The Double Standard of America's China Trade Policy." Project Syndicate, May 10. https://www.project-syndicate.org/commentary/american-trade-policy-double -standard-by-dani-rodrik-2018-05.

Ross, Robert S. 2018. "What Does the Rise of China Mean for the United States?" In *The China Questions: Critical Insights into a Rising Power,* ed. Jennifer Rudolph and Michael Szonyi, 81–89. Cambridge, MA: Harvard University Press.

Ruggie, John. G. 1982. "International Regimes, Transactions, and Change: Embedded Liberalism in the Postwar Economic Order." *International Organization* 36:375–412.

Saxonhouse, Gary R. 1991. "Japan, SII and the International Harmonization of Domestic Economic Practices." *Michigan Journal of International Law* 12:450–71.

Schleifer, Andrei. 1998. "State versus Private Ownership." *Journal of Economic Perspectives* 12:133–50.

Schoppa, Leonard J. 1997. *Bargaining with Japan: What American Pressure Can and Cannot Do.* New York: Columbia University Press.

Scissors, Derek. 2015. "Grading the Trans-Pacific Partnership on Trade." Washington, DC: American Enterprise Institute. https://www.aei.org/research-products/report/grading-the-trans -pacific-partnership-on-trade/.

Segal, Adam. 2011. *Advantage: How American Innovation Can Overcome the Asian Challenge*. New York: W. W. Norton.

Shambaugh, David. 2013. *China Goes Global: The Partial Power*. Oxford: Oxford University Press.

———. 2016. *China's Future*. Cambridge: Polity Press.

Shan, Weijian. 2019. "The Unwinnable Trade War." *Foreign Affairs* 98:99–108.

Slobodian, Quinn. 2018. *Globalists: The End of Empire and the Birth of Neoliberalism*. Cambridge, MA: Harvard University Press.

Smith, Alasdair, and Antony Venables. 1991. "Counting the Cost of Voluntary Export Restraints in the European Market." In *International Trade and Trade Policy*, ed. E. Helpman and A. Razin, 187–220. Cambridge, MA: MIT Press.

Smith, Julianne, and Torey Taussig. 2019. "The Old War and the Middle Kingdom: Europe Wakes Up to China's Rise." *Foreign Affairs* 98 (September–October): 112–24.

Sokol, Daniel D. 2013. "Merger Control under China's Anti-Monopoly Law." *Journal of Law and Business* 10:1–36.

Song, Ligang. 2018. "State-Owned Enterprise Reform in China: Past, Present and Future Prospects." In *China's 40 Years of Reform and Development, 1978–2018*, ed. Ross Garnaut, Ligang Song, and Cai Fang, 345–74. Acton: Australia National University Press.

Staiger, Robert W., and Alan O. Sykes. 2010. "Currency Manipulators and World Trade." *World Trade Review* 9:583–627.

Steil, Benn. 2018. *The Marshall Plan: Dawn of the Cold War*. New York: Simon and Schuster.

Steinberg, Richard. 1997. "Institutional Implications of WTO Accession to China." Berkeley Roundtable on the International Economy, Working Paper No. 110. Berkeley, CA.

Stewart, Terence. 1993. *The GATT Uruguay Round: A Negotiating History (1986–1992)*. Boston: Kluwer Law.

Stiglitz, Joseph, and Andrew Charlton. 2007. *Fair Trade for All: How Trade Can Promote Development*. Oxford: Oxford University Press.

Sykes, Alan O. 2006. *The WTO Agreement on Safeguards: A Commentary*. New York: Oxford University Press.

Szonyi, Michael. 2018. Introduction to *The China Questions: Critical Insights into a Rising Power*, ed. Jennifer Rudolph and Michael Szonyi, 1–8. Cambridge, MA: Harvard University Press.

Thurow, Lester. 1992. *Head to Head: The Coming Economic Battle among Japan, Europe, and America*. New York: Morrow Publishing.

Tolchin, Martin. 1988. "'Japan-Bashing' Becomes a Trade Bill Issue." *New York Times*, February 28.

Toohey, Lisa, Colin Picker, and Jonathan Greenacre, eds. 2015. *China in the International Economic Order: New Directions and Changing Paradigms*. Cambridge: Cambridge University Press.

Trump, Donald J. 2017. "The National Security Strategy of the United States." Washington, DC: The White House.

Tumlir, Jan. 1984. "International Economic Order and Democratic Constitutionalism." *ORDO: Jahrbuch für die Ordnung von Wirtschaft und Gesellschaft* 34:71–83.

Tyson, Laura d'Andrea. 1991. *Who's Bashing Whom? Trade Conflict in High Technology Industries*. Washington, DC: Institute for International Economics.

Vernon, Raymond. 1996. "International Investment and International Trade in the Product Cycle." *Quarterly Journal of Economics* 80:190–207.

Vogel, Ezra F. 2011. *Deng Xiaoping and the Transformation of China*. Cambridge, MA: Belknap Press of Harvard University Press.

———. 2019. *China and Japan Facing History*. Cambridge, MA: Belknap Press of Harvard University Press.

Walker, William O. 2018. *The Rise and Decline of the American Century*. Ithaca: Cornell University Press.

Walter, Carl E., and Fraser J. T. Howie. 2011. *Red Capitalism: The Fragile Financial Foundation of China's Extraordinary Rise*. Hoboken, NJ: John Wiley & Sons.

Wang, Luolin. 2015. *China's WTO Accession Reassessed*. New York: Routledge.

Weiss, Linda, and Elizabeth Thurnbon. 2006. "The Business of Buying American." *Review of International Political Economy* 13:701–24.

Westad, Odd Arne. 2019. "Are Washington and Beijing Fighting a Cold War?" *Foreign Affairs* 98 (September–October): 86–95.

White, Hugh. 2012. *The China Choice: Why We Should Share Power*. Oxford: Oxford University Press.

Wilcox, Clair. 1949. *A Charter for World Trade*. New York: Macmillan.

Williams, Peter John. 2008. *A Handbook on Accession to the WTO*. Cambridge: Cambridge University Press.

Wolf, Martin. 2017. "The Long and Painful Journey to World Disorder." *Financial Times*, January 5.

Wolfe, Robert. 2017. "Sunshine over Shanghai: Can the WTO Illuminate the Murky World of Chinese SOEs?" *World Trade Review* 16:717–32.

World Bank. 2018a. *China—Systematic Country Diagnostic: Towards a More Inclusive and Sustainable Development*. Washington, DC: World Bank Group.

———. 2018b. "Approach Paper—World Bank Group Support for the Reform of State-Owned Enterprises, 2007–2018: An IEG Evaluation." Washington, DC: World Bank Group.

———. 2019a. *Belt and Road Economics: Opportunities and Risks of Transport Corridors*. Washington, DC: World Bank Group.

———. 2019b. *Innovative China: New Drivers of Growth*. Washington, DC: World Bank Group.

Wu, Mark. 2016. "The 'China Inc.' Challenge to World Trade Governance." *Harvard Journal of International Law* 57:261–324.

———. 2018. "Is China Keeping Its Promises on Trade?" In *The China Questions: Critical Insights into a Rising Power*, ed. Jennifer Rudolph and Michael Szonyi, 140–47. Cambridge, MA: Harvard University Press.

Ye Zhang, Zoey. 2019. "China's SOE Reforms: What the Latest Round of Reforms Mean to the Market, China Briefing." May 29. https://www.china-briefing.com/news/chinas-soe-reform-process/.

Yu, Hong. 2019. "Reform of State-Owned Enterprises in China: The Chinese Communist Party Strikes Back." *Asian Studies Review* 43:332–51.

Zeiler, Thomas W. 1999. *Free Trade, Free World*. Chapel Hill: University of North Carolina Press.

Zhang, Chenguo, and Jin Cao. 2019. "How Fair Is Patent Litigation in China? Evidence from the Beijing Court." *China Quarterly*, September 2.

Zhang, Shuguang, Yansheng Zhang, and Zhongxin Wan. 1998. *Measuring the Cost of Protection in China*. Washington, DC: Institute for International Economics.

Zhang, Zhanjiang, and Baiding Wu. 2019. "Governing China's Administrative Monopolies under the Anti-Monopoly Law: A Ten-Year Review (2008–2018) and Beyond." *Journal of Competition Law and Economics* 15:718–60.

Zhou, Weihuan, and Henry Gao. 2020. "U.S.-China Trade War: A Way Out?" *World Trade Review* 19.

Zhou, Weihuan, Henry Gao, and Xue Bai. 2019. "Building a Market Economy through WTO-Inspired Reform of State-Owned Enterprises in China." *International and Comparative Law Quarterly* 68:977–1022.

Zoellick, Robert B. 2005. "Whither China: From Membership to Responsibility?" Remarks to the National Committee on U.S.-China Relations, New York, September 21. https://2001-2009.state.gov/s/d/former/zoellick/rem/53682.htm.

INDEX

Abe, Shinzo, 55
Acheson, Dean, 114n12, 174, 213
administrative guidance, 91n71
Agreement on Agriculture, 39, 120
Agreement on Government Procurement
(GPA): accession to, 108; challenge pro-
cedures, 188–89; China's promise to join,
38–39, 67, 81; SOEs as public bodies and, 81
Agreement on Trade Facilitation (ATF), 34,
36n43
Ahn, Dukgeun, 187n15
Aid for Trade initiative, 34
Albright, Madeleine, 104
Alford, William P., 190n21
Allison, Graham, 30, 58n30, 217
Amiti, Mary, 10, 58n30, 149
Anderson, Robert D., 68
Antidumping Agreement, 39
APEC. See Asia-Pacific Economic Cooperation
(APEC)
Arab countries, protocols of accession for,
123–24
Arrow, Kenneth, 20n16
Asian Infrastructure Investment Bank
(AIIB), 195, 204
Asia-Pacific Economic Cooperation (APEC),
16, 20–22, 175
Austria, 130
Autor, David H., 62–63

Bacchus, James, 54n25
Bach, Christian, 19
Baker, James A., III, 15n2
Baldwin, Robert E., 161
Barfield, Claude E., 133n42
Barker, George, 23
Barshefsky, Charlene, 26–28
Bashan Conference, 20n16
behind-the-border barriers. See non-tariff
barriers (NTBs)
Belgian Family Allowances, 75

Bell, Daniel A., 186n14
Belt and Road Initiative, 195, 204
Benelux countries, 130
Berkowitz, Daniel, 193
bilateral investment treaties (BITs), 91–92,
109n4, 110, 167, 182
Blustein, Paul: China's accession to the WTO,
15; Chinese currency valuation, U.S.
congressional threat regarding, 65; forced
technology transfer, anecdotal evidence
regarding, 91n72; intellectual property
rights, responses to violations of, 45; loyalty
of Chinese courts to the party and the state,
191n24; multilateralism as the correct
response to the China challenge, 215;
reluctance to take action against China,
examples of, 53n22; SASAC, reason for
introduction of, 194; United States' complaints about Chinese noncompliance, 39;
U.S.-China Bilateral Agreement, 25, 26n27;
Xi's esteem for Mao and Deng, 203n15
Bown, Chad P.: export-led growth by China,
142; globalization, cracks in the foundation
of, 12; protectionism following the great
recession, 34–35; Section 301, downgrad-
ing the use of, 56–57; "stick" strategy and
research by, 10; tariffs on Chinese imports
in the U.S., 66n41; unilateralism, reasons
for unworkability of, 149; U.S.-China
showdown, high stakes of, 148
Brandt, Loren, 30, 197
Branstetter, Lee, 47–48, 187n15
Brazil, 6, 33–34, 130, 150, 152
Brazil–Taxation, 122
Brødsgaard, Kjeld Erik, 197–98
Brooke, Sir Alan, 55
Brunnermeier, Marcus, 217–18
Bulgaria, 113
Bush, George H. W., 56, 58, 103, 137
Bush, George W., 15
Buts, Caroline, 216

231

the Czech economy, 110–11; Article XIX, regulation of trade impact on employment by, 63; Article XV.4, regulation of currency manipulation, 64–65; Article XVII, case law under, 74–82, 101, 119; Article XVII, regulation of state-owned enterprises, 60, 74, 89; Article XXXIII, the accession clause, 107–8, 111; Article XXXV, non-application clause, 129; China's original participation in, 1947–1950, 16; China's preparation for rejoining, 21–23; liberal understanding underlying (*see* liberal understanding underlying the GATT); regime neutrality and, 162–66; state involvement in trade/the economy and, 68–70 (*see also* state-owned enterprises (SOEs)); Structural Impediments Initiative (SII) and, 138; Working Party on China's Status as a Contracting Party, 23; world trading system, as umbrella for (*see* GATT/WTO regime)

General Agreement on Trade in Services (GATS): conclusion of extended negotiations under, 34; Mode 3, Chinese obligations under, 92–93, 177; negotiation of, divide between developed and developing countries in, 162; nondiscrimination as a voluntary specific commitment under, 168n11; as product of 1980s unilateralism, 151; technology transfer, as an alternative for regulating, 60–61

Generalized System of Preferences (GSP) schemes, 22

Georgopoulos, Aris, 81, 189n18

Gertler, Jeffrey L., 23, 28

Gewirtz, Julian, 16, 20n16, 27, 28n32

Gilbert, Richard, 180

global financial crisis of 2008–2009, 32

Goldman, Marshall I., 19n14

Gorbachev, Mikhail, 19, 211

GPA. *See* Agreement on Government Procurement (GPA)

Graham, Lindsey, 65

grantback, 180

Greenspan, Alan, 25

"Guiding Opinions of the Central Committee on Deepening the Reform of State-Owned Enterprises," 195, 199

Haass, Richard N., 195

Haddad, Mona, 141–42

Halverson, Karen, 23

Hamada, Koichi, 139

Han Fei Tzu, 196

Hanson, Gordon H., 62–63

Hardwick, Samuel, 21

Harriman, Averell, 114n12

Hearden, Patrick J., 162n4

Herzstein, Robert, 28–29n33

Hillmann, Jennifer, 10, 156

Hoekman, Bernard M., 42n8, 81, 189n18, 192

Holslag, Jonathan, 62n32

Hoopes, Townsend, 213

Horn, Henrik, 51, 171

Howie, Fraser J.T., 71n51

Howson, Nicholas Calcina, 205

Hua Guofeng, 16

Huawei, 50n20

Hudec, Robert E., 166

Hufbauer, Gary C., 63, 70

Huijin, 45

Hu Jintao, 193–94

Hull, Cordell, 174

Hungary, 114n12, 115

Hu Yaobang, 16, 103

IMF. *See* International Monetary Fund (IMF)

India, 6, 33–34, 130–31, 150, 152

Information Technology Agreements (ITA I and II), 34, 36n43

intellectual property (IP) rights: protecting in China's Protocol of Accession, 45–47; size of the problem, 47; in the TRIPS Agreement, 161–62, 179–80

International Monetary Fund (IMF): Chinese currency manipulation, complaints regarding, 65–66; currency manipulation, IMF-WTO agreement regarding, 64–65; membership in as part of Chinese openness strategy, 21

international trade, organization of. *See* GATT/WTO regime

International Trade Organization (ITO): competition law, attempt to enforce and internationalize, 180, 215; failure to approve the Charter, reasons for, 168–69; GATT and, relationship of, 5, 160–61; Havana Charter for, 108, 110n7, 167; liberal content in the Charter of, 167–68, 171; restrictive business practices, multilateral responses to, 9; Russian participation in, divisions within the U.S. administration on, 114n12

IP. *See* intellectual property (IP) rights

Iran, 151

Sager, Eric, 63n34
Samsung, 50n20
Sasahara, Akira, 63
Saudi Arabia, 123
Schell, Orville, 67, 206n20
Schleifer, Andrei, 202
Schumer, Charles, 65
Scissors, Derek, 186n12
SCM. *See* Subsidies and Countervailing
   Measures Agreement (SCM)
Section 301 of the U.S. Trade Act of 1974:
   Japan, use against, 136–37; private parties,
   instrument for, 56n27; Special 301, 150;
   Super 301, 136–37, 150; as Trump's alter-
   native for dealing with China, 52, 55–59;
   use of during the 1980s and 1990s, 56–57
Segal, Adam, 159n3
services, Chinese market for, 67
Shan, Weijian, 58n30
Shanghai Forum, 102
Shepherd, Ben, 141–42
Siemens, 46
SIEs. *See* state-invested enterprises (SIEs)
SII. *See* Structural Impediments Initiative
   (SII) negotiations/agreement
Singh, Manmohan, 6
Skinner, Kiron, 148
Slobodian, Quinn, 162n4
Smith, Alasdair, 134n43, 144n59
Smith, Julianne, 152
Smith, Walter Bedell, 170
SOCBs. *See* state-owned commercial banks
   (SOCBs)
SOEs. *See* state-owned enterprises (SOEs)
Sokol, Daniel D., 196–97
Soviet Union. *See* Union of Soviet Socialist
   Republics (USSR)
Spearot, Alan, 187n15
Special 301, 150
special economic zones (SEZs), 18–19, 209
Spencer, Herbert, 106
Staiger, Robert W., 51, 66, 208n21
state capital investment companies
   (SCICs), 45
state capital operation companies (SCOCs), 45
state-invested enterprises (SIEs): mentioned
   but not defined in China's Protocol of
   Accession, 42, 80; U.S. administration
   adoption of the term, 84n63
State-Owned Assets Supervision and
   Administration Commission (SASAC):
   concerns about at the time of accession,
   45; establishment and functions of, 44, 193;
   obligations regarding state interference to

be addressed by, 100; state control of the
   economy, increase in, 193–94
state-owned commercial banks (SOCBs),
   43, 45, 71, 182, 194
state-owned enterprises (SOEs): antitrust
   and concerns about at the time of accession,
   45; bilateral China-U.S. trade disputes
   related to, 82–89; Chapter 17 of the TPP
   as approach to China's, 55–56; China's
   compared to those in the rest of the world,
   44, 59–60; in China's Protocol of Accession, 41–43, 73–74, 80–82, 100–101; China's
   WTO obligations regarding, 71–82; contract responsibility system for, 43; corporatization and privatization of, 43–44;
   defining, issues associated with, 42, 80–82;
   dual-pricing system of, 18n10; in the European Union, 17n8, 59; existing alternatives
   for regulation of, 60; in former Soviet
   republics, 117–19; "Guiding Opinions of
   the Central Committee on Deepening the
   Reform of State-Owned Enterprises," 195,
   199; international legal framework for
   addressing, 68–71; magnitude of in the
   Chinese economy, 70n50; mergers, scaling
   up through, 196–97; nonviolation complaints as limited option for addressing,
   156–57; outside China, 17n8, 59, 70; as
   "public body" or "private agent," issue of,
   80–89 (*see also* "public body"); renegotiation
   of the WTO, to be addressed in, 176–82;
   technology transfer and, 187; transformation
   of, township and village enterprises (TVEs)
   and, 18; treatment in the U.S.-China Bilateral
   Agreement, confidence about, 25–26;
   uncoordinated response in negotiations with
   China, 101–2; WTO Appellate Body decisions
   and, 183; Xi's reforms and, 195–202
state-owned financial institutions (SOFIs), 45
state-trading countries (STCs), 109–10, 114n13
state-trading enterprises (STEs): Article
   XVII of the GATT Agreement, addressed
   in, 69–70, 163–65; distinguishing between
   STE and non-STE portions for imports of
   grains, 88–89; in former Soviet republics,
   119; as a form of state-owned enterprises
   (SOEs), 59–60; obligations of, case law
   under Article XVII and, 75–82
Steil, Benn, 170
Steinberg, Richard, 28n33
Stiglitz, Joseph, 66
Structural Impediments Initiative (SII)
   negotiations/agreement, 56, 58, 63, 131–32,
   136–39

136–39; Phase One agreement as product of, 153–54; of the 1980s compared to contemporary, 150–53; of the Trump administration, viii, 153; by the U.S., 38, 55, 57–58

Union of Soviet Socialist Republics (USSR): economic policy and the role of the party, differences with China on, 19; GATT and, 110n7, 162n4; Poland's accession to GATT, reaction to, 113. *See also* former Soviet republics, WTO accession of; Russia

United Kingdom (U.K.), 33, 130, 163

United States-Mexico-Canada Agreement (USMCA), 185–86, 212

United States (U.S.): alternatives to the WTO for pursuing complaints against China (*see* Section 301 of the U.S. Trade Act of 1974; Trans-Pacific Partnership (TPP) Agreement); Asian Infrastructure Investment Bank (AIIB), pushback against, 195; *Canada–Softwood Lumber* case, 165; *Canada–Wheat Exports and Grain Imports,* 76–78; as complainant against China in the WTO framework, 52; GATT and WTO, dominant position in, 33; Japan, post-war geopolitical concerns regarding, 170–71; Japan, trade frictions with, 133–39; Japan's accession to the GATT and, 125–28; Poland's accession to GATT, reaction to, 113; proposed renegotiation of the WTO, participation in, 206–7; trade liberalization and national security, link between, 170–71; U.S.-China Bilateral Agreement, signing of and optimism surrounding, 25–28; WTO complaints against, number of, 50–51. *See also* Trump, Donald

Uno, Sōsuke, 137

U.S. Trade Act of 1974, Section 301. *See* Section 301 of the U.S. Trade Act of 1974

U.S. Trade Representative (USTR): Section 301 investigation of China, 57–58; unhappiness with WTO Appellate Body report, 87–88

U.S.–Antidumping and Countervailing Duties (China), 82–88

U.S.-China Bilateral Agreement, 25–28; human rights absent from, 27–28

U.S.-China Business Council, 27

U.S.-China Chamber of Commerce, 27

U.S.-China trade dispute: alternative views of, 159–60; complaints against SOEs before the WTO, 82–89; Economic and Trade Agreement between the United States

of America and the People's Republic of China, Phase One, 153–54; magnitude/significance of, 58–59, 148; timing of, unfortunate, 159; U.S. administration's hubris regarding, 158–59

U.S.-China Trade Policy Working Group, 159–60n3

U.S.–Countervailing Measures (China), 82–88, 213–14

U.S.–Fur Felt Hats, 111n9

U.S.-Japan Semiconductor Pact of 1985, 133, 144n59

USMCA. *See* United States-Mexico-Canada Agreement (USMCA)

Venables, Antony, 134n43, 144n59

Vernon, Raymond, 90

VERs. *See* voluntary export restraints (VERs)

Vietnam: EU-Vietnam Free Trade Agreement, 175, 186; EU-Vietnam Investment Protection Agreement, 175

Vietnam, Protocol of Accession, 112, 124

Vogel, Ezra F.: China-Japan relations, 17n6–7, 125; Deng's pursuit of technology transfer, 90; Deng's reform strategy, 16, 19; economic change, resistance to, 18n12; high-speed railway in China, expansion of, 30; Japan's informal ties with the Asian Infrastructure Investment Bank, 204n18; the Meiji reforms in Japan, survival of, 132; Truman's refusal to divide Japan, 127n30

voluntary export restraints (VERs), 134, 143–44

von Platen, C. H., 115n14

Walker, William O., 170

Walter, Carl E., 71n51

Wan, Zhongxin, 20

Wang Shengjun, 191n22

Wei Jingsheng, 191n24

Weinstein, David E., 10, 58n30, 139, 149

Weiss, Linda, 68

Wen Jiabao, 32n39

Westad, Odd Arne, 148, 204

Whalley, John, 68

White, Hugh, 216

Wilf, Meredith, 113

Wilgress, Dana, 110n7

Will, George F., 174

Williams, Brett, 23

Wolf, Martin, 217

Wolfe, Robert, 187

Working Party on the Accession of China, report of, 23, 73–74, 99–100

A NOTE ON THE TYPE

This book has been composed in Adobe Text and Gotham.
Adobe Text, designed by Robert Slimbach for Adobe,
bridges the gap between fifteenth- and sixteenth-century
calligraphic and eighteenth-century Modern styles.
Gotham, inspired by New York street signs, was designed
by Tobias Frere-Jones for Hoefler & Co.